Savoring the Southwest Again

Roswell Symphony Guild Publications

Roswell, New Mexico

All proceeds from *Savoring the Southwest Again*
benefit the Roswell Symphony Orchestra.

Library of Congress Number 98-065965

ISBN Number
0-9612466-1-8

Additional copies of *Savoring the Southwest Again*
as well as copies of *Savoring the Southwest* may be obtained by contacting:

Roswell Symphony Guild Publications
P.O. Box 3078
Roswell, New Mexico 88202-3078

(505) 623-7477 or 1-800-457-0302

First Edition
First Printing   15,000   October, 1998

Printed in the USA by

WIMMER
The Wimmer Companies
Memphis
1-800-548-2537

PETER HURD
(FEBRUARY 22, 1904 - JULY 9, 1984)

HENRIETTE WYETH HURD
(OCTOBER 22, 1907 - APRIL 3, 1997)

FRONT COVER: PETER HURD—The Oasis, 1945, egg tempera on panel, 47"x47", permanent collection, Roswell Museum and Art Center. Gift of Mr. and Mrs. Donald Winston and Mr. and Mrs. Fredrick Winston, 1947. Photography by Richard Faller.

BACK COVER: HENRIETTE WYETH—Spring Flowers, ca. 1958, oil on linen, 41½"x60½", permanent collection, Roswell Museum and Art Center. Gift of Mrs. Leland L. Fellows in honor of Mrs. Dora Lewis McKnight, 1986. Photograph by Jose Rivera.

IN MEMORIAM

A native of Roswell, Peter Hurd has been compared to John Constable and J.M.W. Turner for his ability to capture the delicate luminescence of the southeastern New Mexico landscape, with its interplay of plains, sky, and mountains. Hurd and his wife, artist Henriette Wyeth, not only draw international attention for their works made in this part of the world, they also left a continuing legacy of succeeding generations of younger artists.

After graduating from New Mexico Military Institute, Peter Hurd attended the U.S. Military Academy at West Point, but decided to pursue a career as an artist. In 1922, he arrived at Chadds Ford, Pennsylvania, to study with noted illustrator Newell Convers Wyeth. Hurd became engaged to Wyeth's oldest daughter Henriette, who was already an accomplished artist, and they were married in 1929. In 1934, the Hurd family moved West to the Sentinel Ranch in the village of San Patricio, New Mexico, just fifty miles west of Roswell in the Hondo River Valley. The ranch became a center of artistic activity for the region and continues as such under the management of their son, artist Michael Hurd. Both Peter Hurd and Henriette Wyeth Hurd are buried there.

Peter Hurd's work includes watercolors done as a World War II correspondent for *Life* magazine, large public murals, and, most notably, his New Mexico landscapes, suffused with atmosphere and light, in egg tempera.

Henriette Wyeth is considered by many art scholars to be one of the great women painters of the 20th century. She began studying with her father at the age of 11 and, like him, preferred to work in oil. Her powerful still life paintings, although realistic, also have a transcendent quality. She is noted for exquisite floral compositions. Her paintings of irises, which flourish in southern New Mexico's arid soil, capture the flowers in their full complexity.

Both artists were distinguished portraitists, and their subjects include family members, friends, and nationally prominent figures. Some of their finest studies are of ordinary people from the village of San Patricio.

The artistic reputations of Peter Hurd and Henriette Wyeth increase every year; their works are displayed throughout the U.S. in famous galleries and private collections. However, their greatest gift to us was to capture the soul and spirit of the Southwest that they loved, and where they lived, painted, and raised their children Peter, Carol, and Michael. We forever honor them.

About the Art

Linda Miller-A PORTION OF SPRING, 1992,
oil on linen, 10˝ x 11˝, private collection.

Bill Wiggins-STRIPES #9, 1993,
oil on canvas, 21¾˝ x 29⅝˝, permanent collection,
Roswell Museum and Art Center.
Photograph by Jose Rivera.

Phillis Ideal-ICON SERIES: THE RED ONE, 1984,
oil on wood panel, 69˝ x 48˝, permanent collection, Roswell Museum and Art Center.
Photograph by Jose Rivera.

Luis Jimenez-THE ROSE TATTOO, 1983,
color lithograph on paper, 22˝ x 30˝, permanent
collection, Roswell Museum and Art Center, 1985.
Photograph by Richard Faller.

Gussie Dujardin-HONEYSUCKLE ROSE, 1987,
oil on canvas, 60˝ x 72˝, collection of the artist.
Photograph by Jose Rivera.

Elmer Schooley-BETWEEN HERE AND SANTA FE, 1974-75,
oil on canvas, 60˝ x 72˝, permanent collection, Roswell Museum and Art Center.
Gift of the artist in honor of Patricia Lubben Bassett.
Photograph by Jose Rivera.

Martha (Martie) Zelt-GREY CAT, 1986,
printed at the Tamarind Institute, ed. 22, assembled by the artist, lithograph,
screenprint on paper, fabric, stick, 38˝ x 30˝, permanent collection,
Anderson Museum of Contemporary Art, Roswell, NM.

Pomona Hallenbeck-EL RIO HONDO, 1996,
watercolor, 8˝ x 11˝, collection of the artist.
Photograph by Jose Rivera.

Ted Robertson-HONDO OASIS,
pastel, 18˝ x 24˝, private collection.

Keith Avery-HOMEWARD BOUND,
oil on canvas, 24˝ x 30˝, private collection.

The Roswell Symphony Guild

A handful of local musicians, goaded by their fearless leader, Glenn Cunningham, decided they were capable of forming a symphony orchestra by incorporating into a nonprofit organization. Free legal services were offered by a music-loving attorney, the proper documents filed, and a Board of Directors was elected.

It was evident that a support group would be necessary to aid this fledgling group, and that a symphony guild was a real necessity. Being the only woman on the Board, and knowing that women would be the most likely source of guild members, I was chosen to organize this effort.

I called upon the women I knew who braved and supported the orchestra's early efforts. The response was very gratifying, and the Roswell Symphony Guild was born in 1961. This small group of women carried on through the lean years, cooking, entertaining, recruiting and fund raising. As the guild grew - now 200 members - men joined, and this year they have taken leadership positions.

The Guild has supported the orchestra with thousands of dollars each year, as well as sponsoring children's concerts and education programs.

Roswell Symphony Guild Publications, the creator of *Savoring the Southwest,* and now, its companion, *Savoring the Southwest Again* is an offspring of the Guild, but still an integral part of it, its membership overlapping and serving dual purposes.

As a parent feels when his or her child flourishes, I am so proud of the Roswell Symphony Guild. May it endure forever.

Dorothy Herring

Acknowledgments

A huge debt of appreciation is due the many friends and friends of friends who so graciously opened their files and shared their most treasured recipes with us. Also thanks to our recipe testers and their families who tested and tested making certain all recipes "worked" as written, tasted really wonderful and were special enough for our book. "Thank you's" must also go to all who served on any cookbook committee and lent suggestions, talent, and time, whether it was one hour or many.

We would be remiss if we did not acknowledge our symphony office staff, as well as the on-going support of the Roswell Symphony Orchestra Board.

Without this faithful, untiring, and conscientious cadre, *SAVORING THE SOUTHWEST AGAIN* could have not come to fruition, and we could have not had the opportunity to share our varied and colorful southwestern cuisine and art with you, the reader.

Gracias! Gracias! Gracias!

The Development Committee

Patricia Eckert, Co-chairman

Billie Michaud, Co-chairman

Anne Owen McCormick, Editor

Dorothy Peterson, Art Consultant

Sandie Davies, Text Development

Hannah Ginsberg, Text Development

Billie Howes, Social Coordinator

Sherry Spartano, Secretary

Millie Whitacker, Food Consultant

Reida Henry, Marketing

The Roswell Symphony Guild Publications, Inc. publishes *SAVORING THE SOUTHWEST AGAIN*. Profits from the sale of this cookbook help fund the Roswell Symphony Orchestra and its music education programs in our community. In purchasing this book, each of you contributes to the Guild's effort in enriching many lives through music.

Table of Contents

Index of Line Drawings

All line drawings by Dorothy Peterson

Appetizers &
Beverages

All line drawings in *Savoring the Southwest Again* by Dorothy Peterson.

Dorothy Peterson began painting and drawing the landscape, the places and the people of the Estancia Valley and the Manzano Mountain Villages of central New Mexico when she was growing up in Moriarty, New Mexico, in the 1940's. A professional artist for many years, she continues to interpret the brooding, mysterious quality of the mountains and the shimmering light of this very special area of the state where the plains of the East meet the mountains of the North. Travels to other parts of the United States and abroad have influenced her work, and the Pecos Valley, where she now maintains a studio, has been incorporated into her imagery, as well.

Dorothy's award-winning work has been displayed in numerous competitive and invitational shows, and is included in corporate and public collections across the United States.

The artist, who is listed in *Who's Who in American Art,* works in a variety of media including watercolor, oil, acrylic and pastel. Many thin layers of translucent color are built upon the surface of the painting, giving her work a richness and vitality that makes one feel the work has a "life of its own".

There is a dialogue between the viewer and the art that sets Dorothy Peterson's work apart as unique—a poetry of color and form.

Featured on page 9 "Roswell Civic Center"

Avocado-Blue Cheese Dip

2   medium-size ripe avocados, peeled and seeded
2   tablespoons chopped onion
1½ teaspoons fresh lemon juice
1½ cups sour cream
¼   cup crumbled blue cheese
½   teaspoon salt
⅛   teaspoon pepper
    Assorted fresh vegetables
    Assorted crackers

Cut avocados into chunks. Place avocado, onion, and lemon juice in blender; puree until smooth. Add sour cream, blue cheese, salt, and pepper; blend until well combined. Cover and chill 1 to 2 hours. Serve with vegetables and crackers.

Makes 2 cups.

Black Bean Nachos

1   (15-ounce) can black beans, rinsed and drained
⅓   cup salsa
1   small tomato, seeded, chopped, and drained
4   green onions, chopped
1   teaspoon grated onion
1½ cups shredded Monterey Jack cheese
¼   cup sliced ripe olives
4   tablespoons sour cream
    Tortilla chips

Preheat oven to 425°. Pat beans gently with paper towels to remove excess moisture. Spread beans in bottom of a pie plate or baking dish. Combine salsa and next 3 ingredients; spoon evenly over beans. Sprinkle with cheese, and top with olives. Bake until thoroughly heated and cheese melts, about 6 minutes. Spoon sour cream around edges, and serve with tortilla chips.

Makes 6 servings.

Cheese-Coated Grapes

10 ounces pecans, walnuts, or almonds
1 (8-ounce) package cream cheese, softened
¼ pound Roquefort cheese

2 tablespoons heavy whipping cream
1 pound seedless red or green grapes, stemmed, washed, and dried

Preheat oven to 275°. Place nuts on a baking sheet; cook, stirring occasionally, until lightly toasted. Let nuts cool; pulse in a food processor until coarsely chopped. Combine cream cheese, Roquefort, and cream; beat until smooth. Gently stir grapes into cheese mixture until coated. Roll coated grapes, 1 at a time, in nuts. Place on a wax paper-lined tray, and chill until ready to serve.

Makes 6 servings.

Brie with Salsa and Roasted Garlic

4 whole garlic bulbs
¼ cup olive oil
⅓ pound tomatillos, husked
½ small white onion, chopped
1 garlic clove
1 serrano chile pepper, chopped

½ teaspoon salt
¼ cup water
½ cup cilantro leaves
8 ounces brie cheese
2 French baguettes, cut into 18 slices

Preheat oven to 375°. Remove white, papery skin from garlic bulbs, and cut a ¼-inch slice from tops. Drizzle bulbs with oil, rubbing oil over garlic bulbs. Wrap garlic bulbs in aluminum foil, and bake 30 minutes or until soft. Process tomatillos and next 6 ingredients in a food processor or blender until smooth. Place cheese on a baking sheet, and bake until it just begins to melt, 3 to 5 minutes. Pour salsa over cheese. Squeeze pulp from garlic bulbs over salsa. Spread mixture on bread slices.

Makes 6 servings.

Chile Canapés

½ cup softened butter
4 cups shredded Cheddar cheese
1 cup mayonnaise

2 (4-ounce) cans diced green chiles
1 garlic clove, crushed
3 loaves party rye bread

Combine first 5 ingredients. Spread mixture on bread slices, and place on baking sheets. Broil 3 to 4 minutes or until cheese mixture is bubbly; serve hot.

Makes 10 servings.

Chile Con Queso

2 (4.5-ounce) cans chopped green chiles
1 large onion, finely chopped
1 (28-ounce) can tomatoes
2 tablespoons vinegar
1 tablespoon sugar
½ teaspoon pepper

2 teaspoons paprika
1½ teaspoons onion salt
½ teaspoon garlic salt
2 pounds processed Cheddar cheese, cubed
   Tortilla chips

Combine first 9 ingredients in a large saucepan; simmer 1½ hours. Add cheese to mixture, and stir until melted. Transfer to a serving container, and serve hot with tortilla chips.

Makes 2 cups.

Mexican Caviar

1 cup chopped black olives
1 cup chopped green chiles
2 tomatoes, peeled and chopped
3 green onions, chopped
2 garlic cloves, mashed

2 teaspoons olive oil
2 teaspoons red wine vinegar
1 teaspoon pepper
⅛ teaspoon seasoning salt
   Tortilla chips

Combine all ingredients, and chill overnight. Serve with tortilla chips.

Makes 8 to 10 servings.

Delicious on pasta or baked potatoes.

Chicken-Jalapeño Nachos

1   whole chicken breast, poached, skinned, boned, and diced
12 ounces cream cheese, softened
2   jalapeño peppers, seeded and minced
3   tablespoons chopped purple onion
2   garlic cloves, minced

1   teaspoon ground cumin
1   teaspoon chile powder
1½ cups shredded Monterey Jack cheese
    Salt and pepper to taste
6   medium-size pita bread rounds, each split into 2 rounds

Preheat oven to 375°. Beat first 8 ingredients at medium speed with an electric mixer until blended; season to taste with salt and pepper. Spread each pita round with chicken mixture. Place on baking sheets, and bake until puffed and bubbly, 5 to 7 minutes. Cut into wedges while hot, and serve.

Makes 98 nachos.

Chile Con Queso with White Cheddar

6   fresh green chiles (New Mexico or Anaheim)
1   yellow onion, chopped
2   garlic cloves, chopped
2   tablespoons vegetable oil

1   pound white Cheddar cheese, shredded
1   tablespoon sour cream
    Tortilla chips

Char chiles; peel chiles, and remove stems, veins, and seeds. Coarsely chop chiles. Sauté onion and garlic in hot oil in a skillet over medium heat until translucent, about 20 minutes. Add chiles, and cook 10 minutes. Reduce heat to medium-low; add cheese, and cook, stirring constantly, until cheese is melted, about 5 minutes. Stir in sour cream; transfer to a serving container, and serve immediately with tortilla chips.

Makes 6 servings.

Chile Rellenos Dip

1 (16-ounce) can tomatoes, drained and chopped
3-4 green onions, chopped
1 (4-ounce) can chopped black olives

1 (4.5-ounce) can chopped green chiles (hot)
3 tablespoons olive oil
1½ tablespoons vinegar
1 teaspoon garlic salt

Tortilla chips

Combine all ingredients well, and chill until ready to serve. Serve with tortilla chips.

Makes 15 servings.

Recipe may be doubled, but do not double amount of olives.

Cilantro Mousse

1 cup mayonnaise
1 bunch cilantro, stems removed
3 tablespoons sweet cream
½ medium-size onion, chopped
1 small serrano chile pepper, seeded and chopped

1 teaspoon chicken consommé granules
2 envelopes unflavored gelatin, dissolved in ½ cup boiling water
Saltine crackers

Process first 6 ingredients in a food processor until blended. Add gelatin, and blend well. Place in a well-greased mold, and chill until set. Unmold onto a serving platter, and serve with saltines.

This recipe, straight from Cuernavaca, Mexico, is delicious and unusual.

Linda Miller

Linda Miller is a native of Snyder, Texas, and has lived in the Hondo Valley of south-eastern New Mexico for a number of years.

A self-taught artist, Linda credits the late Henriette Wyeth as a major inspiration in her development as an accomplished realist painter. The artist's own inner vision, combined with a remarkable mastery of form and technique sets her work apart—a truly personal statement about the world that surrounds her. The adobe house she built; beloved animals and birds; treasures from everyday life in this magical place, find their way into her paintings and become invested with a magic and beauty all their own.

Linda Miller's paintings are included in major collections across the United States.

A Portion of Spring
Artist – Linda Miller
10″ × 11″   1992
oil on linen
Private collection

Feta Torta

½ pound unsalted butter, cut up
¾ pound feta cheese, crumbled
1 (8-ounce) package cream cheese, softened
2 garlic cloves, minced
1 shallot, minced
2-4 tablespoons dry vermouth

Ground white pepper to taste
½ cup toasted pine nuts
8 ounces sun-dried tomatoes, softened and minced
1 cup pesto (see index)
Garnish: fresh basil leaves

Process first 6 ingredients in a food processor until smooth. Add white pepper to taste. Oil a 4-cup mold; line mold with plastic wrap, allowing enough wrap to extend over edge. Layer pine nuts, cheese mixture, tomato, and pesto until mold is full. Fold plastic wrap over top, and press to compact. Chill until firm, about 2 hours. Invert torta onto a serving plate, and remove plastic wrap. Garnish, if desired.

Green Chile Bites

½ cup milk
½ cup water
½ cup margarine
¼ teaspoon salt
⅛ teaspoon pepper
⅛ teaspoon ground nutmeg

1 cup all-purpose flour
4 extra large eggs
2 cups shredded sharp Cheddar cheese
1½ cups drained chopped green chiles

Preheat oven to 400°. Grease mini muffin pans. Bring first 6 ingredients to a boil in a saucepan over medium-high heat. Gradually add flour. Reduce heat to medium-low, and stir mixture until it forms a thick, smooth ball. Remove from heat, and cool slightly. Transfer to a mixing bowl; add eggs, 1 at a time, beating with an electric mixer until smooth after each addition. Stir in chiles and cheese. Pipe mixture into muffin pans. Bake 15 minutes; reduce oven temperature to 350°. (Do not open oven door or bites will flatten.) Bake 20 to 25 more minutes; cool and remove from pans.

Makes about 24 bites.

Hot and Spicy Chix

⅔ cup mayonnaise
⅓ cup sour cream or plain yogurt
3   tablespoons milk
½ teaspoon ground cumin
½ teaspoon onion salt
¼ teaspoon cayenne pepper

¼ teaspoon garlic salt
1   pound chicken breasts, skinned, boned, and cut into 1-inch cubes
¾ cup crushed sesame crackers
½ cup salsa

Preheat oven to 425°. Combine mayonnaise and sour cream; reserve ½ cup mixture. Add milk and next 4 ingredients to remaining mayonnaise mixture. Dredge chicken in milk mixture; coat well with crushed crackers. Place on aluminum foil-lined or greased baking sheet; bake 18 to 20 minutes. Combine reserved mayonnaise mixture and salsa, and serve with chicken as a dip.

Makes 4 servings.

Picante Spinach Dip

1   onion, chopped
2   tablespoons vegetable oil
2   tomatoes, peeled, seeded, and chopped
2   jalapeños, minced
1   (10-ounce) package frozen chopped spinach, thawed and squeezed dry
2   cups shredded Monterey Jack cheese with peppers

1   (8-ounce) package cream cheese, cut into ½-inch cubes
1   cup half-and-half
2   (2.5-ounce) cans black olives, halved
1   tablespoon red wine vinegar
    Salt and pepper to taste
    Tortilla chips, fresh vegetables

Preheat oven to 350°. Sauté onion in hot oil in a skillet over medium-high heat until tender. Add tomato and jalapeños, and cook 2 minutes. Transfer onion mixture to a bowl, and stir in spinach, cheeses, and next 3 ingredients. Season with salt and pepper to taste; serve with tortilla chips and fresh vegetables.

Makes 6 to 8 servings.

Peppered Pecans

1 tablespoon olive oil
1 teaspoon freshly ground black pepper
1 teaspoon freshly ground white pepper
1 teaspoon cayenne pepper
½ teaspoon dried thyme, crumbled

2 egg whites
1 tablespoon Worcestershire sauce
1 teaspoon Tabasco
1 teaspoon salt
1 pound jumbo pecan halves (about 4½ cups)

Preheat oven to 375°. Brush a large, heavy baking pan with olive oil. Combine spices in a small bowl. Whisk egg whites in a medium-size bowl until foamy; whisk in Worcestershire sauce, Tabasco, and salt. Add nuts to egg white mixture, stirring to coat. Sift pepper mixture over nuts, tossing quickly to coat before egg whites dry. Spread nuts onto baking pan; bake in top third of oven for 5 minutes. Stir nuts, breaking up any clumps; bake until crisp and brown, stirring once or twice, about 7 minutes. Transfer to a bowl, and cool completely; store in an airtight container until ready to serve. (These may be prepared up to 4 days ahead.)

Makes 8 servings.

Recipe works well with almonds, cashews, or peanuts.

Roadrunners

2 cans refrigerated crescent rolls
2 (8-ounce) packages cream cheese, softened
½ cup sour cream
¾ cup mayonnaise

1 package Ranch-style dressing mix
3 cups finely chopped vegetables (broccoli, cauliflower, carrot, green onions, green and red bell pepper)

Preheat oven to 350°. Flatten roll dough onto a 15-x 10-inch pan; press out seam lines to make continuous crust. Bake crust 7 minutes; let cool. Combine cream cheese and next 3 ingredients; spread over cooled crust. Sprinkle vegetables over cream cheese mixture; cut into squares, and serve immediately.

Makes about 35 squares.

Chile Verde Empanadas

Cream Cheese Pastry

1   pound unsalted butter, room
    temperature
6   ounces cream cheese, room
    temperature

6   ounces cream cheese with chives,
    room temperature
4   cups all-purpose flour
½   teaspoon salt

Chile Verde Filling

3-4 jalapeño peppers
1   New Mexico green chile, roasted,
    peeled and seeded
2   pounds lean ground pork
5   cloves garlic, minced
1½ large onions, chopped fine

    Salt and freshly ground pepper,
    to taste
1½ large ripe tomatoes, peeled and
    chopped
1   egg
2   tablespoons sugar

In food processor, blend butter and cheeses. Put flour and salt evenly over top and process by pulsing until dough just begins to pull together. Remove and wrap in plastic wrap; refrigerate for several hours before rolling out. Can be frozen for later use.

In heavy skillet, cook pork over medium heat until meat loses red color. Drain off fat. Add peppers, salt and pepper and tomatoes. Cook about 30 minutes over medium heat. Cool to room temperature. In food processor, process mixture until well blended and no large chunks of meat remain.

Roll out ¼ of the pastry to about ⅛-inch thickness. Cut pastry into 3-inch circles with a cookie cutter. Place a generous 2 teaspoons of filling near center of the bottom half of each circle; fold other half over to make half moon shape. Dampen outside edges to seal and crimp edges with a fork. Place on nonstick cookie sheet or one lined with parchment paper.

Preheat oven to 375°.

Beat egg lightly; brush top of each empanada with small amount. Continue with remaining pastry and filling. Bake for 20 to 25 minutes until well browned. As soon as you remove them from oven, sprinkle just a little of the sugar on top. Serve hot or room temperature.

Makes about 100.

These empanadas can be made ahead and frozen unbaked. Brush with egg glaze before baking, not before freezing. They will take a little longer to bake.

Roswell Sweet Pecans

1	egg white, lightly beaten	¼	teaspoon allspice
2	tablespoons cold water	¼	teaspoon ground cinnamon
½	cup sugar	½	teaspoon salt
¼	teaspoon ground cloves	4	cups pecan halves

Preheat oven to 250°. Combine first 7 ingredients in a large bowl, mixing well; let stand 15 minutes. Add pecans to mixture, and stir to coat. Spread evenly on a greased baking sheet; bake 15 minutes, stirring after 5 minutes. Loosen pecans from sheet immediately; store in an airtight container until ready to serve.

Makes about 4 cups.

Pesto Salmon and Olive Torte

36	ounces cream cheese, softened	6	ounces smoked salmon, finely chopped
1	cup unsalted butter, softened		
1	(7-ounce) package pesto or 7 ounces homemade pesto (see index)	1	(4½-ounce) can chopped black olives, drained
			Garnish: fresh basil leaves
			Crackers or French bread slices

Combine 24 ounces cream cheese and butter until blended. Combine 4 ounces cream cheese and pesto in a small bowl. Combine remaining 4 ounces cream cheese and olives in a small bowl. Line a 9- x 5- x 3-inch loaf pan with plastic wrap, overlapping edges of pan. Spread one-fourth butter mixture into bottom of pan; layer with pesto mixture. Drop one-fourth butter mixture over pesto by spoonfuls; spread gently to cover. Sprinkle salmon over butter mixture, followed by olive mixture. Drop and spread remaining butter mixture over olive mixture. Fold plastic wrap over torte to enclose; press firmly to make torte compact. Chill at least 3 hours or up to 3 days. Remove plastic, and invert torte onto a serving platter; garnish, if desired, and serve with crackers or French bread.

Makes 30 servings.

Tumbleweeds

1	pound Italian sausage (hot, mild, or combination), casings removed	1	(8-ounce) can tomato sauce
½	pound fresh mushrooms, thinly sliced	2	teaspoons dried oregano
		2	teaspoons dried basil
¼	pound mozzarella cheese, shredded	2	teaspoons olive oil
1	(2¼-ounce) can sliced ripe olives, drained	1	pound phyllo pastry sheets, thawed overnight in refrigerator
		½	pound unsalted butter, melted

Preheat oven to 375°. Cook sausage in a large skillet over medium heat to render fat, crumbling sausage as you cook. Drain well. Cook mushrooms in a clean skillet over medium-low heat until liquid evaporates; remove from heat. Combine sausage, mushrooms, and next 6 ingredients, adjusting seasonings to taste (mixture will be thick). Cut phyllo sheets crosswise into 4 pieces. Butter 1 phyllo strip; top with a second buttered strip. Place 1 tablespoon filling at 1 end of dough stack, and roll 2 to 3 turns to cover filling. Fold sides of strips in about ½ inch, and continue rolling to end of dough. Repeat procedure with remaining strips and butter. Lightly butter tops of rolls, and place on ungreased baking sheets. Bake for 20 minutes or until golden brown. Serve hot or warm.

Makes 45 to 50 rolls.

Rolls may be frozen in an airtight container before baking. Add 5 to 10 minutes baking time to frozen rolls.

Phyllo Dough

Phyllo is tissue-thin dough used to make a delicate, multi-layered pastry. Frozen dough should be thawed in the refrigerator about 8 hours. Thaw completely, or dough will tear.

For a crispy layered texture, each layer is brushed with butter to ensure layers separate when baking. Olive oil may be used instead of butter in savory recipes. The pastry will not brown as well with oil.

Keep phyllo moist by placing a damp towel over sheets you are not working with. A wide piece of plastic wrap under the towel will keep the dough from getting too wet.

Cover leftover phyllo with plastic wrap, and tightly roll. Seal in the original plastic container, if possible, and chill for up to 2 weeks.

Roasted Garlic-and-Almond Dip

3 garlic bulbs, peeled (about 36 cloves)
¼ cup vegetable oil
2 teaspoons Worcestershire sauce
1½ teaspoons Dijon mustard
1½ cups blanched almonds, toasted and coarsely chopped
1 cup sour cream
1 cup mayonnaise
¼ cup plus 2 tablespoons chopped fresh parsley
2 teaspoons dried rosemary, crumbled
Salt and freshly ground pepper to taste
Crackers, red pepper strips, and snow pea pods

Preheat oven to 300°. Place garlic in a small baking dish, and toss with oil. Bake until garlic is soft and golden, about 30 minutes; transfer to a blender, and add Worcestershire sauce and mustard. Blend until garlic is finely chopped; scrape mixture into a large bowl. Stir in almonds and next 4 ingredients. Season with salt and pepper to taste. Cover and chill at least 2 hours or overnight to meld flavors; let stand at room temperature 1 hour before serving. Serve with crackers, pepper strips, and snow pea pods.

Makes about 4 cups.

Stuffed Jalapeño Peppers

1 (8-ounce) package lite cream cheese or Neufchâtel cheese
2 tablespoons minced fresh parsley or cilantro
4 tablespoons minced onion
¼ teaspoon salt
⅛ teaspoon pepper
2 garlic cloves, minced
17-20 jalapeño peppers, cut lengthwise and seeded
15-20 large corn chips, crushed

Combine first 6 ingredients in a bowl. Fill pepper halves with mixture, and roll in crushed chips. Place in a broiler pan, and broil on middle rack about 15 minutes or until coating turns brown. Serve hot or cold.

Makes 34 to 40 servings.

Savory Pesto Cheesecake

1½ tablespoons butter
¼ cup fine breadcrumbs, lightly toasted
¼ cup grated Parmesan cheese
2½ cups fresh basil leaves
½ cup parsley sprigs, stemmed
¼ cup olive oil
½ teaspoon salt
1 garlic clove, halved

1 pound fresh, whole-milk ricotta cheese, room temperature
2 (8-ounce) packages cream cheese, softened
½ pound Parmesan cheese, grated
4 eggs
⅓ cup pine nuts, lightly toasted
Garnish: fresh basil leaves

Preheat oven to 325°. Butter bottom and sides of a 9-inch springform pan. Combine breadcrumbs and ¼ cup Parmesan; press mixture in pan, and chill. Process basil leaves and next 4 ingredients in a food processor until a smooth paste forms, about 2 minutes, scraping sides of bowl if needed. Transfer basil mixture to a large bowl; process ricotta, cream cheese, and ½ pound Parmesan in processor until smooth, about 2 minutes. Add eggs to ricotta mixture, and stir into basil mixture. Pour into prepared crust; sprinkle with pine nuts. Set pan on a baking sheet; bake 1 hour and 30 minutes. Turn oven off, and cool cheesecake in oven with door ajar. Transfer to a wire rack, and remove pan. Garnish, if desired, and serve at room temperature.

Makes 12 servings.

Skim-milk ricotta may be used instead of whole-milk ricotta.

Savoring the Southwest cookbook received an American Symphony Orchestra League National Conference Award for placing in the top six in the fund-raising category. Guild members spent untold hours developing and testing recipes. Many more hours were spent typing, proofreading, editing, and indexing. More than a cookbook, it reflects not only the rich and colorful heritage and mystique of New Mexico, but also the dedication of those who believe beautiful music should be a part of the cultural legacy of a community. This book is a shining example of some of the Southwest's finest artists and a kaleidoscope of information about Roswell and the Southwest.

*And now here is **Savoring the Southwest Again** for your enjoyment.*

Sun-Dried Tomato-Pine Nut Torta

1	cup unsalted butter, cut up		Ground white pepper to taste
¾	pound feta cheese, crumbled	½	cup toasted pine nuts
1	(8-ounce) package cream cheese, softened	8	ounces sun-dried tomatoes, softened and minced
2-4	garlic cloves, minced	1	cup pesto (see index)
1	shallot, minced		Garnish: fresh basil sprigs
2-4	tablespoons dry vermouth		Crackers

Process first 6 ingredients in a food processor until smooth; stir in pepper. Oil a 4-cup mold, and line with plastic wrap. Beginning with pine nuts, alternate layers of nuts, cheese mixture, tomatoes, and pesto, ending with a layer of cheese mixture. Fold plastic wrap over top, and press to make compact; chill until firm, about 2 hours. Invert onto a serving platter, and remove plastic. Garnish, if desired, and serve with crackers.

Makes about 4 cups.

Susie's Tiny Sandwiches

1	pound lean ground beef	2	tablespoons minced fresh parsley
½	pound hot pork sausage	1	medium onion, grated
1½	pounds processed cheese	4	packages party rye bread
2	teaspoons dried oregano	3	cups shredded mozzarella cheese
½	teaspoon pepper		

Preheat oven to 400°. Brown beef and sausage in a large skillet over medium heat until no longer pink; drain well. Stir in processed cheese, and add oregano, pepper, parsley, and onion; cook until cheese melts. Spread 1 tablespoon mixture on bread slices; top with mozzarella. Place on baking sheets, and bake until cheese is bubbly.

Makes 5 dozen sandwiches.

To make ahead, freeze prepared sandwiches flat on baking sheets; stack sandwiches in freezer containers. Bake as directed.

Carnitas Sabrosa

1 pound boneless pork shoulder
1 clove garlic

¾ teaspoon salt
Freshly ground pepper, to taste

Trim pork of fat and cut into 1-inch cubes. Puree garlic and add salt and pepper, making paste. Rub pork cubes thoroughly with mixture and let stand at room temperature 1 hour.

Preheat oven to 350°. Spread pork cubes on baking sheet and bake 1 hour or until browned and crisp, stirring occasionally and draining off fat as it accumulates. Drain pork on paper towels. Transfer to a heated serving platter and serve hot with cocktail picks, accompanied with Guacamole or a salsa (see index) for dipping.

Makes about 20.

Walnut-Cheese Spread

½ cup chopped walnuts
10 pimiento-stuffed green olives, undrained
1 (8-ounce) package cream cheese, softened

2 teaspoons liquid from olives
4 green onions, chopped (including tops)

Preheat oven to 350°. Spread walnuts in a shallow pan. Bake, uncovered, for 8 to 10 minutes or until lightly browned. Cool slightly. Drain olives, reserving juice. Finely chop olives. Beat cream cheese and reserved olive liquid at medium speed with an electric mixture until fluffy; add walnuts, olives, and green onions. Cover and chill at least 2 hours or up to 2 days. Mound cheese spread on a platter or in a bowl, and surround it with toasted pita halves or unsalted crackers.

Makes 1½ cups.

Valley-of-Fire Pecans

2 cups large pecan halves
¼ cup butter, melted

1½ tablespoons hot red chile powder (or to taste)
1½ teaspoons salt

Preheat oven to 375°. Toss pecans with butter, and place in a single layer in a large cast-iron skillet. Place skillet in oven for about 10 minutes or until pecans begin to toast and release a nutty fragrance. Remove from oven, and allow to cool 5 minutes so chile does not burn when added to pecans. Combine chile powder and salt, and sprinkle over warm pecans.

Makes 2 cups.

These are best if made with butter. However, peanut oil may be substituted (increase oven temperature to 400°). Do not use margarine, because it will burn.

Margaritas For A Crowd

1 fifth tequila
½ pint Triple Sec
1¾ quarts water
4 (6-ounce) cans frozen limeade concentrate

4 ounces fresh lime juice
¼ cup lemon juice
Coarse salt for dipping

The day before serving, combine first 5 ingredients, and chill. Six hours before serving, stir well, and freeze; return to refrigerator until ready to serve. Before pouring, dip rims of margarita glasses in lemon juice, then salt.

Makes 28 (4-ounce) servings.

Margarita-Flavored Punch

1   cup orange juice
¾   cup unsweetened grapefruit juice
1   (6-ounce) can frozen limeade
      concentrate, thawed

2   cups sparkling water or
      lemon-lime soft drink
      Ice cubes
      Orange, lemon, or lime slices
      (optional)

Combine first 3 ingredients in a large pitcher. Just before serving, stir in sparkling water, ice, and, if desired, fruit slices.

Makes 6 servings.

Margaritas

½   cup fresh lime juice, shells
      reserved
      Coarse salt for dipping

1   cup crushed ice

½   cup Cointreau or Triple Sec
1   cup good quality white tequila

Rubs rims of margarita glasses with lime shells; dip rims into salt, and set aside. Process lime juice, Cointreau, tequila, and ice in a blender until well blended; pour into prepared glasses.

There are almost as many recipes for margaritas as there are people who enjoy them. They may be made with or without salt on the rim; on the rocks; blended with crushed ice; shaken with ice and strained; with Triple Sec, Cointreau, or Grand Marnier; pureed with fruit, such as strawberries or peaches. However, the two most important ingredients are fresh (not frozen) lime juice and a good tequila. Tequila comes from the Mexican agave plant and is said to contain vitamins (if one needs a rationale).

Museum Punch

1 large can frozen lemonade
4 cups white grape juice
Ice cubes

1 (3-liter) bottle lemon-lime soft
drink
Garnish: fresh fruit

Combine lemonade and grape juice in a punch bowl or large pitcher. Fill bowl with ice, and add soft drink; garnish, if desired.

Makes 25 servings.

You can add other juices, such as apricot, for color.

This punch was "composed" because the Roswell Symphony Orchestra Guild was admonished not to bring red punch that might, if spilled, stain the Roswell Museum and Art Center's carpets and floors.

Orange Sangría

1 medium-size orange
¼ cup sugar
2 cups fresh orange juice

1 bottle dry red wine
½ cup Cointreau
Garnish: orange slices

Cut orange in half; cut 1 to 2 thin slices from 1 half for garnish. Using a vegetable peeler or zester, remove outer zest from orange, and place in a bowl. Add sugar to zest, and bruise with back of a spoon. Stir in orange juice, wine, and Cointreau; cover and chill, removing zest after 15 minutes. Serve over ice, and garnish, if desired.

Makes 4 to 6 servings.

Sangría

3½ cups chilled dry red wine
½ cup chilled fresh lemon juice
½ cup chilled orange juice
½ cup sugar

¼ cup brandy
1¼ cups chilled sparkling water
1 lemon, thinly sliced
1 orange, thinly sliced

Combine first 5 ingredients in a large pitcher; chill until ready to serve. Just before serving, add sparkling water and fruit. Pour over ice in tall glasses.

Makes 6 servings.

Strawberry Rum Slush

1 (6-ounce) can frozen limeade
   concentrate, thawed
6 ounces rum
1 pint hulled fresh strawberries

1-2 tablespoons sugar (optional)
14 ice cubes
Garnish: lime slices

Process half each of first 4 ingredients in a blender, adding half of ice cubes at a time, until smooth and very thick. Pour mixture into a large pitcher; repeat with remaining half of ingredients, and stir into pitcher. Garnish, if desired.

Makes 7 cups.

The official symphony season begins with a Labor Day Concert held at the Spring River Park and Zoo. This concert, a gift to the community, features the full orchestra and delights and entertains a crowd of all ages. In keeping with the holiday, the orchestra, conducted by Maestro John Farrer, preforms patriotic tunes and traditional favorites while families sit on blankets and picnic. This is a fun day for all that participate—as well as the animal residents at the zoo.

Paul's Golden Punch

1 pint fresh or frozen orange juice	2 cups sugar
2 (46-ounce) cans pineapple juice	6 (12-ounce) cans Sprite
2 (46-ounce) cans apricot juice	Ice cubes

Combine all ingredients in a punch bowl.

Makes 50 servings.

Paul Rodriguez, manager of the New Mexico Military Institute dining room, created this punch. It is served at all N.M.M.I. social events.

Tequila Sunrise

1½ cups tequila	¾ cup club soda
Crushed ice	3 tablespoons grenadine
1½ cups orange juice	Garnish: 6 orange slices

Pour ¼ cup tequila into each of 6 tall glasses. Fill glasses three-fourths full with crushed ice. Pour ¼ cup orange juice and 2 tablespoons club soda over ice in each glass; stir. Spoon ½ tablespoon grenadine into each glass. (Do not stir.) Garnish each glass, if desired; serve immediately.

Makes 6 servings.

_____Southwestern Sunset_____

4½ cups orange juice
1   cup tequila

1   cup prickly pear puree (about 6 prickly pears, peeled, pureed, and strained)
½   cup Triple Sec or Grand Marnier

Combine orange juice and tequila; divide among 6 glasses filled with ice. Combine pear puree and Triple Sec; gently pour 2 tablespoons mixture into each glass. (Do not stir.) Serve immediately.

Makes 6 servings.

The sunsets in New Mexico are absolutely spectacular! The almost ostentatious colors that paint the sky in the evenings are truly one of the joys of living in the Southwest. The Southwestern Sunset cocktail, with its brilliant red and orange combination, resembles these magnificent displays.

_____White Sangría_____

3½ cups chilled dry white wine
½   cup Cointreau, Triple Sec, or Grand Marnier
¼   cup brandy

¼   cup sugar
1¼ cups chilled sparkling water
1   lemon, thinly sliced
2   limes, thinly sliced

Combine first 4 ingredients in a glass pitcher; chill until ready to serve. Just before serving, stir in sparkling water and fruit. Pour over ice in tall glasses, or serve in cocktail glasses without ice.

Makes 6 servings.

This a very cooling drink on a hot evening. White Sangría goes well with spicy Southwestern food.

Breads

The Roswell Symphony Orchestra:
A Unique Organization

In the fall of 1959, a group of musicians in this small city in southeastern New Mexico gathered in a local church to organize a community orchestra to accompany a combined choral performance of Handel's *Messiah*. Their collaboration was the forerunner of the Roswell Symphony Orchestra, a prestigious professional ensemble often favorably compared with some of its counterparts in the country's largest cities.

The arrival of conductor and music director John Farrer in 1972 brought a force to develop the Roswell Symphony Orchestra into a 60-piece ensemble of first-class musicians. Music director of the Bakersfield, California, Symphony Orchestra and cover conductor of the San Francisco Orchestra, Farrer oversaw the expansion of Roswell's orchestra and its season. His reputation attracts the best musicians from Roswell itself and from orchestras and universities in New Mexico, Texas, and Colorado. His musical leadership draws the attention of music lovers throughout the cities and plains of New Mexico and West Texas.

John Farrer, senior guest conductor of the English Sinfonia, holds guest conducting posts with the London Philharmonic and the Royal Philharmonic Orchestras; on more than one occasion he has commuted from California to Europe and back to Roswell. In October of 1997, Maestro Farrer was honored by the entire community with a gala concert and celebration marking his 25th anniversary of the Roswell Symphony.

The Roswell Symphony Orchestra now offers a popular annual Subscription Concert Series of five classical concerts (many featuring world-renowned guest artists), a three-concert Chamber Music Series, a free Labor Day Pops Concert, and a traditional Children's Educational Concert. And while many professional orchestras in the country struggle for financial survival, the Roswell Symphony Orchestra has maintained itself debt-free since its inception in 1959.

RSO's remarkable debt-free status is a tribute to the strong community support it has enjoyed over the years. The RSO Sustaining Fund receives annual contributions from more than 300 individual contributors and a number of Roswell businesses.

The lifeblood of our symphony is truly the mammoth effort by people behind the scenes who genuinely care not only about music, but about maintaining this important community institution. Members of the Roswell Symphony Orchestra Board, together with the RSO Guild are constantly engaged in supporting activities for the orchestra.

RSO Guild Publications oversees one of the organization's most successful and challenging projects: the gathering of culinary information, art, and local lore in the popular cookbooks *Savoring the Southwest* and its sequel *Savoring the Southwest Again*. Not only an important source of funding for the orchestra, the cookbooks also highlight the cultural diversity of the region and provide reliable, tested recipes.

Roswell long ago made the statement that it wants to hear fine music performed by a full orchestra. RSO's unqualified success is due not only to Maestro Farrer and the large number of visiting and local musicians, but also to the support from that community—something that cannot be overemphasized at a time when many metropolitan orchestras cannot meet payrolls or fill seats. Board and Guild members, staff, volunteers and contributors continue to combine energy and commitment to assure that Roswell's prestigious orchestra is sustained not only by its music, but especially by its vital community support.

Shirly Ann Munroe
President, Roswell Symphony Orchestra Board of Directors

Featured on page 33 "Musicians-Roswell Symphony Orchestra"

Almond Puff

½ cup butter, softened	1 teaspoon almond extract
1 cup all-purpose flour	1 cup all-purpose flour
2 tablespoons water	3 eggs
½ cup butter	Powdered Sugar Glaze
1 cup water	Chopped nuts

Preheat oven to 350°. Cut ½ cup butter into 1 cup flour in a large bowl; sprinkle 2 tablespoons water over mixture, and blend with a fork. Shape dough into a ball, and divide in half. Pat each dough portion into a 12- x 3-inch strip on an ungreased baking sheet, keeping strips a few inches apart. Bring ½ cup butter and 1 cup water to a boil in a medium-size saucepan. Remove butter mixture from heat, and quickly stir in almond extract and 1 cup flour. Stir vigorously over low heat until mixture forms a ball, about 1 minute. Remove from heat. Beat eggs into butter mixture all at once until smooth. Divide mixture in half over dough strips, covering completely. Bake for about 1 hour or until topping is crisp and brown. Cool puffs, and frost with glaze; sprinkle generously with nuts.

Powdered Sugar Glaze

½ cup powdered sugar	1½ teaspoons almond or vanilla extract
2 tablespoons butter, softened	1-2 tablespoons warm water

Combine all ingredients, stirring until smooth.

Makes 6 to 8 servings.

New Mexico Spoonbread

1 (16-ounce) can cream-style corn	½ teaspoon salt
¾ cup evaporated skimmed milk	1 teaspoon brown sugar
⅓ cup melted butter	½ cup chopped New Mexico green chiles
2 eggs, lightly beaten	1½ cups shredded low-fat Cheddar cheese
1½ cups cornmeal	
½ teaspoon baking soda	
1 teaspoon baking powder	

Preheat oven to 400°. Combine first 3 ingredients; stir in eggs. Combine cornmeal and next 4 ingredients; fold into corn mixture. Pour half of batter into a greased 9-inch square pan; sprinkle with half of chiles and half of cheese. Top cheese with remaining batter; top with remaining chiles and cheese. Bake for 45 minutes.

Makes 6 to 8 servings.

Coconut-Macadamia Banana Bread

2¼ cups all-purpose flour
¾ teaspoon baking powder
½ teaspoon baking soda
1 teaspoon salt
¾ cup unsalted butter, softened
1 cup firmly packed light brown
   sugar
½ cup sugar
1½ teaspoons vanilla extract

3 large eggs
1 tablespoon freshly grated lemon
   zest
1⅓ cups mashed ripe bananas,
   (about 3 large)
3 tablespoons sour cream
¾ cup chopped macadamia nuts
1 cup lightly toasted sweetened
   flaked coconut, cooled

Preheat oven to 350°. Sift together first 4 ingredients into a bowl. Cream butter and sugars in a large bowl at high speed with an electric mixer; beat in vanilla, eggs (1 at a time), lemon zest, bananas, and sour cream. Add flour mixture to butter mixture, and beat until combined. Stir in macadamias and coconut. Divide batter among 5 (5¾- x 3¼- x 2-inch) buttered and floured loaf pans. Bake on middle rack of oven for 35 to 40 minutes or until a wooden pick inserted in center comes out clean. Remove from pans, and cool, right sides up, on a wire rack. Keep bread wrapped tightly in plastic wrap and foil in refrigerator up to 1 week, or freeze up to 1 month.

Makes 5 small loaves.

Southwest Banana Bread

1⅔ cups whole-wheat flour
1 teaspoon baking soda
½ teaspoon salt
½ cup margarine, softened
¾ cup sugar
2 eggs
1 teaspoon vanilla extract

1 cup mashed ripe bananas
½ cup crushed pineapple
3 green chiles, stemmed, seeded, and
   chopped
¼ cup low-fat milk
1 tablespoon lemon juice
½ cup chopped walnuts

Preheat oven to 350°. Combine first 3 ingredients in a small bowl. Beat margarine, sugar, eggs, and vanilla in a large bowl at medium speed with an electric mixer until fluffy; slowly add flour mixture, beating until blended. Add bananas, pineapple, chile, and milk to batter. Add lemon juice and walnuts; beat 30 seconds longer. Pour batter into a greased loaf pan, and bake for 1 hour.

Makes 1 loaf.

All-Purpose Crêpes

1 cup all-purpose flour	3 large eggs
⅔ cup milk	¼ teaspoon salt
⅔ cup cold water	6 tablespoons clear melted butter

Place flour into a bowl; whisk in milk and water by dribbles to make a perfectly smooth mixture. Pour batter through a fine wire-mesh strainer to remove lumps. Whisk in eggs, salt, and 3 tablespoons melted butter. Let batter rest at least 1 hour in refrigerator. Heat a crêpe pan until drops of water dance on it; brush pan lightly with melted butter. Pour ¼ cup crêpe batter into center of hot pan, and tilt in all directions. Batter should cover pan in a light coating. Pour out any excess batter from pan. Cook until crêpe is lightly browned, about 30 seconds. Turn crêpe with fingers or a spatula, and cook 15 to 20 seconds or until bottom is spotted brown. Transfer crêpes to a rack as done to cool. When cooled completely, stack crêpes (they won't stick). Place into a plastic bag, and store in refrigerator, if desired, up to 2 days, or freeze several weeks.

Makes 20 (5½-inch) crêpes or 8 to 10 (8-inch) crêpes.

Dessert Crêpes

½ cup all-purpose flour	1 tablespoon kirsch, orange liqueur,
1 large egg, plus 1 egg yolk	bourbon, or rum
¼ cup milk	1 tablespoon sugar
¼ cup water	⅛ teaspoon salt
1½ tablespoons melted butter	

Combine all ingredients; let stand in refrigerator 1 hour, and cook as directed for All-Purpose Crêpes.

Makes 8 to 10 (5½-inch) crêpes or 4 to 5 (8-inch) crêpes.

 The recently established "Partners in Education" with fifteen Roswell elementary schools evidence music education as a primary goal of the Guild and the Board of Directors. Symphony Guild members, interested parents, and other local volunteers visit the classrooms and provide teachers and students with outreach music appreciation and "Childrens Concerts" information. They use music education packets, recordings, and musical instruments along with the established curriculum to provide an arts-integrated approach to learning music.

Scones

4	cups all-purpose flour	½	cup currants
2	tablespoons sugar	2	egg yolks
1	tablespoon baking powder	1⅓	cups plus 1 tablespoon half-and-
2	teaspoons baking soda		half
1	teaspoon salt		Jam for serving
½	cup cold butter, cut up		

Preheat oven to 400°. Combine first 5 ingredients in a large bowl; cut in butter with a pastry blender. Stir currants into flour mixture. Combine egg yolks and 1⅓ cups half-and-half in a small bowl; stir into flour mixture. Toss dough with fork, and knead 8 to 10 times. Roll out to ¾-inch thickness; cut into 2-inch rounds, and brush with 1 tablespoon half-and-half. Place scones on greased baking sheets, and bake for 15 minutes. Serve with jam and clotted cream.

Makes 2½ dozen.

Mock Clotted Cream

1	cup whipping cream	¼	cup sour cream

Combine ingredients, and serve on scones.

Spiced Masa Muffins

1	cup all-purpose flour	½	teaspoon baking soda
½	cup masa harina or finely ground yellow cornmeal	½	teaspoon salt
		¼	cup sugar
2	teaspoons baking powder	2	large eggs, lightly beaten
1	teaspoon crushed red pepper flakes	¾	cup sour cream
		½	cup vegetable oil

Preheat oven to 375°. Prepare 8 muffin pans by lining with paper cups or coating lightly with cooking spray. Combine first 7 ingredients; add eggs, sour cream, and oil. Stir just enough to blend. Divide batter evenly among 8 muffin pans; bake for 25 minutes or until golden. Cool muffins in pans 5 minutes; transfer to a wire rack. Serve warm.

Makes 8 muffins

Jalapeño Scones

1½ cups cake flour
½ cup cornmeal
1½ cups shredded Cheddar cheese
1½ teaspoons baking powder
½ teaspoon baking soda
½ teaspoon salt

2 jalapeños, seeded and minced
¼ teaspoon dried red pepper flakes
¼ cup unsalted butter, chilled and cut into ½-inch pieces
½ cup whipping cream (more as needed)

Preheat oven to 350°. Combine flour, cornmeal, 1 cup cheese, baking powder, baking soda, salt, chiles, and red pepper in a large bowl; blend thoroughly. Cut butter into flour mixture with a pastry blender until mixture resembles coarse meal. Sprinkle cream over surface of flour mixture, and blend in until a soft dough forms, adding cream, if needed. Pat dough into a circle on a lightly oiled surface; roll out to ½-inch thickness. Cut into 2-inch rounds, and transfer to a buttered baking sheet. Sprinkle remaining cheese over scones. Bake for 20 to 25 minutes or until firm and golden brown. Cool on a rack wire.

Makes 24 scones.

Serve with Avocado Butter (see index) or jalapeño jelly. These are best served the day they are made. For appetizers, cut in half, and fill with chicken salad or sliced smoked turkey breast. They're also a good base for poached eggs in a Southwestern version of Eggs Benedict.

Zucchini-Basil Muffins

2 eggs, room temperature
¾ cup milk
⅔ cup vegetable oil
2½ cups all-purpose flour
¼ cup sugar

1 tablespoon baking powder
2 teaspoons salt
2 cups shredded zucchini
2 tablespoons minced fresh basil
½ cup grated Parmesan cheese

Preheat oven to 425°. Butter 22 to 24 muffin tins. Beat eggs in a large bowl; whisk in milk and oil. Combine flour and next 3 ingredients; add to egg mixture, 1 cup at a time, stirring until thick and moist. Do not over mix. A few lumps are no problem. Gently stir in zucchini and basil just until combined. Divide batter evenly among muffin pans, filling each half full. Sprinkle Parmesan evenly over batter. Bake for 20 to 25 minutes or until muffins are golden brown and cheese is melted. Turn muffins out, and tap crust to be certain it is hard, not soft.

Makes 22 to 24 muffins.

Pumpkin Muffins

1½ cups whole-wheat pastry flour
1½ cups all-purpose flour
2   teaspoons baking powder
1   teaspoon baking soda
1   teaspoon ground cinnamon
¾   teaspoon salt
⅔   cup sugar

⅓   cup vegetable oil
⅓   cup pure maple syrup
¾   cup skim milk
2   egg whites
1   (29-ounce) can pumpkin (3½ cups)
⅓   cup dried fruit, such as raisins, Bing cherries, or pitted dates

Preheat oven to 375°. Line 18 muffin cups with paper baking cups, or spray with vegetable cooking spray. Combine first 7 ingredients in a large bowl, stirring to blend. Combine oil and next 3 ingredients in a separate bowl. Stir pumpkin into flour mixture; gradually pour in milk mixture, beating with a flexible spatula or at low speed with an electric mixer. Beat just until pumpkin is incorporated and there are no streaks of flour showing. Stir dried fruit into batter. Pour ⅓ to ½ cup batter into each muffin cup. Fill any remaining cups with water to prevent scorching. Bake for 25 to 30 minutes or until muffins are puffed and firm. Cool 15 minutes in pans, and transfer to wire racks to cool completely. Wrap muffins individually, and store in refrigerator 1 week, or freeze up to 2 months.

Makes 18 muffins.

Spicy Vegetable Cornbread

2   cups yellow cornmeal
1   cup all-purpose flour
1½ tablespoons baking powder
1½ teaspoons salt
2   tablespoons dark brown sugar
3   large eggs
1⅓ cups milk
½   cup unsalted butter, melted

1   cup canned or frozen sweet corn kernels, thawed and drained
1   cup shredded Colby cheese
½   cup finely chopped carrot
½   cup grated onion
¼   cup seeded, finely chopped jalapeño

Preheat oven to 400°. Grease a 10-inch cast-iron skillet or muffin pan. Combine first 5 ingredients in a large bowl. Whisk eggs, milk, and melted butter in a medium-size bowl; stir into dry ingredients. Add corn, cheese, carrot, onion, and jalapeño; stir until thoroughly blended. Pour batter into skillet, and bake for 30 to 35 minutes or until a wooden pick inserted in center comes out clean. Cut into wedges.

Makes 8 servings.

Can be made in muffin pans; makes 12 muffins.

Sun-Dried Tomato-and-Olive Bread

3 cups all-purpose flour
2 teaspoons baking powder
1 teaspoon baking soda
1 teaspoon salt
2 tablespoons sugar
2 garlic cloves, minced
1 teaspoon crumbled dried rosemary
1 teaspoon freshly ground pepper
½ cup sun-dried tomatoes packed in oil, drained and chopped, oil reserved

2 large eggs
1½ cups milk
3 tablespoons melted vegetable shortening, cooled
½ cup chopped kalamata olives
2 tablespoons capers, drained and minced
½ cup minced fresh flat-leaf parsley
1 cup freshly grated Parmesan cheese

Preheat oven to 350°. Sift together first 5 ingredients into a large bowl. Heat 2 tablespoons reserved oil from tomatoes in a small skillet; add garlic, rosemary, and pepper, and sauté over medium-low heat until softened but not browned. Whisk together eggs, milk, shortening, and garlic mixture; add flour mixture, and stir just until combined. Add tomatoes, olives, capers, parsley, and cheese to skillet. Divide batter evenly among 4 (5¾- x 3¼- x 2-inch) buttered, floured loaf pans. Bake on middle oven rack for 35 to 40 minutes or until a wooden pick inserted in center comes out clean. Remove bread from pans, and cool, right side up, on wire racks. Bread keeps well wrapped in plastic up to 1 week or frozen up to 1 month.

Makes 4 small loaves

Sweet Potato-Cayenne Dinner Rolls

4¾ cups bread flour
1 tablespoon sugar
1 tablespoon salt
1 teaspoon cayenne pepper
2 envelopes active dry yeast

2 cups water
2 tablespoons vegetable shortening
¾ cup cooked, mashed sweet potatoes
1 egg, lightly beaten with 1 teaspoon water

Preheat oven to 375°. Grease 2 (8-inch) round cake pans. Combine 3½ cups flour, sugar, and next 3 ingredients, blending well. Heat water and shortening in a saucepan until mixture reaches 120° to 130°. Add warm liquid to flour mixture. Stir or use electric mixer to blend in potatoes. Add remaining flour, ½ cup at a time, until dough is smooth and elastic. (Not all flour may be needed.) Divide dough into 16 pieces; shape each piece into a ball, and place 8 balls into each cake pan. Cover loosely with a kitchen towel, and let rise in a warm, draft-free place until doubled in bulk. Brush rolls with egg wash, and bake for 20 to 30 minutes or until golden brown.

Makes 16 rolls.

Basic Yeast Dough

2 cups milk	2 teaspoons salt
1 cup vegetable shortening	1 tablespoon active dry yeast
2 eggs	⅔ cup warm water (115°)
¼ cup sugar	6 cups all-purpose flour

Heat milk in a saucepan to 120°; whisk in shortening and eggs, and cool. Dissolve yeast in ⅔ cup water in a large mixing bowl; stir in sugar. Add milk mixture to yeast mixture, and beat with an electric mixer until blended. Beat in 4 cups flour and salt until blended. Beat in remaining 2 cups flour. Allow dough to rest, covered, 20 minutes. Turn dough out onto a floured surface, and knead 5 minutes.

Dinner Rolls
Preheat oven to 400°. Pat or roll dough to desired thickness; cut with a round cutter. Place on buttered baking sheets, and allow to rise 20 to 30 minutes. Bake for 15 minutes or until lightly browned.

Makes about 48 rolls.

Cinnamon Rolls
Preheat oven to 400°. Divide dough into 4 equal portions. On a floured surface roll 1 portion of dough into a 15- x 10-inch rectangle; repeat with remaining 3 portions. Brush dough with melted butter; sprinkle with cinnamon and sugar (1 part cinnamon, 3 parts sugar). Roll each portion of dough jelly roll style, starting with a long side. Cut rolls into 1-inch slices, and place in a buttered pan with sides touching. Let rolls rise 10 to 15 minutes. Bake for 20 minutes or until lightly brown. Drizzle with Icing.

Makes about 60 rolls.

Icing

3 cups powdered sugar	½ teaspoon almond extract
1 teaspoon vanilla extract	⅓-½ cup milk

Combine all ingredients, whisking until smooth.

Basic Yeast Dough can be used to make pizza crust, doughnuts, or coffee cake. For pizza crust, shape and bake for 20 to 25 minutes (makes 3 to 4 crusts). For doughnuts, deep-fry until golden brown (makes 3 to 4 dozen). For coffee cake, bake 15 to 20 minutes (makes 2 cakes).

Cheddar-Corn Rolls

4½ cups unbleached all-purpose flour
¾ cup cornmeal
3 tablespoons sugar
1 envelope active dry yeast
2 teaspoons salt
1¼ cups buttermilk

3 tablespoons unsalted butter or corn oil
2 tablespoons Dijon mustard
2 eggs, room temperature
1 cup shredded extra-sharp Cheddar cheese

Preheat oven to 375°. Combine 1 cup flour and next 4 ingredients in mixing bowl of a heavy-duty electric mixer (dough can also be mixed by hand). Heat buttermilk, butter, and mustard in a medium-size saucepan to 120° (mixture may appear curdled). Add buttermilk mixture to flour mixture; beat with a dough hook until smooth and creamy. Add eggs and 1 cup flour, and beat until well combined. Beat in cheese, and add enough flour, ½ cup at a time, to form a soft dough that pulls away from sides of bowl. Knead dough on a lightly floured surface until smooth and elastic but slightly sticky, adding flour, if needed, about 10 minutes. Grease a large bowl, and add dough, turning to coat entire surface. Cover loosely with plastic wrap. Let dough rise in a warm, draft-free place until doubled in bulk, about 1 hour and 15 minutes. Line a large baking sheet with parchment paper. Gently punch dough down. Knead on lightly floured surface until smooth. Divide dough into 18 portions, and shape each into a smooth ball. Place on baking sheets, spacing 1 inch apart and pressing to flatten. Slash an "X" in center of each roll. Cover loosely with plastic wrap, and let rise in a warm, draft-free place until almost doubled in bulk, about 45 minutes. Bake rolls about 18 minutes or until golden brown. Cool slightly on a rack before serving.

Makes 18 rolls.

 At least one Children's Concert is presented by the orchestra each year. The education chairs of the Roswell Symphony Orchestra Board and the Symphony Guild create "Music Education Packets" about each performance and distribute them to the public schools for use by teachers prior to the concerts. The students, usually from the fourth grades, are bussed to the auditorium and are treated to a classical concert. For many students, it is their first exposure to classical music.

Herbed Whole-Wheat Bread

1 envelope active dry yeast	1½ teaspoons dried Italian herbs
1 teaspoon sugar	1 teaspoon salt
¼ cup warm water (115°)	2 tablespoons olive oil
2½ cups unbleached all-purpose flour	¾ cup cold water
¾ cup whole-wheat flour	

Preheat oven to 375°. Dissolve yeast in warm water. Pulse 2¼ cups unbleached flour, whole-wheat flour, herbs, and salt in a food processor until blended. Add yeast mixture and oil; turn on processor, and pour cold water through food chute in a slow, steady stream as flour absorbs it. When dough forms a ball, stop machine, and check consistency. Dough should be soft but not sticky. Process in remaining flour, 2 table-spoons at time, until blended. Process 45 seconds to knead. With lightly floured hands, remove dough, and shape into a ball. Place in a lightly floured plastic bag. Squeeze out air, and close with twist tie, allowing room for dough to rise. Let rise in a warm, draft-free place 1 to 1½ hours. Punch dough down in bag. Shape into a loaf, and place in a greased loaf pan. Cover with oiled plastic wrap, and let rise 1 hour. Bake on middle rack of oven for 35 to 40 minutes. Makes great sandwiches or hamburger buns.

Makes 1 loaf.

Super-Easy Dinner Rolls

3 eggs	1¼ cups warm water (115°)
½ cup sugar	1¼ cups unsifted whole-wheat flour
½ cup vegetable oil	2½ cups unsifted all-purpose flour
1½ teaspoons salt	3-4 cups unsifted all-purpose flour
2 envelopes active dry yeast	

Preheat oven to 375°. Beat first 8 ingredients at medium speed with an electric mixer 2 minutes. Change mixer to dough hook, or mix by hand. Add 3 to 4 cups all-purpose flour. Beat well. Dough should be stiff, not hard. Remove dough hook; leave dough in same bowl. Grease top of dough, and cover bowl with plastic wrap. Let rise in a warm, draft-free place until doubled in bulk, about 1 hour. Grease a 13- x 9- x 2-inch pan. Pinch off plum-size balls of dough (about 24); roll in hands until smooth. Place in pan. Let rise another hour or until rolls reach top of pan. Do not jiggle pan, or rolls with flatten. Bake for 14 minutes or until browned on top. Cool in pan on a wire rack. Brush tops of rolls with melted butter while hot. Cool completely in pan.

Makes 24 rolls.

Roadrunner

Beans, Grains, & Rice

The Roadrunner

The roadrunner, also known as the Chaparral Bird, is the state bird of New Mexico. A familiar and amusing bird of the deserts, it lives among the sands and cacti of the southwestern U.S. and Mexico. The name comes from its habit of dashing along desert roads at a speed that automobiles have clocked at 15 mph. The roadrunner flies very little, preferring to travel by running and taking fast, gliding jumps.

The bird presents a comical appearance as it sprints along with neck and head stretched forward, crest raised, short wings outspread, and long tail jerking up and down. When the roadrunner tires, it abruptly turns aside into the brush and brakes to a sudden stop by throwing its tail over its back.

The roadrunner is about two feet long, including the foot-long tail. Snakes are an important food, and many tales are told in the Southwest about this bird's battles with rattlesnakes.

Featured on page 45 "Roadrunner"

_____Baked Polenta with Onions and Bacon_____

2 cups chicken broth
1 cup water
½ teaspoon dried sage, crumbled
1 cup cornmeal

2 tablespoons unsalted butter, cut into bits
½ cup freshly grated Parmesan
3 bacon slices, chopped
2 onions, thinly sliced

Preheat oven to 400°. In a heavy saucepan bring broth, water, and sage to a bare simmer. Whisk in cornmeal gradually, whisking vigorously for 5 minutes. Whisk in butter, ¼ cup Parmesan, and salt and pepper to taste. Divide polenta mixture between 4 buttered 1½-cup gratin dishes, or spread in a buttered 6-cup baking dish. Bake in middle of oven for 25 minutes. Cook bacon over medium heat until crisp. Transfer bacon to paper towels to drain, and pour off all but 2 tablespoons drippings. Cook onion in skillet over medium-low heat, stirring occasionally, until softened but not browned. Stir in bacon. Top polenta with onion mixture, spreading onion mixture evenly; sprinkle with remaining ¼ cup Parmesan, bake for 5 minutes or until Parmesan is melted.

Makes 4 servings.

_____Baked Rice with Pine Nuts_____

2½ tablespoons butter
2 tablespoons minced onion
¼ teaspoon minced garlic
1 cup uncooked rice
1½ cups chicken broth
2 sprigs parsley

1 sprig fresh thyme or ¼ teaspoon dried thyme
½ bay leaf
⅛ teaspoon cayenne pepper or ⅛ teaspoon Tabasco
¼ cup toasted pine nuts

Preheat oven to 400°. Melt 1 tablespoon butter in a heavy, ovenproof saucepan; add onion and garlic, and sauté until onion is soft. Add rice, stirring over low heat until all grains are coated with butter. Stir in chicken broth, stirring until smooth. Add parsley, thyme, bay leaf, and cayenne. Cover with a close-fitting lid, bake rice exactly 17 minutes. Remove cover, and discard parsley, bay leaf, and thyme sprig. Using two-pronged fork, stir in remaining butter and pine nuts.

Makes 4 servings.

To Toast Pine Nuts
Heat oven to 350°. Spread a single layer of nuts on a baking sheet, and toast until golden and fragrant, about 3 to 5 minutes. Check often for pine nuts burn easily.

Bill Wiggins

Bill was born in Roswell on September 24, 1917, to M.B. and Mona Wiggins, pioneer ranchers in this area. He attended Roswell schools, including New Mexico Military Institute, and also Abilene Christian College, Abilene, Texas, and American Shrivenham University in Shrivenham, England, where he studied under Frances Speight, a professor of art from the Pennsylvania Academy of Fine Arts. Following his army service during World War II Bill worked on his father's ranch while he continued to paint, and for a period of ten years taught art at the Roswell Museum and Art Center.

Bill's work has been exhibited locally, nationally and internationally, including a joint show with his brother, Walt, a photojournalist, at the Territorial Gallery in Roswell in 1975, and one with his nephew, K. Douglas Wiggins at the Cline Gallery of Fine Arts in Santa Fe in 1994. *Wiggins - A Thirty Year Retrospective* was published in 1982 by Walt Wiggins Pintores Press, and *A Fifty-Five Year Retrospective* of his works from 1940 to 1995 was on exhibition at the Roswell Museum and Art Center March through May, 1995.

Stripes #9
Artist – Bill Wiggins
21³/₄″ × 29⁵/₈″   1993
oil on canvas
Permanent collection, Roswell Museum
and Art Center. Photograph by Jose
Rivera.

Brown Rice-and-Pine Nut Casserole

½	cup pine nuts	1	tablespoon finely minced fresh chives or scallions
¼	cup butter		
1	cup brown rice, rinsed and drained	¼	teaspoon salt
½	cup bulgur (cracked wheat)	¼	teaspoon pepper
1	large onion, chopped	3	(14-ounce) cans beef or chicken broth
1	cup minced fresh parsley		

Preheat oven to 375°. Sauté pine nuts in a medium-size skillet with 2 tablespoons butter over medium heat until browned, about 5 minutes. Remove from skillet. Melt remaining butter in skillet. Add rice, bulgur, and onion; brown, stirring often, 10 minutes. Spoon mixture into a 2-quart baking dish. Add ¾ cup parsley, chives, salt, and pepper. Bring broth to a boil in a saucepan, and stir into rice mixture. Bake, uncovered, for I hour and 15 minutes. Garnish with remaining parsley.

Makes 8 servings.

Corn-Chile Rice

1	tablespoon olive oil		Freshly ground pepper to taste
1	cup chopped red bell pepper	1	cup fresh or frozen corn kernels
1	cup chopped onion	2-3	jalapeño peppers, seeded and chopped, or 1 (4.5-ounce) can diced green chiles
2	cups long-grain rice		
2	cups water		
1¾	cups chicken broth	½	cup light sour cream
1	teaspoon ground cumin	1½	cups shredded Monterey Jack cheese
½	teaspoon salt		

Preheat oven to 350°. Heat oil in a large saucepan over medium heat; add bell pepper and onion, and sauté until soft, about 5 minutes. Add rice, and stir to coat. Stir in water, broth, cumin, salt, and pepper; bring to boil, then reduce heat, and cook, covered, until liquid is absorbed, about 25 minutes. Remove lid, and cool slightly. Stir in corn, chiles, and sour cream. Put rice mixture into a lightly oiled 4-quart baking dish; top with cheese. Bake uncovered, until heated through and cheese is melted, about 20 minutes.

Makes 10 to 12 servings.

If made ahead, bring to room temperature before baking.

Black Bean Torta

3 cups cooked black beans
¼ cup chicken stock
1 tablespoon corn oil
2 cups finely chopped purple onion
2 red bell peppers cored, seeded, and julienned
2 zucchini, halved and thinly sliced
2 garlic cloves, minced
1 cup corn kernels
1 teaspoon cumin seed, ground to a powder, or ¾ teaspoon ground cumin
¼ teaspoon cayenne pepper
Salt to taste
6 (8-inch) flour tortillas
2 cups Salsa Fresca
2 cups shredded asadero or Monterey Jack cheese

Preheat oven to 375°. Puree beans and chicken stock in a food processor. Set aside. In a large skillet, heat corn oil over medium heat; add onion, bell pepper, zucchini, and garlic, and sauté until tender, about 10 minutes. Add corn, cumin, cayenne, and salt; cook another 2 to 3 minutes. Lightly oil an 8-inch springform pan with 3-inch sides. Place 1 tortilla in bottom of pan. Spread ½ cup bean puree over tortilla; top with 1 cup sautéed vegetable mixture. Spoon ¼ cup Salsa Fresco over vegetables, and sprinkle ⅓ cup cheese over salsa. Repeat with remaining ingredients, ending with cheese. Bake for 45 minutes, or until torta is warmed through; let stand 5 minutes before cutting into wedges. Note: This torta can be made with pinto beans rather than black beans.

Makes 10 to 12 servings.

Salsa Fresca

3 ripe tomatoes, finely chopped
½ cup finely chopped onion
1-3 serrano chiles, cored, seeded, and minced
1 New Mexico green chile (or Anaheim chile) cored, seeded, and finely chopped
2 tablespoons minced fresh cilantro
1 teaspoon sugar
1 tablespoon fresh lime juice
Salt and freshly ground pepper to taste

Mix all ingredients together in a non-aluminum bowl, and allow flavors to blend at room temperature for at least 1 hour. The salsa will keep in the refrigerator for up to 2 weeks.

Makes about 1½ cups.

Brown Rice Puff

3	beaten egg yolks	1	cup cooked brown rice
½	cup milk	½	cup shredded cheddar cheese
2	tablespoons butter, melted		(2 ounces)
¼	teaspoon dry mustard	½	cup shredded Monterey Jack cheese
⅛	teaspoon ground red pepper	3	egg whites

Preheat oven to 300°. Combine egg yolks, milk, butter, mustard, and pepper; stir in rice and cheeses. Beat egg whites at high speed with an electric mixer until stiff peaks form. Fold whites into rice mixture. Turn into 4 greased 8-ounce baking dishes. Bake for 30 minutes or until a knife inserted 1 inch from center comes out clean.

Makes 4 servings.

This can be baked in an 8- x 1½-inch round baking dish. Add 5 minutes to baking time.

Chickpeas with Spinach

⅔	cup plain non-fat yogurt	1	(16-ounce) can garbanzos, with
1	garlic clove, minced		liquid reserved
1	tablespoon chopped fresh mint	10	ounces spinach leaves, rinsed and
½	teaspoon salt		coarsely chopped
2	tablespoons olive oil	2	tablespoons fresh lemon juice
1	medium-size onion, chopped		Salt and pepper
1	red bell pepper, seeded and cubed		Steamed white or brown long-
2	teaspoons ground coriander		grain rice or orzo
1	teaspoon ground cumin		Garnish: fresh mint sprigs
⅛	teaspoon saffron		

Combine yogurt, garlic, mint, and salt in a bowl; set aside to allow flavors to blend. Heat olive oil in a skillet over medium heat; add onion, and sauté until soft, about 6 minutes. Add bell pepper, coriander, cumin, and saffron, and continue to cook and stir for another few minutes. Stir in garbanzos and about ¼ cup of their liquid; simmer 5 minutes or until bell peppers are just tender, adding more of the reserved liquid, if necessary. Add spinach, and cook, stirring often, until spinach is wilted, 2 to 3 minutes. Stir in lemon juice, and season with salt and pepper to taste. Serve immediately on rice or orzo. Spoon on spiced yogurt sauce and, if desired, garnish.

Makes 4 to 6 servings.

Green Chile Rice

3 tablespoons olive oil
1 small onion, finely chopped
1 cup white rice, uncooked
1 small jalapeño pepper, seeded and minced, or 1 small fresh green chile pepper, seeded and minced
¾ cup small broccoli florets
2 garlic cloves, minced

1¾ cups chicken stock or water
½ cup fresh spinach leaves, coarsely chopped
2 tablespoons finely chopped fresh parsley
1 tablespoon freshly grated Parmesan cheese

Heat 2 tablespoons oil in a large skillet or deep frying pan over medium heat; add onion, and sauté until lightly browned, about 5 minutes. Add rice, and stir to coat; cook over medium heat until rice begins to brown. Add pepper, broccoli, garlic, and chicken stock. Increase heat, and bring to a boil. Reduce heat to low; cover and cook 15 minutes. Stir spinach into rice mixture; cover and cook over low heat until rice and spinach are tender and water is absorbed, about 5 minutes. Remove from heat, and let stand 10 minutes. Just before serving stir in remaining 1 tablespoon oil, parsley, and Parmesan.

Makes 4 to 6 servings.

Mexican Blush Rice

1 tablespoon olive oil
½ yellow onion, chopped
1 garlic clove, chopped
3 small canned peeled tomatoes, drained
1 cup white rice

1½ cups chicken broth
¼ teaspoon ground cumin
¼ teaspoon salt
Freshly ground pepper to taste
¼ cup chopped fresh cilantro or parsley

Heat oil in a saucepan over medium heat; add onion and garlic, and sauté until tender, about 5 minutes. With a slotted spoon, transfer onion and garlic to a food processor or blender; add tomatoes, and process until smooth. In the same saucepan, add rice, and stir until coated with oil. Add broth, cumin, salt, pepper, and tomato mixture; bring to a boil. Reduce heat to low, and cook, covered, until rice is tender, about 20 minutes. Fluff with a fork, and transfer to a warm bowl. Sprinkle cilantro or parsley on top, and serve immediately.

Makes 4 servings.

Jalapeño Pilaf

2	tablespoons unsalted butter	1	cup basmati rice
½	cup chopped purple onion	2	cups chicken stock
2	jalapeño chiles, seeded and minced	2	cups chopped, seeded tomato
½	teaspoon cumin seed, crushed, or ¼ teaspoon ground cumin	1	teaspoon chopped fresh cilantro
			Salt to taste

Melt butter in a large saucepan; add onion, chiles, cumin, and rice. Cook, stirring constantly, until onion is soft and rice is lightly browned, about 8 minutes. Add chicken stock, and bring to a boil. Add tomato, cilantro, and salt; stir once to mix. Cover, reduce heat, and simmer 20 to 25 minutes or until all liquid has been absorbed and rice is tender.

Makes 6 servings.

Adding diced cooked chicken, beef, or pork could make this a main dish.

Refried Black Beans

1	pound dried black beans, washed and picked over	3	green onions, white and green parts, chopped
¼	large white onion, peeled	3	tablespoons vegetable oil
2	garlic cloves, chopped		Salt and freshly ground white pepper
2	cups chicken stock		
½	pound bacon, minced	¾	pound white cheese (Monterey Jack or feta), shredded
3	jalapeños, stemmed and chopped		

Place beans in a stockpot with water to cover; bring to a boil. Reduce heat, and simmer beans, partially covered, 1 hour. Add half of onion and garlic, along with chicken stock, to beans; simmer another 30 minutes or until beans are very tender. Cook bacon in a skillet until almost burned; remove with a slotted spoon. Pour off drippings, reserving ¼ cup. Sauté remaining onion with jalapeños and green onions in reserved drippings over medium heat until onions are translucent. Drain cooked beans, reserving broth. Place beans, bacon, and jalapeño mixture in a blender or food processor, along with 3 cups bean broth; process until mixture is pureed but consistency is still chunky. Heat vegetable oil in a deep, heavy skillet; add bean mixture. Cook over low heat, stirring constantly, until beans are thick and some of liquid has evaporated, about 10 minutes. Season with salt and pepper to taste. To serve, sprinkle cheese over each portion.

Makes 8 servings.

Nutted Wild Rice

1   cup golden raisins
½   cup dry sherry
1   cup wild rice
4⅔ cups chicken stock, boiling
6   tablespoons unsalted butter

1   cup brown rice
1   cup slivered almonds
½   cup chopped fresh parsley
Salt and freshly ground black
pepper to taste

Bring raisins and sherry to a boil in a small saucepan; reduce heat, and simmer 5 minutes. Set aside. Place wild rice, 2 cups boiling stock, and 2 tablespoons butter in top of a double boiler over simmering water; cook, covered, for 1 hour. Place brown rice, remaining 2⅔ cups boiling stock, and 2 tablespoons butter in a medium-size saucepan. Heat to boiling; reduce heat to low, and cook until all stock is absorbed, about 50 minutes. Sauté almonds in remaining 2 tablespoons butter in a small skillet over low heat until lightly toasted. Combine wild rice, brown rice, raisin mixture, almonds, and parsley in a large mixing bowl. Season to taste with salt and pepper; remove to a serving bowl, and serve immediately.

Makes 8 to 10 servings.

Sagebrush Beans

2   cups dried lima beans (small
    or large), washed and sorted
    Salt to taste
2   tablespoons butter
2   medium onions, thinly sliced
    Freshly ground black pepper to
    taste

1   teaspoon dried crumbled sage
    (not ground)
1   cup shredded Cheddar cheese
½   cup whipping cream
4   bacon slices

Soak beans in water to cover in a large pot overnight. Bring beans to a boil over medium-high heat; skim off any foam. Reduce heat, and simmer 2 hours or until tender. Add salt toward the end of cooking. Drain beans. Preheat oven to 350°. Melt butter in a skillet over medium heat; add onion, and sauté until limp. Place half of beans in a lightly greased 8-inch baking dish; sprinkle with pepper, half of sage, and onion. Top with remaining beans, more pepper, and remaining sage. Sprinkle with cheese; pour cream over cheese, and top with bacon. Bake, uncovered, for 30 minutes or until bacon is crisp.

Makes 4 servings.

Spicy Southwest Avocado Rice

1	cup white rice	½	teaspoon ground cumin
½	cup chopped onion	1	avocado, diced
¼	cup chopped jalapeños	½	cup salsa (see index)
2	tablespoons butter		Garnish: 2 tablespoon chopped
2	cups chicken broth		fresh cilantro

Sauté rice, onion, and jalapeño in butter in a skillet over medium heat until rice turns opaque. Heat broth to boiling; add cumin and rice mixture. Reduce heat, cover, and simmer until rice is tender, about 25 minutes. Add avocado and salsa; mix well. Garnish, if desired.

Makes 4 servings.

Red and Green Rice

1	cup uncooked rice	½	cup red wine
1	cup chopped tomato	2	teaspoons salt
½	pound mushrooms, sliced	⅛	teaspoon pepper
½	cup chopped onion	1	cup green peas, cooked
½	cup butter	¼	cup grated Parmesan cheese

Cook first 4 ingredients in butter in a large saucepan over medium heat, stirring occasionally, 10 minutes. Add wine, broth, and seasonings; mix well. Cover and simmer about 30 minutes or until rice is tender and liquid is absorbed. Stir in peas, and cook until heated through. Sprinkle with cheese.

Makes 6 to 8 servings.

Santa Fe Hominy

2	garlic cloves, minced	2	New Mexico green chiles (or poblanos), roasted, peeled, cored, seeded, and diced
1½	cups chopped purple onion		
2	tablespoons corn oil		
2	(15-ounce) cans hominy, rinsed and drained	1	jalapeño chile, seeded and minced
3	large ripe tomatoes, diced	1	cup shredded asadero or Monterey Jack cheese

Sauté garlic and onion in hot oil in a large, heavy skillet over medium heat until onion is translucent. Stir in hominy, tomato, and chiles; cover and simmer over low heat until all ingredients are blended and vegetables are tender, about 15 minutes. Uncover and sprinkle with cheese. Stir just until cheese is melted; serve immediately.

Makes 6 servings.

West of the Pecos Hominy

2 tablespoons vegetable oil	2 small jalapeños, seeded, deveined, and minced
1 onion, chopped	
1 garlic clove, minced	1 (4.5-ounce) can mild green chiles, drained and chopped
1 large tomato, peeled, seeded, and chopped	
	1 (29-ounce) can whole hominy, rinsed and drained
⅛ teaspoon sugar	
½ teaspoon chopped fresh thyme or ¼ teaspoon dried thyme	½ teaspoon salt
	¼ teaspoon freshly ground pepper
1 teaspoon tomato paste	2 cups shredded Monterey Jack cheese

Preheat oven to 375°. Heat oil in a large, heavy skillet; add onion, and sauté 1 minute. Add garlic, and sauté 4 minutes. Stir in tomato, sugar, thyme, and tomato paste; cook 5 minutes. Add jalapeños and green chiles, and cook 5 minutes. Stir in hominy, salt, and pepper; remove from heat. Stir in 1½ cups cheese, and transfer mixture to a greased baking dish. Sprinkle with remaining cheese, and place in oven. Immediately reduce temperature to 350°. Bake for 45 minutes; let stand 5 minutes before serving.

Makes 4 to 6 servings.

Black Bean Cakes

2 cups black beans, drained and rinsed	½ red bell pepper, chopped
	½ cup breadcrumbs
1 cup cooked brown rice	1 egg, beaten
1 teaspoon ground cumin	2 tablespoons olive oil
1 teaspoon chile powder	1 (4.5-ounce) can green chiles (optional)
½ cup chopped fresh cilantro	
2 green onions, chopped	Salt and pepper to taste

Process rice and beans in a food processor until blended. Add remaining ingredients. Shape mixture into patties, and chill 15 minutes. Fry on both sides; serve as you would a hamburger patty (can be made ahead, but do not freeze).

Makes 5 to 8 servings.

Eggs & Cheese

Bottomless Lakes State Park

The beautiful and unique area known as Bottomless Lakes State Park comes as a complete surprise after the flat country surrounding Roswell, New Mexico. These seven lakes, actually sinkholes ranging in depth from 17 feet to 90 feet, were formed when circulating underground water dissolved salt and gypsum deposits to form subterranean caverns. When the roof of the caverns collapsed from their own weight, sinkholes resulted and soon filled with water. The greenish blue color and illusion of great depth are created by algae and other aquatic plants covering the lake bottoms.

In the 1800s, the lakes were a stopover for cowboys herding cattle through New Mexico. After the cowboys tried without success to find the bottom of the lakes, with their lariats tied together, they dubbed the lakes "bottomless." The lariats were actually swept aside by underwater currents.

Dairy and Cheese

Plentiful water, fertile soil, and a mild climate contribute to the $329 million agricultural economic base in Chaves County, New Mexico. Dairy cattle lead the list in income production, followed by beef cattle, sheep, and Angora goats. More wool is sold from Roswell than any single community in the United States.

The availability of sun-drenched land at a reasonable price and seven crops of hay a year lured dairy families from the East to the Roswell area. In 1997, there were 42 dairies and 80,000 dairy cows in the county. The growing dairy and alfalfa industries maintain a strong cheese industry. Leprino Foods is the nation's largest producer of mozzarella cheese. Four million pounds of milk are utilized daily.

New Mexico ranks 11th in total milk production in the U.S., 8th in cheese production, and 3rd in average annual yield per cow—evidently Bossy is very contented in New Mexico!

"Cheese—milk's leap towards immortality." Clifton Fadiman

Featured on page 57 "Bottomless Lakes"

Breakfast Burrito

4   large flour tortillas
8   ounces chorizo sausage
10 eggs
¼   cup water
½   teaspoon chile powder

Salt and pepper to taste
Tomatillo Salsa
⅓   cup sour cream
⅓   cup shredded sharp Cheddar
    cheese

Cover tortillas with a damp towel, and place in a warm oven while you cook eggs. Crumble sausage into a medium-size skillet, and sauté until just cooked through; pour off all but 2 teaspoons drippings. Whisk together eggs and next 3 ingredients in a large bowl; add to sausage in skillet, and cook, stirring often, just until eggs are set, 3 to 4 minutes. Spoon egg mixture onto middle of warm tortillas; fold sides of tortillas over, and roll up like egg rolls. Top with salsa, sour cream, and shredded Cheddar cheese; serve warm.

Makes 4 servings.

Tomatillo Salsa
8   husked tomatillos
3   garlic cloves
1   small purple onion, minced
1   jalapeño, diced
    Juice of 1 lime

3   tablespoons vegetable oil
1   teaspoon ground cumin
½   teaspoon ground coriander
1   teaspoon chopped cilantro
    Salt and pepper to taste

Preheat oven to 425°. Place tomatillos in a roasting pan, and cook 20 minutes. Remove from oven, and cool about 10 minutes; process in a food processor with garlic until smooth. Pour tomatillo mixture into a medium-size bowl, and add onion and next 7 ingredients.

 An extensive music library is maintained and stored at the Roswell Symphony Office. These books, recordings, musical instruments and other materials are available to be checked out by any teacher in the area. A catalog of the library has been made available to all schools.

Buenos Dias Eggs

6   hard-cooked eggs, shelled
½   cup melted butter
½   teaspoon Worcestershire sauce
¼   teaspoon prepared mustard
2-3 green onions, finely chopped,
     including tops

1   tablespoon minced fresh parsley
3-4 ounces sliced cooked ham, finely
     chopped
     Salt and pepper to taste

White Sauce
4   tablespoons butter
4   tablespoons all-purpose flour

2   cups milk

Topping
1   cup shredded Cheddar cheese
     Minced fresh parsley

     Minced onion

Preheat oven to 325°. Cut eggs lengthwise, and remove yolks. Mash yolks with butter, Worcestershire sauce, and mustard in a bowl. Add green onions, parsley, and ham to egg mixture; season with salt and pepper to taste. Spoon filling into egg whites; arrange in a buttered baking dish. For sauce, melt butter in a saucepan over medium heat; add flour and milk. Cook, stirring occasionally, until sauce thickens. Pour warm sauce over eggs. Sprinkle cheese over sauce, and top with minced parsley and onion. Bake, uncovered, for 25 to 30 minutes.

Makes 3 to 4 servings.

Baked Chiles Rellenos

12   fresh or canned whole green chiles
½   pound Cheddar cheese, shredded
½   pound Monterey Jack cheese,
     shredded

2   eggs
1   cup milk
1   cup cracker crumbs
¼   cup butter, melted

Preheat oven to 325°. Roast chiles, and peel (if using canned chiles, omit roasting). Place chiles in a buttered baking dish. Layer cheeses over chiles. Whisk together eggs and milk; pour mixture over cheese, and top with cracker crumbs. Pour melted butter over top; bake for 45 minutes.

Makes 6 servings.

This dish freezes well, before or after baking.

Chile Corn Quiche

2 cups finely crushed cheese crackers
3 tablespoons melted butter
3 tablespoons canola oil
1 serrano chile pepper, seeded, stemmed, and minced
½ cup minced onion
2 tablespoons all-purpose flour
½ teaspoon salt
⅛ teaspoon ground white pepper
1¼ cups low-fat milk
2 eggs, beaten
¾ cup diced New Mexico green chiles
1 cup diced zucchini
2 cups fresh corn kernels or 1 (17-ounce) can whole kernel corn, drained

Preheat oven to 400°. Combine 1½ cups crumbs, 2 tablespoons melted butter, 2 tablespoons oil, and serrano chile. Set aside ½ cup crumbs for topping. Press crumb mixture into a 9-inch glass pie plate. Combine remaining 1 tablespoon melted butter, remaining 1 tablespoon oil, and onion in a small saucepan; cook over medium heat, stirring constantly, 30 seconds. Sprinkle flour over hot mixture, and add salt, celery seed, and white pepper; reduce heat to low, and stir until blended, 20 to 30 seconds. Add milk, all at once, and stir constantly with a wire whisk until mixture starts to thicken. Whisk ¼ cup milk mixture into beaten eggs. Add egg mixture in a slow, steady drizzle to remaining hot mixture, whisking constantly. Remove from heat; stir in green chiles, zucchini, and corn. Slowly pour mixture into prepared crust; sprinkle with reserved crumbs. Bake for 15 to 20 minutes; remove from oven, and let stand at least 5 minutes. Cut into 6 wedges, and serve.

Makes 6 servings.

Fiesta Tortilla Quiche

12 medium-size flour tortillas
18 eggs
9 cups shredded Monterey Jack cheese
1 cup evaporated milk
⅓ cup dry onion flakes
4 ounces diced green chiles
¼ cup diced red bell pepper
½ teaspoon seasoning salt
¼ teaspoon garlic powder
⅛ teaspoon pepper
Salsa, sour cream, chopped chives

Preheat oven to 325°. Line 12 (4-inch) pie pans with tortillas, folding to fit. Combine eggs and next 8 ingredients in a large bowl. Fill each shell with ¾ cup egg mixture. Bake for 30 to 40 minutes or until knife inserted in center comes out clean. Serve with salsa, sour cream, and chives.

Makes 12 servings.

_____Chiles Rellenos Casserole_____

4	(6- to 7-inch) corn tortillas	1	(7-ounce) can whole green chiles, drained
½	cup finely chopped onion		
2	tablespoons vegetable oil	½	cup chopped fresh cilantro
¾	pound Monterey Jack cheese with peppers	4	eggs, separated
		2	tablespoons all-purpose flour

Preheat oven to 375°. Stack tortillas, and cut into ½-inch strips. Sauté onion in 1 tablespoon hot oil in a skillet until limp; add tortilla strips and remaining oil, and cook over high heat, stirring constantly, until strips start to brown, 8 to 10 minutes. Scatter tortilla mixture in a 12- x 8- x 2-inch baking dish. Shred 1 cup cheese, and sprinkle over mixture in dish; cut remaining cheese into ¼-inch-thick sticks. Stuff chiles with cheese sticks; lay chiles in single layer over tortilla mixture, and sprinkle cilantro over top. Beat egg whites at high speed with an electric mixer until soft peaks form; set aside. Beat yolks and flour at high speed until blended; fold in egg whites, and spread egg mixture over casserole. Bake for about 15 minutes or until golden brown.

Makes 5 to 6 servings.

_____Eggs Diablo_____

6	hard-cooked eggs	2	tablespoons taco sauce
1	green New Mexico or Anaheim chile, roasted, peeled, cored, seeded, and diced	2	tablespoons mayonnaise
			Salt and freshly ground pepper to taste
2	tablespoons finely chopped green onions		Garnish: 24 strips roasted red pepper or pimiento
2	tablespoons finely shredded Monterey Jack cheese		

Cut eggs in half lengthwise; place yolks in a bowl, and mash with a fork. Blend in remaining ingredients except garnish. Fill egg whites with yolk mixture. Garnish each egg with 2 red pepper strips, if desired.

Makes 12 servings.

For more picante flavor, use Monterey Jack with peppers.

Huevos Con Papas

1	tablespoon vegetable oil	2	teaspoons minced fresh basil or
1	small onion, sliced		1 teaspoon dried basil
1	pound potatoes, unpeeled and	1	egg
	thinly sliced	6	egg whites
½	cup water		Picante sauce or pico de gallo
	Pepper to taste		(see index)
½	teaspoon minced fresh thyme or		
	¼ teaspoon dried thyme		

Heat oil in a nonstick skillet until hot. Sauté onion and potato in hot oil about 5 minutes or until lightly browned. Stir in water; cover and cook over low heat 10 minutes or until potato is tender. Sprinkle potato mixture with pepper, thyme, and basil. Process whole egg and egg whites in a blender 1 minute; pour over potato mixture, patting down firmly. Cover and cook until set, 5 to 10 minutes. Brown under broiler, and cut into 4 pieces. Serve with picante sauce or fresh pico de gallo.

Makes 2 to 4 servings.

Huevos Oaxaca

	Corn oil	¼	cup chopped fresh cilantro
6	corn tortillas, halved	1½	teaspoons ground cumin
12	eggs	4	ounces feta cheese, crumbled
4	large green onions, sliced		Salt and pepper to taste
2	jalapeños, very thinly sliced	2	tablespoons corn oil
½	red bell pepper, diced		Garnish: fresh cilantro sprigs

Heat oil in a heavy saucepan to 375°. Add tortilla halves, and fry, turning occasionally, until golden brown and crisp, about 2 minutes. Transfer to paper towels to drain. Beat eggs, next 5 ingredients, and half of cheese in a large bowl until blended; crumble 6 tortilla halves into mixture, and season with salt and pepper to taste. Let mixture stand 5 minutes. Heat 2 tablespoons oil in a large, heavy skillet over medium heat; add egg mixture, and cook, stirring often, until just set, about 3 minutes. Divide egg mixture among 6 serving plates; sprinkle remaining cheese over eggs. Stand a tortilla half in each serving, and garnish, if desired.

Makes 6 servings.

Green Chile Tart

Crust

1 cup all-purpose flour	¾ cup unsalted butter, chilled and cut into ¼-inch pieces
¾ cup blue or yellow cornmeal	
1 teaspoon salt	4 tablespoons ice water

Filling

1 cup shredded Gruyère cheese	¾ cup crumbled, soft, fresh goat cheese, room temperature
1 cup shredded mozzarella cheese	
3 large fresh poblano or New Mexico chiles, charred, peeled, seeded, and chopped	¼ cup butter, softened
	¾ teaspoon salt
	¼ teaspoon pepper
4 large eggs	1 cup shredded Colby or Cheddar cheese
¾ cup whipping cream	

For Crust, combine flour, cornmeal, and salt in a food processor; cut in butter using on/off turns until mixture resembles coarse meal. Pulse in water, 1 tablespoon at a time, until mixture forms moist clumps. Gather dough into a ball; flatten into a disk, and wrap in plastic wrap. Chill 1 hour. Preheat oven to 375°. Lightly butter an 11-inch tart pan with removable bottom. Press dough onto bottom and up sides of pan, trimming edges to fit and reserving scraps. Place pan on a heavy baking sheet. Bake crust for 20 minutes or until set and edge begins to brown. (If crust cracks, gently press small bits of reserved dough scraps into cracks.) Transfer pan to a wire rack to cool. Sprinkle Gruyère and mozzarella over bottom of crust. Sprinkle chiles over cheese. Process eggs and next 5 ingredients in food processor until well blended. Pour mixture into crust. Sprinkle Colby cheese over top. Bake for 25 minutes or until filling is golden brown and set. Transfer to a wire rack to cool slightly. Serve warm or at room temperature.

Makes 8 servings.

Tart may be made 8 hours ahead. Cover and chill. Bring to room temperature before serving.

Hacienda Eggs

10 tablespoons unsalted butter
2 cups coarse fresh breadcrumbs
1¼ pounds fresh mushrooms, sliced ¼-inch thick
8 large hard-cooked eggs, sliced
1 medium-size onion, diced
½ cup all-purpose flour
4 cups whole milk
3 tablespoons Dijon mustard
1¼ teaspoons salt
Freshly ground black pepper to taste
½ teaspoon ground nutmeg
1 bunch tarragon, stemmed and chopped
4 English muffins, split and toasted

Preheat oven to 325°. Melt 2 tablespoons butter in a saucepan over low heat; add breadcrumbs. Spread breadcrumbs on a baking sheet, and bake until crumbs are lightly browned, about 10 minutes. Increase oven temperature to 375°. Spray a 13- x 9-inch baking dish with cooking spray. Heat 2 tablespoons butter in a heavy skillet; add mushrooms, and sauté until liquid evaporates. Spread dry mushrooms evenly over bottom of baking dish; top with sliced eggs. Melt remaining 6 tablespoons butter in a heavy saucepan; add onion, and sauté until soft but not browned, about 5 minutes. Reduce heat, and add flour; stir carefully, breaking up any lumps, and cook until mixture is faintly colored, about 5 minutes. Add milk to flour mixture, stirring constantly until mixture thickens; bring to a boil, reduce heat, and cook 5 minutes. Stir mustard and next 4 ingredients into flour mixture. Pour sauce evenly over egg slices in dish; top with toasted breadcrumbs. Bake 25 minutes or until bubbly. Serve over English muffin halves.

Makes 8 servings.

Use an egg slicer for uniform slices of mushrooms.

 "The Story of Babar the Elephant," by Jacques Brel, an American Symphony Orchestra League National Conference Award Winner, placed in the top six educational activities of all symphony guilds. This event, still much in demand in our community, featured a puppet show with narration and music composed especially for this story by Francis Poulenc. Guild members made and dressed 14 elephant puppets. These delightful creations brought applause from children and adults that fell in love with these whimsical lovable creatures.

Huevos Rancheros

12 large eggs
1   tablespoon vinegar
    Vegetable oil

6   (6- to 8-inch) corn or flour tortillas
1½ cups Ranchero Sauce
1   cup shredded Monterey Jack cheese

Poach eggs, in batches if necessary, in a skillet of boiling water with vinegar. Heat ½ inch oil in a skillet over high heat; fry corn tortillas, 1 at a time, a few seconds on each side until soft. Place 2 eggs on each tortilla; top with ¼ cup Ranchero Sauce, and sprinkle with 2 tablespoons cheese. Transfer to a baking sheet, and broil 3 inches from heat until cheese melts.

Makes 6 servings.

Ranchero Sauce

2   tablespoons vegetable oil
1   cup finely chopped onion
1   garlic clove, minced
4   cups finely chopped fresh or
    canned tomatoes

2   Anaheim or other mild chiles,
    cored, seeded, and chopped
1   teaspoon sugar
    Salt and pepper to taste
2   tablespoons minced fresh cilantro

Heat oil in a large skillet; add onion, and sauté 2 minutes. Add garlic, and sauté 2 minutes or until onion is translucent. Add tomatoes and next 3 ingredients; simmer until slightly thickened, about 15 minutes. Stir in cilantro. Store in refrigerator up to 1 week.

Makes about 4 cups.

Eggs may be fried or poached in red chile sauce. All versions of Huevos Rancheros include tortillas, eggs, sauce or salsa, and cheese.

To heat flour tortillas, wrap in aluminum foil, and place in a 350° oven for 15 to 20 minutes or until heated through.

Polenta Torte

1 garlic clove, minced
½ cup chopped leek, white part only
½ cup chopped purple onion
2 tablespoons olive oil
4 cups vegetable broth
1 teaspoon butter
1 cup yellow cornmeal

1½ ounces fresh white goat cheese
1 ounce smoked Gouda cheese, cut into ¼-inch cubes
1 ounce Parmesan cheese, grated
Salt to taste

Preheat oven to 450°. Sauté first 3 ingredients in hot oil in a skillet until golden. Heat broth and butter in a saucepan until butter melts; whisk in cornmeal, and simmer, stirring constantly with a wooden spoon, until thick, 10 to 15 minutes. Remove polenta from heat, and stir in onion mixture and goat cheese; stir in Gouda and Parmesan. Add salt to taste. Pour hot polenta into a buttered deep-dish pie plate or round baking dish. Smooth top. Cover and chill for 45 minutes or longer. Loosen polenta from pan; invert on a buttered baking sheet. Bake for 12 to 15 minutes or until heated through and just crisping on outside. Cut into wedges, and serve with roasted tomato sauce (see index).

Makes 4 servings.

Mexican Brunch Casserole

1 pound ground beef
½ cup chopped onion
2 teaspoons salt
¼ teaspoon pepper
2 (4-ounce) cans whole green chiles, cut in half crosswise and seeded

1½ cups shredded sharp Cheddar cheese
¼ cup all-purpose flour
4 eggs, beaten
1½ cups milk
¼ teaspoon Tabasco

Preheat oven to 350°. Brown beef and onion in a large skillet over medium heat; drain. Add salt and pepper to beef. Place half of chiles in a 10- x 6- x 1½-inch baking dish, and sprinkle with cheese. Top cheese with beef mixture; arrange remaining chiles over top. Combine remaining ingredients, and mix until smooth; pour over casserole. Bake for 45 to 50 minutes; cool 5 to 10 minutes, and cut into squares to serve.

Makes 6 servings.

Scrambled Egg Casserole

2   tablespoons butter
2   tablespoons all-purpose flour
1¼ cups milk
6   ounces sharp Cheddar cheese,
    shredded
12 eggs, slightly beaten
1   cup frozen peas, cooked and
    drained

1   (6-ounce) can sliced mushrooms,
    drained
½   cup chopped pimiento
2   tablespoons snipped chives
6   bacon slices
3   bread slices, cut into ¼-inch cubes
    Garnish: fresh chives, tomato
    wedges

Melt butter in a medium saucepan over medium heat; blend in flour. Add milk, stirring constantly until thickened and bubbly. Reduce heat to low, and stir in cheese until melted. Set mixture aside. Combine eggs and next 4 ingredients in a bowl. Cook egg mixture in a lightly greased skillet over medium heat, gently lifting edges so uncooked portion flows underneath. When eggs are set, fold in cheese mixture. Turn into an 11- x 7-inch baking dish. Cover and chill overnight. Preheat oven to 350°. About 30 minutes before serving, uncover casserole, and bake for 20 minutes. Cook bacon in a large skillet over medium heat until crisp; remove from skillet, reserving drippings in skillet. Cook bread cubes in reserved drippings until crisp. Top casserole with bread cubes and bacon, and bake 10 more minutes or until heated through. Garnish, if desired.

Makes 6 to 8 servings.

Stuffed French Toast

1   (8-ounce) package cream cheese,
    softened
1   teaspoon vanilla extract
½   cup chopped walnuts
1   (16-ounce) loaf French bread
4   eggs, beaten
1   cup whipping cream

½   teaspoon vanilla extract
½   teaspoon ground nutmeg
    Butter for cooking
1   (12-ounce) jar apricot or orange
    marmalade
½   cup orange juice

Stir cream cheese and vanilla until blended; add walnuts. Cut bread into 1½-inch slices; cut a pocket into side of each slice. Fill each pocket with 1½ tablespoons cheese mixture. Combine eggs and next 3 ingredients in a bowl; dip stuffed bread into mixture. In large skillet melt butter over medium heat until it foams and coats bottom of pan. Cook bread in batches until golden. Combine marmalade and juice, and serve with French toast.

Serves 6 to 8

Southwest Frittata

1 egg
2 egg whites
½ teaspoon salt
Freshly ground pepper to taste
4 tablespoons plus 1 teaspoon canola or vegetable oil
2 medium-size potatoes, peeled, grated, rinsed 3 times, and squeezed dry
1 cup sliced fresh mushrooms
2 garlic cloves, minced
½ teaspoon dried thyme or 1½ teaspoons fresh thyme

3 green onions, chopped
2 jalapeños, minced
1 small red bell pepper, diced
½ cup frozen corn kernels, thawed and rinsed
1 teaspoon fresh lemon juice
2 tablespoons grated Parmesan cheese
1 cup shredded Monterey Jack cheese
Garnish: 2 to 3 tablespoons chopped fresh cilantro

Whisk egg and egg whites together in a bowl; add half of salt, pepper, and 1 teaspoon oil. Set aside. Heat 2 tablespoons oil in a large nonstick skillet over medium-high heat. Add potato, and cook, stirring occasionally, until crisp and browned. In a separate non-stick skillet, sauté mushrooms and next 5 ingredients in 2 tablespoons oil 2 to 3 minutes; add corn, remaining ¼ teaspoon salt, and lemon juice. Cook mixture, stirring until vegetables are tender and all liquid has evaporated, about 5 minutes; stir in Parmesan. Reduce heat under potato to low, and pour egg mixture over potato; cook until egg begins to set, about 1 minute. Spread vegetable mixture evenly over egg mixture; sprinkle Monterey Jack cheese over top, and cover. Cook just until cheese melts; slide frittata onto a warm plate, and cut into wedges. Serve immediately. Garnish, if desired.

Makes 6 servings.

Pueblo Baked Eggs

¾ cup chopped mushrooms
⅓ cup chopped shallot
3 tablespoons unsalted butter
3 tablespoons chopped cooked ham

½ cup beef broth
⅛ teaspoon pepper, or to taste
4 large eggs, room temperature

Preheat oven to 350°. Sauté mushrooms and shallot in butter in a skillet over high heat 2 minutes. Add ham, and sauté over medium-high heat 3 minutes; add broth, and cook 3 minutes. Add pepper, and divide mixture among 4 well-greased ¾-cup ramekins. Crack 1 egg into each ramekin, and bake 15 minutes or until eggs are opaque on top.

Makes 4 servings.

Southwestern Puffed Omelet

6	eggs, separated	1	tablespoon butter
⅓	cup water	1	cup shredded Monterey Jack
½	teaspoon salt		cheese
¼	teaspoon pepper	1	cup salsa (see index)

Preheat oven to 375°. Place egg yolks and whites in separate mixing bowls. Add water, salt, and pepper to yolks, and whisk until blended. Beat egg whites at high speed with an electric mixer until soft peaks form. Pour yolk mixture over beaten egg whites, and gently fold together. Heat butter in an ovenproof 12-inch skillet until foamy; pour in egg mixture, smoothing top. Cook, uncovered, over low heat 2 minutes; place skillet in center of oven, and cook 8 to 10 minutes or until omelet is set and top just begins to color. Remove from oven, and cover with cheese. Using a spatula, make a crease down center of omelet, and fold omelet in half, pressing gently but firmly for a few seconds. Transfer to a serving platter, and spoon salsa over top. Cut into 4 wedges, and serve with extra salsa.

Makes 4 servings.

Sunset French Toast

3	eggs	½	cup butter, softened
3	tablespoons peach preserves	2	fresh peaches, peeled and sliced
¾	cup half-and-half		Powdered sugar
6	French bread slices		Toasted almonds
⅓	cup peach preserves		

Whisk eggs and 3 tablespoons preserves in a small bowl; whisk in half-and-half. Place bread slices in a single layer in an 11- x 7-inch baking dish. Pour egg mixture over bread; cover and chill several hours or overnight until moisture is absorbed. Beat ⅓ cup preserves and 4 tablespoons butter at high speed with an electric mixer until fluffy; set aside until ready to serve. Just before serving, melt 2 tablespoons butter in a large skillet over medium-high heat; add 3 bread slices, and cook until browned, turning once. Remove from skillet, and keep warm. Repeat procedure with remaining bread slices and 2 tablespoons butter. Serve French toast topped with about 1 tablespoon peach butter and peach slices; sprinkle with powdered sugar and almonds.

Makes 4 to 6 servings.

Beef, Lamb, & Pork

The dictionary describes hospitality as "given to generous and cordial reception of guests."

The southwest farmers and ranchers are the most hospitable hosts in the world. A custom of ranchers in the southwest is to make a hand in helping your neighbor when a herd of cattle needs branding and working. All of this hot and heavy work is gratis, and a tip of the sombrero is all that is expected. The rancher's wife is delighted to welcome a cheery and hungry group of neighbors to her table. Thick slabs of roast beef, hot cream gravy, mashed potatoes and biscuits topped off with hot apple pie were reward enough. The farmers and ranchers of the southwest are hearty eaters and seconds were the order of the day. I sympathize with the city dwellers who have never washed up in a tin pan, rolled up his sleeves, and joined the happy throng. Warm hospitality and fine food were a treat, a treat to all. The reader will find a treasure trove of excellent recipes in this new book on Southwest Cooking. I am sure you will strike the mother load of superb cooking.

Rogers Aston

Featured on page 71 "West of the Pecos Cowboy"

Beef Fillets Stuffed with Blue Cheese

3 ounces blue cheese, at room
 temperature
4 tablespoons dry breadcrumbs
6 strips bacon, cooked and crumbled

6 beef tenderloin steaks
 (about 6 ounces each)
 Salt and pepper to taste
2 tablespoons vegetable oil
 Béarnaise Sauce

Process cheese and breadcrumbs in a food processor until smooth. Add crumbled bacon, stirring just to mix. Insert a small sharp knife into side of each steak, not quite through to other side; carefully angle knife to 1 side and then the other to form a pocket in meat. Gently stuff steaks with cheese mixture. (You will use all of the stuffing if patient.) Just before cooking, salt and pepper steaks. Grill steaks outside, or if grilling indoors, add oil to a heavy skillet over medium heat. Add steaks to hot oil (do not crowd), and cook until medium-rare, about 4 minutes per side. Place 2 tablespoons Béarnaise Sauce in center of each serving plate. Place a fillet on top of sauce, and serve immediately.

Makes 6 servings.

Béarnaise Sauce

1 cup dry vermouth or dry white
 wine
⅛ teaspoon freshly ground black
 pepper
2-3 tablespoons minced shallot or
 onion

1 tablespoon chopped fresh parsley
1 tablespoon minced fresh tarragon
 or 1 teaspoon dried tarragon
3 eggs yolks
8 ounces unsalted butter, melted and
 kept hot

Place wine, pepper, shallot, parsley, and tarragon in a small, non-aluminum saucepan; bring to a boil, and cook until mixture is reduced to 2 or 3 tablespoons, almost syrup. In a food processor, place yolks and wine mixture. With machine running, slowly pour in hot butter until it combines with egg yolks and thickens. When all butter has been added, adjust seasoning with salt and pepper, and, if necessary, add a little white wine vinegar to raise acidity a bit.

Beef Fillets with Cream-Mushroom Sauce

8	ounces fresh mushrooms, sliced		¼	cup Madeira
2	tablespoons butter		¾	cup beef stock
1	tablespoon vegetable oil		1	cup whipping cream
3	tablespoons minced shallot		2	teaspoons cornstarch blended with
¼	teaspoon salt			1 tablespoon whipping cream
⅛	teaspoon pepper			Salt and pepper to taste
2½	pounds fillet of beef		2	tablespoons butter, softened
2	tablespoons butter			Garnish: fresh parsley sprigs
1	tablespoon vegetable oil			

Sauté mushrooms in a skillet in 2 tablespoons hot butter and 1 tablespoon oil 4 to 5 minutes to brown lightly. Stir in shallot, and cook 1 minute longer. Season mushrooms with salt and pepper, and set aside. Remove all fat and filament, and cut fillet into pieces about 2 inches by ½-inch-thick. Dry thoroughly on paper towels. Place 2 tablespoons butter and 1 tablespoon oil in skillet over medium-high heat. When butter foam begins to subside, sauté beef, a few pieces at a time, 2 to 3 minutes on each side to brown on exterior only. Drain drippings from skillet. Pour wine and stock into skillet, and boil rapidly until liquid is reduced to about ⅓ cup. Whisk in cream, then cornstarch mixture; simmer 1 minute. Add sautéed mushrooms, and simmer 1 minute more or until slightly thickened. Lightly salt and pepper beef, and return to skillet along with any juices. Cover skillet, and heat to below a simmer 3 to 4 minutes, being careful not to overcook beef. Just before serving, tilt skillet, and add softened butter to sauce a bit at a time while basting meat until butter has been absorbed. Garnish, if desired, and serve at once over rice or pasta.

Makes 6 to 7 servings.

 Since Roswell has a very vigorous senior citizen population, the Roswell Symphony Board developed a program to give free concert tickets to seniors on a first come, first served basis. "Send A Senior to the Symphony" is underwritten by local businesses, professionals and individuals and provides more than 150 senior citizens with free tickets for each concert.

Beef with Port

3   cups beef stock
1   cup Tawny Port
1   (3½- to 4-pound) boneless first-
    cut sirloin roast or fillet, tied
    (room temperature)
2   tablespoons minced shallot

2   tablespoons Tawny Port
2   tablespoons red wine vinegar
8   tablespoons unsalted butter
½   teaspoon salt
¼   teaspoon freshly ground pepper

Preheat oven to 450°. Combine stock and 1 cup Port in a saucepan; boil until reduced to ¾ cup, about 1 hour. Reserve mixture. Place roast on a rack over a shallow roasting pan. Set in oven, and immediately reduce temperature to 375°. Roast until meat thermometer registers 125° (for rare), about 1 hour and 15 minutes. Set meat aside on a carving board. Drain off all but 1 tablespoon fat from roasting pan; add shallot, remaining Port, and vinegar, and bring to boil over medium heat, scraping up any browned bits clinging to bottom of pan. Let boil about 1 minute. Transfer sauce to skillet. Add reserved ¾ cup stock, and bring to boil. Reduce heat, and simmer 2 minutes. Whisk in butter, 1 tablespoon at a time, making sure each piece is fully incorporated before adding the next. Add salt and pepper. Adjust seasoning. Serve with roast beef.

Makes 8 servings.

Chaves County Cube Steak

1   pound cube steaks
    Salt to taste
1   teaspoon cracked or coarsely
    ground black pepper
2   tablespoons olive oil

1   garlic clove, minced
1½ teaspoons Dijon mustard
¼   cup red or white wine or beef stock
2   tablespoons water

Sprinkle both sides of steaks with salt, then press pepper into meat with your finger-tips. Heat olive oil in a large skillet over medium heat; add steaks, and cook until medium-rare, about 2 minutes per side. Remove meat from skillet, and reduce heat. Add garlic to skillet, and cook 30 seconds; add mustard, wine, and water, and simmer about 45 seconds, stirring up browned bits clinging to bottom of skillet. Add meat juices that have accumulated from cube steaks to skillet, and adjust seasoning. Spoon sauce over steaks to serve.

Makes 4 servings.

Beef Roast with Onion Sauce

1 rolled sirloin tip roast, about 4 pounds	Salt and pepper to taste
3 garlic cloves, sliced	Onion Sauce

Preheat oven to 450°. Make slits in meat, and insert garlic slices. Season with salt and pepper. Place roast in a shallow roasting pan. Cook until well browned, about 15 minutes. Reduce oven temperature to 350°. Spoon about 3 tablespoons Onion Sauce over meat. Roast 25 minutes to the pound for medium-rare, about 2½ hours, basting with sauce several times during roasting. Remove from oven, and let stand about 15 minutes before carving. Pour remaining Onion Sauce over meat, and serve.

Makes 6 servings.

Onion Sauce

⅓ cup butter	2 tablespoons chopped fresh parsley
1 cup chopped onion	½ teaspoon salt
¾ cup dry white wine	

Melt butter in a skillet over medium heat; add onion, and sauté until soft, about 5 minutes. Add wine, parsley, and salt; simmer 1 minute longer. Remove from heat, and use for basting beef.

Makes about 1¼ cups.

Elegant Fillet

3 tablespoons butter	2 tablespoons Madeira
½ pound sliced fresh mushrooms	1 teaspoon all-purpose flour
Salt and pepper to taste	4 tablespoons butter, softened
2 tablespoons brandy, warmed	1 tablespoon Dijon mustard
2 tablespoons dry sherry, warmed	4 beef tenderloin fillets, ¾ inch thick

Melt butter in a large skillet over medium heat; add mushrooms, and sauté 5 minutes. Add salt, pepper, brandy, sherry, and Madeira. Ignite mixture with a long match, and shake skillet until flame dies out. Cream flour with 2 tablespoons butter and mustard; stir into mushroom mixture. Cook until mixture is slightly thickened. Pan broil tenderloins in remaining 2 tablespoons butter, 2½ to 3 minutes per side for rare. Spoon sauce over fillets, and serve.

Makes 4 servings.

Beef Tenderloin Steaks
with Roquefort Sauce

4 tablespoons butter
⅓ cup finely chopped shallot
2 teaspoons all-purpose flour
½ cup dry white wine

⅔ cup crumbled Roquefort cheese
   (about 3 ounces)
¼ cup whipping cream
4 beef tenderloin steaks, about 1
   inch thick (6 to 8 ounces each)

Melt 2 tablespoons butter in a heavy saucepan over medium heat; add shallot, and sauté until just beginning to brown. Add flour, and stir 1 minute; gradually mix in wine. Boil until liquid is reduced to ¼ cup, stirring often, about 5 minutes. Reduce heat to low; gradually add Roquefort, and stir until melted and smooth. Add whipping cream, and simmer until thickened, about 2 minutes. Season to taste with salt and pepper. Cover and chill (sauce can be prepared 1 day ahead). Melt remaining 2 tablespoons butter in a large, heavy skillet over medium-high heat. Season steaks with salt and pepper; add to skillet, and cook to desired doneness, about 4 minutes per side for rare. Remove sauce from refrigerator, and bring to a simmer over low heat, stirring constantly and thinning with a little more cream, if needed. Stir in any juices from steaks. Spoon sauce over steaks, and serve.

Makes 4 servings.

New Mexico Flank Steak

2 pounds flank steak
1 onion, coarsely chopped
2 garlic cloves, finely chopped

2 teaspoons ground cumin
2 teaspoons freshly ground pepper
½ cup fresh lemon juice

Place steak in a shallow pan. Process remaining ingredients in a food processor until blended. Pour mixture over steak, and marinate 2 hours at room temperature or 4 hours in refrigerator. Prepare grill or broiler. Remove meat from marinade, discarding marinade. Grill or broil about 5 minutes per side. Slice on the diagonal, and serve with Avocado Salsa (see index).

Makes 4 servings.

Bloody Mary Pot Roast

1	(3- to 4-pound) boneless bottom round roast	1	tablespoon prepared horseradish
3	garlic cloves, sliced	1	garlic clove, minced
	Salt and pepper to taste	1	tablespoon Dijon mustard
1	cup spicy tomato juice (Bloody Mary mix)	1	teaspoon Worcestershire sauce
		1	tablespoon vodka
		1	tablespoon cornstarch
		¼	cup water or vodka

Preheat oven to 400°. Place roast in a roasting pan. With a sharp knife, cut slits in meat, and insert garlic slices. Season with salt and pepper to taste, and roast, uncovered, 15 minutes. In a small bowl, stir together juice, horseradish, garlic, mustard, and Worcestershire sauce. Pour sauce over meat. Reduce oven temperature to 350°, and bake roast, covered, 2½ hours, basting with sauce several times. Remove meat to a platter, and let stand 10 minutes before carving. Combine 1 tablespoon cornstarch and ¼ cup water (or vodka). Stir into roasting pan with drippings. Place over high heat, and bring to a boil, stirring constantly, until thickened, about 2 minutes. Serve gravy with roast.

Makes 4 to 5 servings.

Oven-Roasted, Deviled Country Ribs

¾	cup all-purpose flour	2-2½	pounds lean, boneless country beef ribs
1	tablespoon hot paprika		
½	teaspoon salt	1	cup Dijon mustard
1	teaspoon freshly ground black pepper	1	tablespoon brown sugar
		1	cup dry breadcrumbs
3	garlic cloves, minced	⅓	cup chopped fresh parsley

Preheat oven to 325°. Put flour, paprika, salt, pepper, and garlic in a paper bag, and shake to blend. Drop ribs into seasoned flour, and shake to coat. Place ribs on a rack in a roasting pan, and bake for 1½ hours. Remove ribs, and cut into individual portions. Cool to room temperature. (The ribs can be prepared up to this point up to 2 days ahead and refrigerated. Return to room temperature before continuing.) Preheat oven to 425°. Combine mustard and brown sugar. Using a brush, paint ribs generously with mustard mixture. Combine breadcrumbs and parsley, and roll mustard-painted ribs in crumb mixture. Place ribs on a shallow baking pan lined with foil. Bake for 45 minutes or until brown and crispy.

Makes 8 servings.

Bourbon Beef Tenderloin

1 whole beef tenderloin, about
  4 pounds
  Bourbon Baste

Garnish: fresh parsley sprigs
Horseradish Sauce

Prepare grill. Place meat in a foil pan; spread with Bourbon Baste. Grill with lid down for 1 hour and 15 minutes for medium-rare. Add ½ cup water, if necessary to keep meat moist. Transfer to a platter; slice and serve with Horseradish Sauce. Garnish, if desired.

Bourbon Baste

2 tablespoons bourbon
3 tablespoons soy sauce
1 tablespoon Dijon mustard
1 tablespoon vegetable oil

1 tablespoon honey
1 teaspoon prepared horseradish
2 cloves garlic, minced
  Freshly ground pepper to taste

Combine all ingredients.

Makes about ½ cup.

Horseradish Sauce

1 tablespoon peeled, grated fresh
  horseradish or 2 tablespoons
  prepared horseradish

½ cup light sour cream
¼ cup plain nonfat yogurt
¼ teaspoon dry mustard

Combine all ingredients in a bowl; cover and chill until ready to use. Serve at room temperature.

Makes ¾ cup.

Phillis Ideal

Phillis Ideal is a true Roswellite having been born in Roswell, New Mexico in 1942, though she spent most of her art career in New York City and now lives in Albuquerque. She received her Bachelor of Fine Arts degree from the University of New Mexico, Albuquerque in 1964 and a Masters of Fine Arts degree from the University of California at Berkeley in 1976.

Ideal's exhibition record includes shows from the West Coast to the East Coast, including the San Francisco Art Institute, the Museum of Fine Arts in Santa Fe, and the Richard Green Gallery in New York, New York. Her work is included in collections at the Roswell Museum and Art Center and the Anderson Museum of Contemporary Art in Roswell; Crocker National Bank in San Francisco; Skidmore, Owings and Merrill, Chicago, Illinois; and Prudential Insurance Collection, Newark, New Jersey.

One reviewer summarized an exhibit of Ideal's work by saying, "Overall, one is left with a strong sense of Ideal's personal iconography, one that is able to strike a chord in every viewer. Greatly enhanced by their tactile, fresco-like surfaces, their simplicity and honesty, these paintings offer access to the delight that can be found in the commonest of objects."

The Red One
Artist – Phillis Ideal–Icon series
69″ × 48″   1984
oil on wood panel
Permanent collection, Roswell
Museum and Art Center.
Photograph by Jose Rivera.

Corn Pie in Ground Beef Crust

1 tablespoon olive oil
1 cup chopped yellow onion
½ cup chopped celery
½ cup chopped red bell pepper
2 tablespoons minced fresh hot chile pepper
1½ cups peeled, seeded, and chopped ripe or canned tomato
1 tablespoon minced garlic
½ cup golden raisins
1 teaspoon ground cumin
1 tablespoon chile powder, preferably from ancho or pasilla peppers
Salt to taste

Crushed dried red pepper to taste
1 pound ground round or other lean tender beef
¼ cup fine, dry whole-wheat breadcrumbs
2¾ cups fresh corn kernels (about 4 large ears)
1 tablespoon all-purpose flour
2 eggs, lightly beaten
½ cup milk
2 green onions, including green tops, thinly sliced
Garnish: fresh cilantro sprigs

Preheat oven to 350°. Heat oil in a large skillet over medium heat; add onion and next 4 ingredients, and sauté until juices have evaporated and vegetables are soft. Add garlic and next 5 ingredients; stir and remove from heat. Combine ground beef and breadcrumbs, and add to vegetable mixture, stirring until well mixed. Spoon into a greased 9-inch square baking dish; smooth top with back of a spoon, creating an even layer. Combine corn and next 4 ingredients; stir to mix well. Pour over meat layer, spreading evenly. Bake until center feels set when lightly touched , about 35 minutes. Remove from oven, and let stand 15 minutes. Cut into squares, and garnish, if desired.

Makes 4 to 6 servings.

Corn-Stuffed Steak

2 pounds boneless beef sirloin or top round, in a single piece about 2 inches thick

Marinade

¾ cup dry red wine
2 tablespoons olive oil
1 tablespoon Dijon mustard
1 tablespoon minced fresh oregano or 1 teaspoon dried oregano, crumbled

1 teaspoon minced garlic
Salt and freshly ground pepper to taste

Combine all ingredients, stirring until well blended. Set aside.

Stuffing

2 tablespoons unsalted butter
½ cup chopped yellow onion
¼ cup finely chopped red bell pepper
2 tablespoons minced fresh green hot chile pepper
½ cup fresh corn kernels

¾ cup crumbled cornbread (your favorite recipe)
½ cup shredded sharp Cheddar cheese
1 tablespoon minced fresh cilantro or parsley
Salt, freshly ground black pepper, and cayenne pepper to taste

Cut a horizontal pocket in center of 1 side of steak, cutting as deeply and as long as possible without piercing the other side or the ends. Place steak in a shallow dish; pour Marinade over steak, and turn to coat all sides and inside of pocket. Let stand at room temperature 1 hour, or cover and chill as long as overnight (bring to room temperature before stuffing). Melt butter in a large skillet over medium heat; add onion and bell pepper, and sauté until soft but not browned, about 5 minutes. Stir in chile pepper and corn, and sauté about 3 minutes. Transfer to a bowl. Stir in crumbled cornbread, cheese, minced cilantro, and salt and peppers to taste. Remove meat from marinade, and pat dry; reserve marinade. Stuff meat pocket with cornbread mixture, and close with skewers or sew tightly with cotton thread. Sprinkle steak with salt and pepper to taste. Prepare grill. Bring reserved marinade to a boil in a small saucepan over medium-high heat. Remove from heat. Place steak on grill rack over a drip pan; cook about 10 minutes per side for medium-rare, basting occasionally with reserved marinade. Let steak stand about 15 minutes. Discard skewers or thread, and cut into slices about ½ inch thick. Arrange slices on individual plates, and spoon drip pan juices over steak.

Makes 8 servings.

Fiesta Skirt Steak

2   pounds skirt steak

Marinade

1   tablespoon dried oregano
2   tablespoons ground cumin
1   tablespoon chile powder

2   garlic cloves, finely minced
⅓   cup red wine vinegar

Sauce

3   tablespoons olive oil
2   large onions, sliced
2   green bell peppers, seeded and cut
      into ½-inch slices
2   red bell peppers, seeded and cut
      into ½-inch slices
2   fresh jalapeños, seeded and
      minced

1   tablespoon minced garlic
1   tablespoon dried oregano
3   cups peeled, seeded, and diced
      tomatoes
¼   cup fresh lemon juice
4   tablespoons chopped fresh cilantro
      Salt and pepper to taste

Cut skirt steak into 4 uniform portions (save very thin parts for another use). Place steak in a shallow dish. Combine all marinade ingredients in a bowl; pour over meat, and let stand at room temperature 2 to 3 hours, or chill 6 hours. Heat oil in a large skillet over medium heat; add onion, and sauté until softened, about 5 minutes. Add green and red bell peppers, and cook 5 minutes. Stir in jalapeños and next 3 ingredients; stir for a few minutes. Add lemon juice and cilantro; simmer 2 minutes. Season sauce mixture with salt and pepper to taste. Prepare broiler or grill. Broil or grill steaks 3 minutes per side for rare. Place steaks on a serving platter; reheat sauce, and pour over steaks.

Makes 4 to 6 servings.

Individual Beef Wellingtons

4	beef fillets (4 ounces each)	4	tablespoons brandy
1	garlic clove, halved	½	cup fresh mushrooms, minced
	Salt and pepper to taste	1	(4-ounce) tin liver pâté (optional)
4	tablespoons butter		

Rub each fillet with garlic, and sprinkle with salt and pepper to taste. Melt butter in a large skillet over medium heat; add fillets, and sauté 3 minutes on each side. Ignite brandy with a long match, and pour over fillets. Remove fillets, and chill. Sauté mushrooms in same skillet; remove and chill. If using pâté, mix with chilled mushrooms, and spread over fillets. Chill. Keep skillet for mushroom sauce.

Pastry

1	package frozen patty shells, thawed, or pie crust dough enough for a two-crust pie	1	egg, beaten
			Butter

Preheat oven to 425°. Roll out patty shells or dough, and trim into 4 (6-inch) squares. Brush squares with egg. Place each fillet, pâté side down, on a pastry square. Fold dough completely over fillets, and seal edges with butter. Place, seam side down, on a greased baking sheet, and brush again with egg. Bake 20 to 25 minutes or until crust is richly browned. Serve with heated Mushroom Sauce.

Mushroom Sauce

¼	cup minced onion	½	cups beef broth
6	large mushrooms, sliced	1	bay leaf
3	tablespoons all-purpose flour	1	teaspoon Worcestershire sauce
½	cup red wine		Salt and pepper to taste

Sauté onion and sliced mushrooms in reserved skillet; stir in flour. Gradually add wine, broth, and bay leaf; stir until sauce bubbles and is thickened. Add Worcestershire sauce and salt and pepper to taste.

Makes 4 servings.

Mushroom-Garlic Skillet Steak

16 garlic cloves, unpeeled
2 teaspoons olive oil
3 tablespoons olive oil
  Salt and pepper to taste
4 (8-ounce) boneless top loin steaks (New York strip) about 1½ inches thick, trimmed of fat

½ pound small wild mushrooms (chanterelles, cremini, and shiitake), cleaned, or ½ pound white mushrooms, sliced
2 tablespoons Scotch whiskey or a good bourbon whiskey
1 cup defatted beef stock
2 teaspoons arrowroot, mixed with a little stock
2 teaspoons fresh thyme leaves

Preheat oven to 375°. Place garlic on a large piece of foil; drizzle with 2 teaspoons olive oil, and sprinkle with salt and pepper. Fold edges of foil over garlic, and crimp to enclose completely. Place foil packet in center of oven, and roast 30 minutes. Open foil, and roast 10 minutes or until garlic is lightly browned and tender. Remove from oven, and let cool. Carefully peel garlic, keeping cloves whole; set aside. Dry steaks thoroughly on paper towels, and set aside. Heat 2 tablespoon olive oil in a 12-inch nonstick skillet over medium-high heat. Add mushrooms to skillet, and sauté quickly until lightly browned; season with salt and pepper; transfer to a dish, and set aside. Add remaining 1 tablespoon olive oil to skillet. When almost smoking, add steaks without crowding pan. Sear steaks quickly on each side until nicely browned; season with salt and pepper. Reduce heat, and continue to cook, covered, 3 minutes per side for rare. Remove steaks to a dish, and keep warm. Discard all fat from skillet; add whiskey, and reduce to a glaze. Add stock; bring to a boil, and reduce by one-third. Whisk in arrowroot mixture, enough to coat a spoon. Add mushrooms, garlic, and thyme; cook just until heated through. Adjust seasonings. Slice each steak crosswise into thin slices, and place on plates. Spoon sauce over steaks.

Makes 6 servings.

New Mexico Beef Stew

½ cup cornmeal
½ teaspoon freshly ground black pepper
½ teaspoon dried thyme
1¾ pounds well-trimmed eye of round, cut in 1½-inch cubes
2-3 tablespoons vegetable oil
3 garlic cloves, minced
1½ cups water, approximately

2⅓ cups fresh corn kernels (about 3 ears)
2 cups chopped onion
2 jalapeños, seeded and chopped
1 (16-ounce) can garbanzos, drained
1 (28-ounce) can whole tomatoes with juice
2 cups 1½-inch cubes celery root (optional)
1 chipotle pepper

Mix cornmeal, black pepper, salt, and thyme. Roll beef lightly in cornmeal mixture, shaking off any excess. Heat oil in heavy, flameproof Dutch oven over high heat. Add beef to oil, and sauté until browned, 4 to 5 minutes. Reduce heat to medium-high, and add garlic. Cook, stirring for a few seconds; add water to come halfway up sides of beef. Cover and bring to a boil. Reduce heat, and simmer 20 to 30 minutes. Add corn and next 6 ingredients. Cover and return to a boil. Reduce heat, and simmer 25 to 30 minutes or until vegetables and meat are tender. Adjust seasonings.

This stew can be cooked in the oven at 350° for 1½ hours.

Makes 6 servings.

Spring River Flank Steak

½ cup pineapple juice
¼ cup soy sauce
1 garlic clove, minced

1 teaspoon ginger
1½ pounds flank steak

Combine first 4 ingredients. Place steak in a shallow dish; score with a sharp knife, and pour marinade over top. Chill 24 hours. Prepare grill; grill steak 8 minutes per side for medium-rare. Slice thinly across the grain.

Makes 4 to 6 servings.

Picadillo Stuffed Peppers

4 tablespoons olive oil
1 pound minced beef chuck
2 onions, chopped
4 celery ribs, chopped
6 garlic cloves, minced
½ cup seeded, diced green chile pepper
2 teaspoons ground cumin
¼ teaspoon ground cinnamon
½ cup dry red wine
1 cup diced canned plum tomatoes

⅔ cup raisins, soaked in hot water to cover 20 minutes, then drained
¼ cup pimiento-stuffed green olives, halved
Beef stock as needed
Salt and pepper to taste
5-6 bell peppers (red, yellow, or green)
1 hard-cooked egg, chopped (optional)
½ cup lightly toasted almonds

Meat Mixture
Heat 2 tablespoons oil in a large skillet over high heat; add beef, and cook, breaking it up with a spoon until browned, 10 to 15 minutes. Transfer meat and juices to a bowl. Heat remaining oil in skillet over medium heat; Add onion, celery, garlic, and chile pepper, and cook, stirring occasionally, until vegetables soften, about 10 minutes. Add beef with juices, cumin, cloves, cinnamon, wine, tomatoes, raisins, and olives. Reduce heat to low, and cook, uncovered, about 15 minutes. (If mixture seems dry, add a little more wine or beef stock.) Add salt and pepper to taste.

Peppers
Preheat oven to 350°. Cut off a thin slice from stem end of each pepper; scoop out seeds. Stuff cooked meat mixture into peppers, and stand them upright in a baking dish just large enough to hold them. Add a little water to dish; cover tightly with foil, and bake until peppers are tender when pierced with a fork, about 30 minutes. Sprinkle tops with egg and almonds.

Makes 5 to 6 servings.

Roast Fillet of Beef with Chipotle Sauce

2 tablespoons vegetable oil
3½ pounds fillet of beef, at room temperature

Salt and pepper to taste

Heat oil in a heavy, flameproof roasting pan over medium-high heat until hot but not smoking. Pat beef dry, and season with salt and pepper to taste. Add beef to oil, and brown, turning every 12 to 15 minutes or until a meat thermometer registers 130°. (Narrow end of beef will be medium-rare; wide end will be rare.) Serve beef with sauce.

Makes 8 servings.

Chipotle Sauce

2 tablespoons olive oil
3 cups thinly sliced red bell pepper (about 3 large peppers)

1 canned unseeded chipotle chile in adobo
2 teaspoons Worcestershire sauce
Salt to taste

Heat oil in a heavy skillet over medium heat; add bell pepper, and cook, covered, over medium-low heat, stirring occasionally, 25 to 30 minutes or until soft. Process bell pepper, chipotle, Worcestershire, and salt in a blender until pureed. (Sauce may be made 2 days in advance and kept covered and chilled.) Transfer sauce to a sauce boat, and serve warm or at room temperature.

Makes about 1 cup.

Veal Loretto

1 pound veal medallions
4 tablespoons olive oil
6 tablespoons butter

¼ cup pine nuts, roasted
2 teaspoons fresh basil
¼ cup Frangelico liqueur

Lightly salt and flour veal. Heat oil in a skillet over medium-high heat; add veal, and sauté on each side until cooked and golden brown. Drain drippings from skillet, and add butter, pine nuts, and basil, stirring over high heat. Add Frangelico, and ignite with a long match. Serve drippings over veal.

Makes 4 servings.

Special Beef Brisket

1 (4- to 5-pound) beef brisket, flat cut
2 tablespoons soy sauce
2 tablespoons red wine
2 tablespoons red wine vinegar
2 cloves garlic, minced
2 teaspoons Worcestershire sauce
1 cup beef broth
1 tablespoon prepared horseradish sauce
1 tablespoon Dijon mustard
   Freshly ground black pepper to taste
1 yellow onion, sliced

Preheat oven to 350°. Remove excess fat from brisket, and place in a non-aluminum baking dish. Combine soy sauce and next 8 ingredients. Pour soy sauce mixture over brisket; cover and chill 4 to 5 hours or overnight, turning once. Remove brisket from refrigerator, and let stand 1 hour before baking. Bake brisket in marinade, covered, for 2 hours, basting several times. Place onion rings on top of brisket, and baste again. Bake, covered, 1 more hour. Remove brisket from dish, and let stand 10 minutes before carving. Slice thinly across grain to serve. Reheat pan juices, and spoon a little over meat.

Can be served with Spicy Mustard Sauce or with noodles or rice and a little of pan juices.

Spicy Mustard Sauce
1 tablespoon brown sugar
1 teaspoon cider vinegar
½ teaspoon dill weed
¼ cup Dijon mustard
¼ cup prepared mustard
2 teaspoons vegetable oil

Combine sugar and vinegar in a small bowl until sugar is dissolved. Stir in remaining ingredients, and mix well. Cover and chill. Serve at room temperature.

Makes ½ cup.

_____Steak Au Poivre_____

5 tablespoons coarsely cracked
   peppercorns
4 beef fillets, about 1½ inches thick,
   at room temperature
   Salt to taste
¼ cup unsalted butter

1 tablespoon olive oil
½ cup Cognac or brandy
½ cup beef stock
2 tablespoon Dijon mustard
1 cup whipping cream

Spread peppercorns on a plate or cutting board. Press fillets into peppercorns, turning to coat both sides and pushing peppercorns into fillets with heel of your hand. Let fillets stand at room temperature 30 minutes. Sprinkle fillets with salt. Heat butter and oil in a heavy skillet over high heat. When pan is hot, add fillets; sear, turning once, 3 minutes per side for rare. Transfer to a warmed platter; keep warm. Pour drippings from skillet. Pour Cognac in skillet over high heat, stirring to dislodge any browned bits. Add stock, mustard, and cream; reduce mixture by half over high heat. Pour over fillets, and serve.

Makes 4 servings.

_____Veal with Lemon_____

8 thin slices veal scaloppine, about
   1½ pounds
   Salt and freshly ground pepper to
   taste
2 tablespoons all-purpose flour
¼ cup olive oil
4 tablespoons butter

⅓ cup dry white wine
½ cup chicken broth
   Juice of 1 lemon
2 tablespoons chopped fresh parsley
   Garnishes: thin lemon slices, fresh
   parsley sprigs

Pound veal pieces with a meat mallet; sprinkle with salt and pepper. Dredge veal in flour. Heat oil in a large, heavy skillet over high heat; add as many pieces of veal as skillet will hold in 1 layer. Cook over high heat until browned, 2 minutes on each side. Transfer veal to a hot platter. Drain drippings from skillet, and return skillet to heat. Melt butter in skillet; return veal to skillet, cooking on both sides and adding any liquid accumulated on platter. Add wine, broth, lemon juice, and parsley; cook, turning veal in skillet so it cooks evenly, until sauce has a nice consistency. Garnish, if desired.

Makes 4 servings.

Breaded Veal with Chile and Cheese

4 slices veal scaloppine, about
¼ pound each
Salt and freshly ground pepper to
taste
¼ cup all-purpose flour
1 egg
2 tablespoons water
2 cups fresh breadcrumbs
¾ cup grated Parmesan cheese

4 tablespoons peanut, vegetable, or
corn oil
1 tablespoon butter
4 whole fresh green chiles, roasted
and peeled
4-8 slices Monterey Jack cheese
Garnishes: lemon wedges, chopped
fresh parsley and cilantro

Pound veal pieces lightly with a meat mallet; sprinkle with salt and pepper to taste. Dredge veal in flour. Beat egg with water in a flat dish; add salt and pepper to taste. Coat veal on all sides in egg, patting with fingers. Dip veal in breadcrumbs blended with Parmesan cheese to coat on all sides. Press on sides of meat lightly with the flat side of a heavy knife to help crumbs adhere. Heat oil and butter in a skillet over medium heat; add veal. Cook until golden brown, about 3 minutes on each side. Arrange green chiles neatly on top of each scaloppine; cover with cheese. Cover skillet, and cook until veal is cooked through and cheese is hot and melted, 3 to 5 minutes. Garnish, if desired.

Makes 4 servings.

Chimayo Marinated Lamb Chops

16 loin lamb chops

Marinade
¼ cup balsamic vinegar
1 cup fresh orange juice
1 teaspoon ground fennel
1 teaspoon ground mace
1 teaspoon ground allspice
1 teaspoon ground cinnamon

1 teaspoon ground cloves
½ cup Chimayo chile, medium-hot
2 tablespoons fresh rosemary
2 tablespoons fresh thyme leaves
Salt and pepper to taste
3-4 cups vegetable oil

Process first 7 ingredients in a blender until blended. Add oil in a slow, steady stream to make an emulsion. Place lamb chops in a large, heavy-duty plastic bag; add marinade, and chill 24 hours. Prepare grill. Grill chops over hot coals 3 minutes per side or until done.

Makes 4 to 6 servings.

Anasazi Lamb Chops

24 loin lamb chops

Marinade
1 cup olive oil
2 tablespoons chopped garlic
1 tablespoon chopped fresh cilantro

2 limes, juiced and zested
1 teaspoon chopped fresh thyme
1 teaspoon chopped fresh rosemary

Combine oil, garlic, herbs, and lime juice and zest in a shallow dish. Coat each lamb chop in mixture; cover and chill overnight. Remove chops from marinade, discarding marinade. Prepare grill or broiler; grill or broil until rare or medium-rare. Serve with Tomato-Mint Jelly.

Makes 6 to 8 servings.

Tomato-Mint Jelly
1 bunch fresh mint, chopped
1 cup sun-dried tomatoes, chopped
2 limes, juiced and zested
1 (8-ounce) jar apple jelly
2 chipotle chiles, cracked

1 purple onion, diced
2 ancho chiles, cut into strips
   Salt, ground white pepper, and
   cayenne pepper to taste

Combine all ingredients in a small bowl, stirring just until combined. Serve as a salsa.

Grilled Lamb Chops

3 tablespoons Dijon mustard
2 teaspoons minced garlic
2 tablespoons balsamic vinegar
½ teaspoon salt
⅛ teaspoon freshly ground black
   pepper

½ cup olive oil
2 teaspoons water
¼ cup chopped fresh basil
12 (1½-inch-thick) rib lamb chops,
   trimmed of extra fat

Combine first 7 ingredients in a bowl; whisk in oil until mixture is creamy. Stir in basil, and pour mixture into a shallow dish. Add chops to mixture, tossing to coat. Cover and chill chops 1 to 3 hours. Shake excess marinade from chops. Prepare grill; grill chops 4 to 5 minutes per side for medium-rare, or slightly longer for well done.

Makes 4 servings.

Balsamic-Marinated Lamb Chops

½ cup balsamic vinegar
3 garlic cloves, coarsely chopped
3 shallots, coarsely chopped
¾ teaspoon crumbled dried thyme
¾ teaspoon salt

½ teaspoon freshly ground pepper
6 (1½-inch-thick) loin lamb chops
Vegetable oil
Pimiento Butter

Whisk first 6 ingredients in a large bowl. Place chops in a large, heavy-duty plastic bag; add marinade, and chill, turning several times, at least 8 hours or overnight. Drain chops, and pat dry with paper towels; bring to room temperature. Brush chops well with oil. Prepare grill. Grill chops on a well-oiled rack set 5 to 6 inches over glowing coals 8 minutes on each side for medium-rare or until just springy to the touch. Transfer chops to a platter, and let stand 5 minutes. Top each chop with a dollop of Pimiento Butter from a spoon or from a pastry bag fitted with a fluted tip.

Makes 6 servings.

Pimiento Butter

6 tablespoons unsalted butter, softened
¼ cup drained bottled pimiento or roasted red pepper, patted dry and chopped

½ teaspoon fresh lemon juice
Salt and pepper to taste

Process all ingredients until pimiento is minced and butter is orange. Season with salt and pepper to taste.

Makes ½ cup.

 The Chamber Concert Series are a very popular addition to the five annual subscription concerts. These three programs are held at the beautiful Roswell Museum and Art Center and feature chamber groups and multi-cultural programs. These more intimate concerts are always a "sell out".

Lamb Chops

⅓ cup fresh sourdough breadcrumbs
½ cup finely minced fresh parsley
2 garlic cloves, minced
1 shallot, minced
3 tablespoons butter, melted

1 teaspoon dry mustard
⅛ teaspoon cayenne pepper
4 (1½-inch-thick) lamb chops, about 4 ounces each
Salt and black pepper to taste

Preheat oven to 500°. Place breadcrumbs on a small baking sheet, and bake until dry but not brown, about 4 minutes. Remove from oven. Place a rack on a baking pan; combine breadcrumbs, parsley, garlic, and shallot in a pie plate. Combine melted butter, mustard, and cayenne pepper in a shallow dish. Season lamb with salt and pepper to taste; dip both sides of chops in butter mixture, then in parsley mixture, coating evenly. Place chops on rack on pan. Bake until coating is golden brown and lamb is cooked to desired doneness, about 14 minutes for medium-rare.

Makes 2 servings.

Braised Lamb Shanks with Rosemary

8 meaty lamb shanks (about 10 pounds)
6 garlic cloves, slivered
3 tablespoons chopped fresh rosemary or
   1 tablespoon crumbled dried rosemary

Salt and pepper to taste
1½ cups all-purpose flour
1 cup vegetable oil
1 quart dry red wine
¼ cup butter
3 large onions, thinly sliced
2 cups beef stock

Preheat oven to 350°. Make incisions in shanks with a sharp knife, and insert garlic slivers. Sprinkle shanks with 1 tablespoon rosemary, pressing rosemary into meat. Sprinkle with salt and pepper to taste, and dust each shank with flour. Heat oil in a large, flameproof baking dish; add shanks in batches, and brown evenly over medium-high heat. Transfer shanks to a platter. Add wine to dish; bring to a boil, and reduce to about 2 cups, scraping dish to loosen browned bits. Heat butter in a large skillet; add onion, and sauté over medium heat 5 minutes. Add onion to wine mixture; top with shanks and stock. Add salt and pepper and remaining rosemary. Bring mixture to a boil; reduce heat, and braise in oven 2 to 2½ hours or until shanks are fork tender.

Makes 8 servings.

Lamb Korma (Rich Curry)

½ cup vegetable shortening
2 medium-size onions, chopped
8 garlic cloves
10 slices fresh ginger root
2 tablespoons ground coriander
2 teaspoons ground cumin

1 teaspoon ground turmeric
Salt to taste
2 pounds cubed lean stewing lamb
2 tablespoons tomato paste
1 cup plain yogurt

Melt shortening in a skillet over medium heat; add onion, and sauté until golden. Add garlic and next 5 ingredients to onion. Add meat, stirring to coat well. Cook 2 minutes; add tomato paste and yogurt. Cook over low heat until meat is tender. (If necessary to add water to gravy, do so after meat is half cooked.) Serve with desired condiments.

Makes 6 servings.

Suggested Sides and Condiments

Fresh mint ground with coconut and green chiles; add lemon juice and salt

Chopped tomato with chopped onion, chopped green chiles, lemon juice, salt, and pepper

Mashed potatoes with chopped onion, green chiles, vinegar, and salt

Fried bacon in rice

Apple ground with mint and green chiles; add lemon juice and salt

Coconut, grated and browned; add salt

Chopped cucumber (seeded), onion, lemon juice, and salt

Green mangoes, onion, coconut, lemon juice, pepper, and salt, all ground to paste

Quarters of banana, tossed in melted butter

Currants, sultanas, almonds, onion rings, all fried in butter

Chopped hard-cooked egg with minced green chiles, salt, and lemon juice

Lamb with Sautéed Peppers

1¾ cups dry white wine
⅓ cup packed fresh oregano leaves, chopped, or 2 teaspoons dried oregano
3 tablespoons extra virgin olive oil
4 bay leaves, crumbled
2 garlic cloves, crushed
1 tablespoon shredded lemon peel
3½ pounds boneless leg of lamb, trimmed and cut into 1-inch pieces
6 tablespoons extra virgin olive oil
1 large onion, finely chopped

1½ tablespoons minced fresh flat-leaf parsley
2 jalapeños, seeded and thinly sliced
2 garlic cloves, minced
1 cup drained Italian-style plum tomatoes, crushed
1 cup chicken stock
 Salt and freshly ground pepper to taste
2 red bell peppers, cut into strips
2 yellow bell peppers, cut into strips

Combine first 6 ingredients in a large bowl. Add lamb, and toss well. Cover and chill overnight. Remove lamb, scraping herbs clinging to lamb back into bowl; reserve marinade. Pat lamb dry with paper towels. Heat 2 tablespoons oil in a large, heavy Dutch oven over medium-high heat; add half of lamb, and brown well. Transfer lamb to a bowl. Repeat procedure with 2 tablespoons oil and remaining lamb. Add onion and parsley to pan, and sauté 3 minutes. Add jalapeños, and sauté until onion begins to brown, about 5 minutes. Add minced garlic and reserved marinade to onion mixture, and bring to a boil, scraping any browned bits loose from pan. Return lamb to pan with onion mixture, and add tomatoes. Reduce heat, cover partially, and simmer until lamb is tender and sauce is very thick but not dry, about 1 hour and 30 minutes. Season with salt and pepper. Heat remaining 2 tablespoons oil in a large, heavy skillet over high heat; add bell peppers, and sauté until tender but firm. Add lamb mixture, and simmer 10 minutes. Serve hot.

Makes 8 servings.

Navajo Lamb Stew

2 tablespoons vegetable oil (more if needed)
1½ pounds lamb, cut into cubes
1 cup finely chopped onion
2 garlic cloves, minced
4 large tomatoes, chopped, or 1 (16-ounce) can tomatoes, undrained
1½ cups corn kernels

1 teaspoon cumin seed, crushed to a coarse powder
1 teaspoon salt
½ teaspoon freshly ground pepper
1 green serrano chile, seeded and minced
1 yellow chile, seeded and minced
1 New Mexico green chile, roasted, peeled, seeded, and finely chopped (or Anaheim, seeded and chopped)

Heat oil in a large skillet over medium-high heat; add lamb in batches, and sauté until browned (add oil, if needed). Remove lamb to a plate. Add onion and garlic to skillet, and sauté until onion is translucent. Add remaining ingredients, including lamb, to skillet; add water to cover, and bring to a boil. Reduce heat, and simmer, covered, 1½ to 2 hours or until meat is tender. Serve with rice or beans.

Makes 6 servings.

Nut-Crusted Lamb Chops

½ cup blanched slivered almonds
½ cup pine nuts
½ cup pistachios
½ cup walnuts
½ cup breadcrumbs
Salt and pepper to taste

½ cup all-purpose flour
2 large eggs
1 teaspoon milk
8 (1½-inch-thick) loin lamb chops (about 4 ounces each)
2 tablespoons olive oil

Preheat oven to 425°. Process all nuts in a food processor until finely chopped; transfer to a medium-size bowl. Add breadcrumbs to bowl. Season mixture with salt and pepper to taste. Place flour in a separate medium-size bowl. Whisk eggs and milk in another bowl. Coat lamb chops with flour, dip into egg mixture, and dredge in nut mixture, coating completely. Heat olive oil in a large, heavy skillet over medium heat; add lamb in batches, cooking until golden brown, about 2 minutes per side. Transfer lamb to a baking sheet. Bake lamb to desired doneness, about 12 minutes for medium-rare.

Makes 4 servings.

You can use chicken breasts instead of lamb in this recipe.

Orange-Herb Roasted Leg of Lamb

2 garlic cloves, minced
2 teaspoons finely chopped grated orange zest
1 tablespoon finely chopped fresh flat-leaf parsley
1 teaspoon finely chopped fresh rosemary
1 teaspoon finely chopped fresh thyme
⅛ teaspoon ground cumin
⅛ teaspoon salt

⅛ teaspoon pepper
3 tablespoons plus 1 teaspoon olive oil
1 (8- to 9-pound) leg of lamb, trimmed of excess fat
½ cup fresh orange juice
¾ cup dry white wine
4 medium-size onions, halved crosswise
8 small carrots, halved lengthwise

Preheat oven to 450°. Combine first 8 ingredients and 1 teaspoon olive oil. Make 25 evenly spaced 1-inch incisions in meaty sections of lamb, using a sharp knife. Stuff each incision with ½ teaspoon orange-herb mixture. Turn lamb, fat side up, and rub with 1 tablespoon oil and 2 tablespoons orange juice. (At this point, lamb may be refrigerated 1 day.) Combine ½ cup wine and 2 tablespoons oil in a large roasting pan. Arrange onion and carrot, cut sides down, in pan. Set lamb atop vegetables, and season with salt and pepper to taste. Bake in center of oven for 20 minutes. Pour ½ cup wine and ½ cup water into pan, and reduce temperature to 325°. Bake 1 hour and 20 minutes, basting occasionally with pan juices and adding water, if needed. Pour 2 tablespoons orange juice over lamb, and increase temperature to 400°. Bake about 30 minutes or until an instant-read thermometer registers 135°. Transfer lamb to a carving board; cover loosely with foil, and let stand 10 minutes. Transfer carrot and onion to a plate, and keep warm. Set roasting pan on 2 burners over medium-high heat. Add ¼ cup orange juice; bring to a boil, and boil 3 minutes, scraping browned bits loose from pan. Add 1 cup water, and reduce sauce about 5 minutes. Skim fat, and pour into serving bowl. Add any juices from lamb; season gravy with salt and pepper. Carve lamb, and serve with roasted carrot and onion.

Makes about 8 servings.

Peppered Lamb

1 cup whipping cream
3 ounces soft fresh goat cheese
¼ cup dried cranberries
Salt and coarsely ground pepper
to taste

4 lamb shoulder chops (about 8
ounces each), trimmed of excess fat
1 tablespoon butter
½ cup pine nuts, toasted
2 tablespoons thinly sliced fresh
basil leaves

Whisk cream, goat cheese, and cranberries in a heavy saucepan over medium-low heat until cheese melts. Simmer, stirring occasionally, until sauce is reduced to 1¼ cups, about 8 minutes. Season sauce with salt and pepper to taste; cover and keep warm. Press pepper onto both sides of lamb; sprinkle with salt. Melt butter in a heavy skillet over medium heat; add lamb, and cook to desired doneness, about 4 minutes per side for medium-rare. Transfer lamb to serving plates. Add pine nuts to sauce, and reheat, if needed. Stir in basil, and pour sauce over lamb to serve.

Makes 4 servings.

Marinated, Grilled Leg of Lamb

Marinade
½ cup olive oil
⅓ cup fresh orange juice
2 teaspoons finely grated orange peel
1 tablespoon Grand Marnier
1½ teaspoons minced fresh thyme or
½ teaspoon dried thyme, crumbled
1 teaspoon cumin seed, crushed to a
coarse powder

1 tablespoon minced fresh cilantro
Salt and freshly ground pepper to
taste
1 leg of lamb (about 5 pounds),
boned, butterflied, and trimmed of
fat
1½ cups Green Chile Sauce (see index)

Combine all marinade ingredients in a large, non-aluminum pan. Add lamb, cover, and chill overnight or up to 2 days, turning occasionally. Prepare grill. Remove lamb from refrigerator, and let stand at room temperature about 30 minutes. Remove lamb from marinade, reserving marinade. Bring marinade to a boil in a small saucepan; remove from heat. Grill lamb over hot coals, about 3 inches from heat, basting often with marinade and turning once, about 20 minutes or until medium-rare. Slice lamb across grain, and serve with Green Chile Sauce.

Makes 6 servings.

Southwestern Grilled Leg of Lamb

2 medium-size yellow onions, chopped

6 garlic cloves, chopped

3 fresh jalapeños, stemmed and chopped

½ cup olive oil

⅓ cup fresh lime juice

3½ tablespoons mild chile powder

1½ tablespoons cumin seed, toasted

1½ tablespoons dried oregano, crumbled

2½ teaspoons salt

1 boneless, butterflied leg of lamb (about 7 pounds)

3 cups mesquite or hickory wood chips, soaked in water 30 minutes and drained

Process first 3 ingredients in a food processor until partially pureed; add oil and next 5 ingredients, and process until smooth. Pour puree over lamb in a large pan; cover and chill 24 hours, turning occasionally. Remove lamb from refrigerator, and let stand until room temperature. Prepare grill, burning until coals are white. Scatter wood chips over coals or grill stones. Lay lamb on grill, 6 inches above fire; grill, turning occasionally and basting with puree, until thickest portion of meat is medium-rare, about 50 minutes. Let lamb sit before carving across grain into thin slices.

Makes 8 to 10 servings.

You may also bake lamb on a rack on a jelly roll pan in upper one-third of oven at 400° for same amount of time. The leg will not be quite as crusty and will lack the smoky flavor, but it will be delicious.

Toasted cumin has a rich, mellow, and nutty flavor that is distinct and delicious. To toast cumin seeds, spread about ½ cup (prepare a quantity since they keep indefinitely in an airtight container) in a small, heavy, ungreased skillet over low heat, stirring often, until seeds are fragrant and brown, 7 to 10 minutes. Remove seeds from skillet, and cool. Grind in a spice mill or mortar and pestle just before using.

Carne Adovado

3	pounds boned pork loin or beef flank steak		Water
			Vegetable oil
2	cups Red Chile Sauce		Garnish: avocado slices, sour
¼	teaspoon ground coriander		cream, or shredded lettuce and
⅛	teaspoon ground cumin		diced tomato
2	tablespoons vinegar		

Preheat oven to 325°. Cut pork into bite-size cubes or strips; place in a bowl. Stir in chile sauce and next 3 ingredients; cover and chill 24 hours. Spread meat and chile mixture in a baking dish or roasting pan; add ¼ inch water. Cover pan with foil, and bake 1 hour and 30 minutes, checking after 1 hour. If meat seems dry, add more water (if using beef, drizzle a little oil over meat). Garnish, if desired.

Makes 6 servings.

Red Chile Sauce

½	pound dried red chiles (New Mexico, ancho, or pasilla)	2	garlic cloves, peeled
		2	teaspoons dried oregano
3	cups chicken stock		Salt to taste

Remove stems and veins from chiles using rubber gloves. Simmer chiles in water to cover in a saucepan 15 minutes; drain. Process chiles, stock, garlic, and oregano in a blender until pureed. Place chile mixture into saucepan, and simmer 15 minutes. Adjust salt.

This is a basic red enchilada sauce and can be made ahead and frozen in batches. Ground cumin can be added to taste, as well as allspice and additional garlic.

Carnitas

15½ ounces pork tenderloin, cut into ¼-inch slices
Salt and pepper to taste
1 garlic clove, minced
½ cup julienned bell pepper
½ cup julienned onion
1 cup Green Chile Sauce (see index)
½ cup shredded Cheddar cheese
¼ cup shredded Monterey Jack cheese
Garnish: avocado slices

Tenderize meat using a meat mallet until slices are doubled in width. Add salt, pepper, and garlic; place on a hot griddle. When tenderloin reaches medium done, add bell pepper and onion, and sauté until pork is well done. Remove to serving plates, and top with sauce and cheeses. Place inside a hot oven 5 to 7 minutes or until cheese melts. Garnish, if desired.

Makes 4 servings.

Green Chile Pork

3 large green New Mexico or Poblano chiles
½ cup bacon drippings
2½ pounds boneless pork shoulder, cut into ½-inch cubes
2 large onions, chopped
2 garlic cloves, minced
2 tablespoons all-purpose flour
4 (4.5-ounce) cans mild green chiles, drained and chopped
4 cups chicken stock
Salt and pepper to taste
Hot cooked rice

Roast, peel, seed, and chop fresh chiles. Set aside. Heat drippings in a large, heavy pan over medium heat; add pork, and sauté in batches until lightly browned. Transfer to a plate. Add onion to drippings, and sauté 1 minute. Add garlic, and cook 2 minutes. Return meat to pan, and reduce heat to medium-low. Sprinkle pork with flour; cook, stirring constantly, 2 minutes. Stir in roasted chiles, canned chiles, and stock; bring to a boil. Reduce heat, and simmer, partially covered, until pork is tender, about 1 hour and 15 minutes. Raise heat slightly if chile is too thin. Add salt and pepper to taste, and serve with rice.

Makes 6 servings.

Classic Pork Chop Casserole

2	tablespoons butter	1	(14-ounce) can tomatoes
4	pork chops	½	(14-ounce) can water
	Salt and pepper to taste	2	teaspoons salt
1	cup uncooked brown rice		Freshly ground pepper to taste
½	cup chopped green bell pepper	1	onion, chopped

Preheat oven to 350°. Melt butter in a large skillet; add pork chops, and cook over medium heat until browned. Season with salt and pepper to taste. Remove chops from skillet, reserving 6 tablespoons drippings in skillet. Wash and drain rice. Heat reserved drippings in skillet; add rice, and cook, stirring often. Add green pepper, tomatoes, water, 2 teaspoons salt, and onion. Sprinkle with pepper to taste. Remove rice mixture from skillet, and place in a baking dish. Layer chops on top. Bake, covered, for 1 hour.

Makes 4 servings.

Green Peppercorn Pork Roast

2-3	teaspoons canned green pepper-corns, rinsed and drained	1	tablespoon Madeira
1	garlic clove, minced	1-2	tablespoons olive oil
½	teaspoon ground coriander	1	(3- to 4-pound) boneless pork loin, well-trimmed of excess fat
½	teaspoon ground cardamom	1	carrot, diced
½	teaspoon ground cinnamon	1	medium-size onion, diced
⅛	teaspoon ginger	1	celery stalk, diced
⅛	teaspoon ground nutmeg	1	cup beef broth, preferably home-made
½	teaspoon salt		
½	teaspoon freshly ground black pepper		

Preheat oven to 375°. Process first 10 ingredients in a food processor until pureed. Add only enough oil to make a paste. Make 1- to 1½-inch-deep holes in meat with sharp point of a knife. Spread spice mixture over meat, packing it into holes. Let stand 30 minutes to 1 hour. Place carrot, onion, and celery in bottom of a roasting pan. Set a rack over vegetables, and place meat on rack. Add broth to bottom of pan. Roast 1½ hours or until a meat thermometer registers 155°. Let roast rest 15 minutes. Strain vegetables from pan juices, and discard. Skim fat from juices, and bring to a boil in a saucepan over high heat. Cook until reduced to a thick glaze, about 10 minutes. Slice roast, and serve with glaze.

Makes 10 to 12 servings.

Grammo Lola's Tamales

5-10	pounds pork butt	4	garlic cloves, chopped
	Salt and pepper to taste	10	pounds masa, coarsely ground
	Water	2	pounds pure lard
1	quart red chile sauce (or more, depending on size of pork butt)	¾	cup baking powder
		½	cup salt
½	pound dried red chile pods	10	dozen corn husks (ojas)
5	cups water		

Place meat in a large kettle with water to cover; season with salt and pepper to taste, and cook slowly until meat is falling-apart tender. Cool meat, and reserve juices. Clean chile pods, and place in a saucepan with 5 cups water; add garlic. Bring to boil, and boil gently about 30 minutes. Process chile mixture in a food processor until blended. Set aside. Shred meat, or coarsely grind in food processor; return to kettle, and add chile sauce. Cook until spreading consistency, about 30 minutes. Adjust seasonings. Beat lard in a large bowl until fluffy; beat in baking powder, salt, and enough reserved meat juices to make a thick batter. Knead masa until soft, shiny, and greasy. Clean corn husks in warm water; soak 30 to 45 minutes. Hold each corn husk flat on 1 hand, rough side up. (Depending on size of husks, you may have to overlap 2 husks to make 1 tamale.) Spread a thin layer of masa (about 1 tablespoon) the width of the husk and three-fourths the length. Top masa with meat mixture (about 1 tablespoon) lengthwise down center. Roll tightly, folding excess at broad end under. Tie together. Repeat procedure with remaining husks and filling. Place tamales, pointed end up, folded end down, side by side in a steamer. Cover with a layer of husks; pour water around sides of pan, and cover tightly. Steam until masa does not stick to husks, about 1 hour.

Makes 10 dozen.

History of Tamale Recipe
Everyone who knows this spry 105-year-old woman calls her Grammo Lola. This tamale recipe was generously shared by this young lady who, on race days, made 100 dozen tamales for the Jockey Club at Ruidoso Downs. After the tamales were prepared, they were taken to the Greyhound bus station in Roswell and put on the bus to make the trip to Ruidoso, arriving by noon unless Grandpa could be persuaded to take them. (Usually there was not too much complaining from him, however, for this meant getting to watch the races.) The 100 dozen Garcia Tamales did not last long, for they were a favorite with the racing crowd.

Since getting this recipe from Grammo Lola, and before going to press, we were saddened by her peaceful death at her home on February 24, 1998. Our community will miss her.

Delores Garcia
December 26, 1892-February 24, 1998.

Gingered Pumpkin Pork

2 garlic cloves, minced
1 tablespoon grated fresh ginger
1 tablespoon vegetable oil
1 pound lean ground pork sausage
   (not Italian)
⅓ cup soy sauce
⅓ cup sugar

½ cup water
1 tablespoon rice, cider, or white
   wine vinegar
1 medium pumpkin, butternut, or
   other winter squash, peeled and
   cut into 1-inch cubes
   Hot cooked rice

Heat first 3 ingredients in a wok or large skillet over medium-high heat until aromatic and sizzling. Add sausage, and cook, stirring to crumble, until no longer pink. Add soy sauce and next 3 ingredients; bring to a boil. Place squash cubes on top, and cover. Reduce heat, and simmer until squash is tender, about 20 minutes. Serve with steamed white rice, adding Tabasco to taste, if desired.

Makes 4 servings.

New Mexican Pork Roast

1 (3- to 4-pound) pork loin

Marinade
½ cup flat beer
   Juice of 1 large lime
2 garlic cloves, minced
½ teaspoon dried thyme, crumbled
½ teaspoon dried oregano, crumbled

¼ teaspoon ground coriander
¼ teaspoon ground cumin
1 teaspoon Worcestershire sauce
   Ground pepper to taste

Place pork loin in a shallow glass dish. Combine remaining ingredients, and pour over pork loin. Cover and chill 8 hours, turning once or twice. Preheat oven to 325°. Remove pork from marinade, and place in a shallow roasting pan. Bring marinade to a boil in a saucepan over medium-high heat. Remove from heat. Bake pork loin for 1 hour and 45 minutes or until done, basting with marinade several times during cooking. Let stand 10 minutes before cutting.

Makes 6 servings.

_____Pork Chops with Caramelized Onions_____

¾	cup all-purpose flour	2	tablespoons butter
2	teaspoons fresh rosemary, minced	2	large onions, sliced
½	teaspoon salt	2	garlic cloves, minced
¼	teaspoon pepper	⅓	cup dry white wine
4	boneless pork chops	⅓	cup beef broth

Combine first 4 ingredients in a shallow dish. Dredge chops in flour mixture. Melt butter in a large, heavy skillet; add chops, and brown on both sides. Remove chops from heat. Add onion and garlic to skillet, and sauté until brown, about 10 minutes. Add wine, and boil until reduced to a glaze. Stir in beef broth. Return pork to skillet; cover and simmer 15 minutes. Remove pork to a platter, and boil juices and onion until liquid coats back of a spoon, 3 to 5 minutes. Spoon onion and sauce over chops.

Makes 4 servings.

_____Pork Chops with Mushrooms_____

3	tablespoons unsalted butter	1	medium onion, diced
3	tablespoons all-purpose flour	1	pound fresh mushrooms, sliced
½	cup vegetable oil	¼	cup plus 2 tablespoons chicken stock
½	cup all-purpose flour		
	Salt and ground white pepper to taste	1	cup milk
		½	tablespoon dried thyme
6	center-cut pork loin chops (½ inch thick)		

Preheat oven to 350°. Make a roux by melting butter in a saucepan over medium-low heat and adding 3 tablespoons flour. Simmer flour mixture, stirring constantly, 5 minutes; remove from heat, and set aside. Heat oil in a skillet until hot. Combine ½ cup flour and salt and pepper; dredge chops in mixture, and cook in hot oil in batches over medium-high heat until golden brown. Place chops in a large baking dish. Drain excess oil from skillet; reduce heat to medium, and add onion and mushrooms. Sauté until wilted. Add chicken stock to deglaze skillet, scraping skillet to loosen browned bits. Bring stock mixture to a boil. Reduce heat to simmer, and whisk in roux, milk, and thyme; whisk constantly until gravy forms. Pour gravy over chops. Bake for 40 minutes or until chops are tender.

Makes 6 servings.

Mexican Stuffed Pork Chops

Marinade

1   tablespoon olive oil
½   teaspoon freshly ground pepper
1   garlic clove, minced

2   teaspoons dried oregano
6   double pork chops, well trimmed of excess fat

Stuffing

1   tablespoon olive oil
½   cup chopped onion
1   garlic clove, minced
2   tablespoons chopped fresh or canned green chiles
1   jalapeño, seeded and chopped
¼   cup chopped fresh parsley

½   teaspoon dried oregano
½   teaspoon chile powder
1   (14-ounce) can whole tomatoes with liquid
¾   cup crushed corn chips
1   tablespoon olive oil
¼-½ cup beef broth

Combine first 4 ingredients in a shallow dish. Cut pockets in sides of chops, and add chops to marinade mixture. Cover and marinate 1 hour at room temperature, or 6 hours in refrigerator. Heat 1 tablespoon oil in a skillet over medium heat; add onion and garlic, and sauté until onion is soft and translucent. Add green chiles, jalapeño, parsley, oregano, and chile powder to onion; cook about 5 minutes. Stir in tomatoes and corn chips, and mix well; adjust seasonings. Add juice from tomatoes, a little at a time, until mixture holds its shape in a spoon. Reserve ¼ cup tomato juice for later use. Set stuffing aside to cool. Remove chops from marinade, and pat dry with paper towels. Stuff each chop with about 1½ teaspoons stuffing. (Leftover stuffing can be chilled or frozen.) Press edges of chops together to seal. Sauté chops in a large skillet coated with olive oil 3 to 4 minutes on each side. Remove from pan, and deglaze skillet by adding ¼ cup broth and scraping browned bits loose. Add ¼ cup juice from tomatoes. Return chops to skillet; cover and bring to a boil. Reduce heat, and simmer until tender, about 30 minutes. Add more broth if needed. Transfer chops to a platter. Increase heat, and reduce juices in skillet until thickened. Spoon sauce over chops.

Makes 6 servings.

Pork Chops with Raspberry Vinegar Sauce

4	large boneless pork chops	1	garlic clove, pressed
2	tablespoons flour	½	cup beef stock
	Salt to taste	½	cup dry vermouth
¼	teaspoon ground white pepper	¼	cup raspberry vinegar
½	teaspoon dried rosemary	¼	cup whipping cream
2	tablespoons vegetable oil		

Dredge pork in flour, shaking off excess; season both sides with salt, peppers, and rosemary. Heat oil in a skillet over medium heat; add garlic, and sauté 1 minute. Add chops to skillet, and brown on both sides. Pour off drippings, and stir in stock and vermouth. Cover and simmer 20 to 30 minutes. Remove chops from skillet, and keep warm. Increase heat to high, and reduce sauce in skillet until thickened. Add vinegar, and continue cooking until thickened. Add cream, and simmer until thick enough to coat chops. Spoon sauce over chops.

Makes 4 servings.

Sautéed Chorizo

1	pound chorizo sausages, cut into ¼-inch slices		Salt and pepper to taste
		2	bay leaves
2	garlic cloves, minced	8	(6-inch) corn tortillas
2	cups canned chopped tomatoes, with juice		Fresh cilantro leaves
			Chopped green onions

Heat a large cast-iron skillet to medium-hot; add sausage, and cook until it begins to brown and render some fat. Add garlic and next 3 ingredients; reduce heat, and simmer gently until liquid is reduced by about one-third and sauce is viscous, about 20 minutes. Remove and discard bay leaves. Dip tortillas in water, and steam briefly on rack of a hot oven. Serve chorizo mixture on 2 overlapping tortillas, and top with cilantro and green onions.

Makes 4 servings.

Pork Fajitas

1 teaspoon chile powder
½ teaspoon ground cumin
½ teaspoon salt

¼ teaspoon cayenne pepper
2 pork tenderloins (8 ounces each)

Salsa
8 ounces plum tomatoes, seeded and chopped
1 medium-size onion, chopped
3 tablespoons minced fresh cilantro
1 jalapeño, minced
1 garlic clove, minced

1 tablespoon vegetable oil
2 teaspoons lime juice
Salt and pepper to taste
4 flour tortillas
4 tablespoons sour cream
1 ripe avocado, peeled and diced

Preheat oven to 450°. Combine first 4 ingredients, and sprinkle evenly over pork, patting it in on all sides. Place pork on a rack in a shallow pan, and bake for 25 to 30 minutes or until an instant-read thermometer registers 155°. Combine tomato and next 7 ingredients. Cool pork about 5 minutes, and slice crosswise into thin slices. Wrap tortillas in foil, and heat in still-warm oven. Spread 1 side of each tortilla with 1 tablespoon sour cream; top evenly with pork, salsa mixture, and avocado. Fold tortillas over, and serve.

Makes 4 servings.

Pork Medallions with Marsala

1 (1½-pound) pork tenderloin, cut into ½-inch slices
½ cup all-purpose flour
8 tablespoons butter
2 shallots, minced

6 large mushrooms, very thinly sliced
⅔ cup dry Marsala
⅓ cup chicken stock
Salt and pepper to taste

Preheat oven to 200°. Place pork between 2 sheets of wax paper; flatten to ¼-inch thickness using a meat mallet. Dredge pork in flour, shaking off excess. Melt 4 table-spoons butter in a skillet over medium-high heat; add pork, in batches, and sauté until golden, 2 to 3 minutes per side. Transfer pork to a platter, and keep warm. Pour off drippings from skillet; add 2 tablespoons butter, and sauté shallot 2 minutes. Add mushrooms, and sauté over high heat until lightly browned. Stir in wine and stock; bring to a boil over high heat until reduced by one-third. Remove from heat, and swirl in remaining butter. Season with salt and pepper to taste. Spoon sauce over pork.

Makes 6 servings.

Pork Loin Beaujolais with Cherries

1   (4-pound) pork loin, trimmed of
    excess fat
2   teaspoons mixed whole
    peppercorns (pink, green, black,
    and white)
20 whole cloves
1   tablespoon ground cinnamon
6   tablespoons unsalted butter, room
    temperature

Salt to taste
1   large onion, coarsely chopped
1   cup red Beaujolais
    Cherry Sauce
⅓   cup plus 2 tablespoons kirsch or
    other cherry liqueur
2   tablespoons cornstarch, dissolved
    in 3 tablespoons Beaujolais

Preheat oven to 375°. Combine peppercorns, 10 cloves, and cinnamon. Grind together in a mortar and pestle or small spice grinder. Combine ground spices with butter to make a paste. Make 10 (½-inch-deep) incisions in pork with tip of a sharp knife. Insert remaining cloves in incisions. Smear spiced butter over pork, and sprinkle with salt. Scatter chopped onion over bottom of a roasting pan; place pork over onion. Pour wine into bottom of pan. Bake pork 1½ to 1¾ hours or until an instant-read thermometer registers 155°, basting occasionally with wine and accumulated pan juices. Add more wine if pan gets dry.

Cherry Sauce
1½ pounds pitted Bing cherries
2   tablespoons light brown sugar
2   tablespoons balsamic vinegar

3   tablespoons fresh rosemary,
    coarsely chopped
1½ cups Beaujolais

Place cherries and next 4 ingredients in a large saucepan. Bring to a boil; reduce heat, and simmer, uncovered, stirring occasionally, 20 minutes. When pork is done, pour ⅓ cup kirsch over top. Ignite roast in pan with a long match; when flames subside, transfer pork to a platter, and keep warm. Stir remaining 2 tablespoons kirsch into Cherry Sauce. Place roasting pan on a burner over medium heat; stir in cornstarch mixture, and cook to thicken pan juices. Pour Cherry Sauce into pan, and continue cooking until all liquid is blended and slightly thickened, about 5 minutes. Carve pork into ½-inch-thick slices, and arrange on platter, surrounded by sauce.

Makes 6 to 8 servings.

Pork Ribs in Green Chile Sauce

4 pounds country-style pork ribs
6½ cups water
2 white onions, coarsely chopped
4 garlic cloves
2 teaspoons salt
2 Poblano or Anaheim chiles, roasted and peeled
2 (6-inch) corn tortillas, toasted in a dry skillet and torn into small pieces

½ cup chopped fresh cilantro
2-4 tablespoons lime juice
  Freshly ground black pepper to taste
1 small head green cabbage, coarsely chopped
2 tablespoons olive oil

Place pork ribs, 6 cups water, onion, garlic, and salt in a Dutch oven; bring to a boil, reduce heat, and simmer, covered, 1 hour and 30 minutes. When ribs are tender, remove from pan. Return liquid to a boil, and reduce to 3 cups, about 10 to 15 minutes. Transfer liquid and solids to blender; add chiles and tortillas, and blend to a coarse puree. Transfer puree to pan; bring to a boil, reduce heat, and simmer. Add ribs to pan; simmer, covered, 15 minutes. If sauce is too thick add water. Stir in cilantro; season with lime juice, pepper, and additional salt, if needed. Keep hot. Combine cabbage, olive oil, and remaining ½ cup water in a large skillet; bring to a boil, reduce heat, and steam, covered, until tender, 3 to 5 minutes. Season with salt and pepper. Cut ribs into serving pieces. Place cabbage on serving plates; top with ribs and sauce.

Makes 4 servings.

These ribs are also wonderful served with any dried beans that have been cooked and seasoned.

Luis Jimenez

It would take a book to list the accomplishments of Luis Jimenez, which is why *New Mexico Magazine* published *Howl, the Artwork of Luis Jimenez,* the second in its series of fine art books featuring the work of important New Mexico artists.

The most famous of the residents of Hondo, New Mexico, Jimenez's career has spanned three decades and continues to flourish. His drawings, prints and sculptures have been exhibited widely in galleries and museums across the United States and abroad, including the National Museum of American Art, Smithsonian Institution.

Jimenez's larger-than-life fiberglass sculptures have been commissioned by public artwork committees in such major cities as New York, Houston, Albuquerque, Oklahoma City, Los Angeles, El Paso, San Diego, Pittsburgh, Cleveland and coming soon to Denver. His work is included in more than 50 important collections throughout the United States including the Hirshhorn Museum and Sculpture Garden in Washington, D.C., the Metropolitan Museum of Art and the Museum of Modern Art in New York, and locally, the Roswell Museum and Art Center and the Anderson Museum of Contemporary Art which houses four major Jimenez sculptures.

Jimenez's numerous grants and awards include the Roswell Artist-in-Residence Program, which brought him to this area; a fellowship grant from the National Endowment for the Arts (NEA); a Mid-Career Fellowship Award from the American Academy in Rome and NEA; the State of New Mexico Governor's Award and the City of Houston's Goodwill Ambassador Award.

Born in El Paso, Texas, in 1940, Jimenez worked in his father's sign shop for numerous years before his formal art training began. He studied at Texas Western College in El Paso and received his Bachelor of Science degree from the University of Texas at Austin. Jimenez continued study at Ciudad Universitaria in Mexico City before returning to the States to assist artist Seymour Lipton in New York. Currently Jimenez is a Distinguished Professor at the University of Houston.

The Rose Tattoo
Artist – Luis Jimenez
22″ × 30″   1983
color lithograph on paper
Permanent collection, Roswell
Museum and Art Center, 1985.
Photograph by Richard Faller.

Pork Tenderloin with _____.
_____Raisins and Hazelnuts

1 (1½-pound) pork tenderloin	2 tablespoons chopped, roasted hazelnuts
½ cup all-purpose flour	¼ cup golden raisins, soaked in red wine vinegar to cover 20 minutes, and drained
½ teaspoon salt	
½ teaspoon finely ground black pepper	⅛ teaspoon dry mustard
2 tablespoons olive oil	1 teaspoon chopped fresh parsley
1 yellow onion, thinly sliced	1 teaspoon chopped fresh thyme
2 shallots, finely chopped	⅛ teaspoon cayenne pepper
1 garlic clove, mashed and chopped	⅛ teaspoon grated lemon zest
¼ cup Riesling or other fruity white wine	1 tablespoon balsamic vinegar
	Garnish: fresh parsley sprigs

Cut tenderloins into ¾-inch slices; place between 2 sheets of wax paper, and gently pound to ½-inch thickness using a meat mallet. Combine flour, salt, and pepper in a shallow dish; dredge pork in mixture. Heat olive oil in a heavy skillet over medium heat; add pork, and brown on all sides. Remove pork to a warm platter. In same skillet, sauté onion, shallot, and garlic just until soft (do not brown). Add Riesling and next 8 ingredients to skillet; simmer until sauce thickens, 2 to 3 minutes. Spoon sauce over pork, and garnish, if desired.

Makes 4 to 6 servings.

_____Pork Tenderloin with
Cranberry-Chipotle Sauce_____

1   tablespoon unsalted butter
1   tablespoon olive oil
1   (½-pound) pork tenderloin

Salt and freshly ground pepper to taste

Cranberry-Chipotle Sauce
2   tablespoons minced shallot
2   garlic cloves, minced
2   cups fresh or frozen cranberries, thawed
3   tablespoons sugar
1   cup dry red wine
2½ cups chicken stock

1   canned chipotle chile in a adobo sauce, pureed
1   teaspoon minced fresh sage or ½ teaspoon crumbled dried sage
3   tablespoons unsalted butter, room temperature
Salt and freshly ground pepper to taste

Preheat oven to 375°. Melt butter and olive oil in a skillet over medium heat; season pork with salt and pepper, and brown in butter on all sides. Reserve drippings in skillet. Remove pork to a rack in a roasting pan, and cook until a thermometer reaches 155°, about 40 minutes. Sauté shallot and garlic in reserved drippings 30 seconds; add cranberries and sugar, and cook, stirring constantly, 30 seconds. Add wine to skillet, scraping browned bits loose from pan; boil mixture over high heat until reduced to ¾ cup. Add chicken stock, chipotle puree, and sage to skillet; bring to a boil over high heat until reduced to 2 cups. Strain mixture into a clean saucepan, and bring to a boil. Whisk butter, salt, and pepper into sauce, and keep warm. When pork is done, remove from oven, cover loosely with foil, and let stand 10 minutes. Cut pork into ½-inch slices; place on serving plates, and top with sauce.

Makes 6 servings.

Red Pork Chile with Black Beans

6	tablespoons olive oil	2	teaspoons cayenne pepper
2	large yellow onions, diced	4	teaspoons salt
8	garlic cloves, minced	1	(28-ounce) can Italian-style plum
5	pounds boneless pork butt or		tomatoes, crushed with liquid
	shoulder, cut into ½-inch cubes	7	cups chicken stock
⅔	cup mild chile powder	4	(16-ounce) cans black beans,
3	tablespoons ground cumin, from		rinsed and drained
	toasted seeds		Garnish: sour cream and minced
3	tablespoons dried oregano		cilantro

Heat 3 tablespoons oil in a skillet over low heat. Add onion and garlic; cook, covered, stirring occasionally, until very tender, about 20 minutes. Heat remaining oil in an 8-quart Dutch oven over medium heat. Add pork; cook, without browning, stirring occasionally, until meat is uniformly colored, about 20 minutes. Stir chile powder and next 4 ingredients into pork, and cook 5 minutes. Stir in onion mixture, tomatoes with liquid, and chicken stock. Bring mixture to a boil; reduce heat, and simmer, uncovered, stirring occasionally, 1 hour. Adjust seasonings, and simmer until chile is thick and pork is tender, 35 to 45 minutes. (Chile can be made up to 3 days in advance. Cover and chill. Warm over low heat, stirring often until hot.) Stir in beans, and simmer 3 to 5 minutes or until beans are heated through. Garnish, if desired, and serve immediately.

Makes 8 servings.

Southwest Spaghetti Pie

8	ounces spaghetti	½	teaspoon ground cumin
½	cup milk	½	teaspoon dried oregano
1	egg	½	teaspoon salt
1	pound ground pork	¼	teaspoon ground black pepper
1	cup chopped onion	1	(16-ounce) can tomato sauce
1	medium-size green bell pepper, chopped	1	cup shredded Monterey Jack cheese with jalapeños
1	garlic clove, minced	1	cup shredded Cheddar cheese
1	tablespoon chile powder		

Preheat oven 425°. Cook pasta in a pan of boiling salted water until al dente, about 8 minutes; drain. Whisk together milk and egg; stir into hot pasta. Spread pasta mixture into a buttered 13- x 9- x 2-inch baking dish. Cook pork, onion, bell pepper, and garlic in a large skillet over medium heat until pork is cooked through, about 6 minutes. Pour off drippings. Add chile powder and next 4 ingredients to pork mixture, and cook 2 minutes. Stir in tomato sauce, and cook 2 minutes. Spread pork mixture over pasta, and sprinkle with cheeses. Bake in lower one-third of oven until cheese melts and is bubbly, about 10 minutes. Let stand 5 minutes, and cut into squares

Makes 4 to 6 servings.

Spicy Pork Stew

1	tablespoon vegetable oil	1½	tablespoons chopped jalapeño
2½	pounds pork shoulder or boneless country-style ribs, cut into 1-inch cubes	2	(14½-ounce) cans Mexican-style stewed tomatoes with liquid
	Salt and pepper to taste	1	tablespoon ground cumin
1	large onion, chopped	1	tablespoon dried oregano
6	garlic cloves, chopped	2	(15-ounce) cans kidney beans, rinsed and dried

Heat oil in a large, heavy Dutch oven over high heat; season pork with salt and pepper, and add to pan. Sauté until no longer pink, about 10 minutes. Add onion, garlic, and jalapeño to pork, and cook 5 minutes. Add tomatoes with liquid, cumin, and oregano; cover, reduce heat to medium-low, and simmer until pork is tender, 1 hour. Stir beans into stew, and simmer until heated through, about 10 minutes. Adjust salt and pepper.

Makes 6 servings.

Southwestern Grilled Pork Tenderloin

Marinade

1	teaspoon chile powder	3	garlic cloves, minced
1	teaspoon ground coriander		Juice of 3 limes (about ½ cup)
1	teaspoon salt	⅓	cup olive oil
1	teaspoon freshly ground black pepper	4	pork tenderloins (about ¾ pound each)
¼	cup dried chile peppers, crushed (or less to taste)		

Combine first 8 ingredients in a shallow, non-reactive dish; add pork, cover and chill 8 hours. Bring pork to room temperature before grilling. Prepare grill. Remove pork from marinade, discarding marinade. Grill pork over hot coals, turning often, until seared, 5 to 10 minutes. If using a gas grill, reduce heat; otherwise, move pork to cooler area of grill, and cook about 12 minutes, turning often, or until an instant-read thermometer registers 155°. Pork is done when there is still a hint of pink in center. Let pork rest on a plate 10 to 15 minutes. Slice pork, and arrange on a platter; drizzle with juices from plate.

Makes 8 servings.

*On concert weekend, many of our musicians leave their "day" work early and drive as much as 200 miles to arrive in Roswell in time for the first symphony rehearsal. "Backstage Buffets" are prepared by Guild members and served the first night of rehearsals allowing more time (which is limited) for practice. The musicians really appreciate this hospitality. This year, the orchestra members made their contribution to **Savoring the Southwest Again** by being some of our willing recipe tasters.*

Stuffed Loin of Pork

1   (4½-pound) boneless pork loin
¼   cup chopped dried apricot
¼   cup chopped pitted prunes
¼   cup peeled, chopped apple
¼   cup chopped cranberries
½   cup all-purpose flour

¼   teaspoon ground ginger
¼   teaspoon ground cinnamon
¼   teaspoon freshly grated nutmeg
    Salt to taste
1½ cups Vouvray or other dry white wine

Preheat oven to 350°. Make a hole lengthwise through center of pork using a thick larding needle or a long sharpening steel. Combine apricot and next 3 ingredients; stuff mixture into center of pork. Combine flour and next 4 ingredients in shallow dish; dredge pork in flour mixture. Place pork in a roasting pan; add wine to pan. Bake for 1 hour and 30 minutes or until an instant-read thermometer registers 155°. Transfer pork to platter, and let stand, loosely covered with foil, 15 minutes. Thinly slice pork to serve.

Makes 8 servings.

Chicken

Roswell

Will Rogers called Roswell "the prettiest little town in the West." Building on this natural beauty and the unique aspects of its geography, Roswell has grown from a rowdy cow town to a thriving center of education, economic development, and culture.

A crossroads in the 1860's and 70's, Roswell was a stopover for cowboys moving cattle up the Chisum and Goodnight-Loving Trails between Texas and Colorado. Roswell incorporated in 1891 and developed quickly with plentiful artesian water for both commercial and agricultural uses. The agricultural industry has in turn provided a stable economic base for the area.

Roswell residents have a well-defined sense of self-reliance. In 1978 it was designated an All American City for its "citizenship, effective organizations, and community involvement."

Our citizens have overwhelmingly demonstrated a commitment to arts organizations and their endeavors; the community has a strong track record of support for high caliber performances, artistic diversity, and steady growth of arts activities. This small city rightfully boasts of its 37 years of symphony orchestra and community theatre; 59 years of established art exhibitions; and 29 years of an artist-in-residence program.

Featured on page 119 "Leering Rooster-Worried Pullet"
Eastern New Mexico State Fair

Baked Chicken Breasts
with Scallions and Lime

4	(5-ounce) skinless, boneless chicken breast halves
½	cup all-purpose flour
5	tablespoons unsalted butter
⅔	cup minced scallions (white and tender green parts only)
1	garlic clove, minced

½	cup dry white wine
¼	teaspoon salt
¼	teaspoon freshly ground pepper
1	tablespoon fresh lime juice
2	teaspoons minced lime zest
1	tablespoon chopped fresh parsley
1	tablespoon fine, dry breadcrumbs

Preheat oven to 400°. Trim any fat from chicken; pound any thicker ends to flatten to even thickness. Dredge chicken in flour, shaking off excess. Melt 4 tablespoons butter in a large skillet; add chicken, and sauté over medium-high heat until golden brown, about 3 minutes on each side. Remove from skillet. Reduce heat to low, and add scallions and garlic; sauté until soft, about 5 minutes. Increase heat to medium-high, and add wine; bring to a boil, scraping any browned bits loose. Boil until reduced by half, 2 to 3 minutes. Spread half of scallion mixture into a buttered baking dish just large enough to hold chicken in a single layer. Add chicken, and season with salt and pepper; drizzle with lime juice. Cover with remaining scallion mixture. Sprinkle with lime zest, parsley, and breadcrumbs. Dot with remaining 1 tablespoon butter. Bake chicken in top third of oven for 15 minutes or until chicken is white throughout but still juicy. Serve immediately.

Makes 4 servings.

Breast of Chicken with
Green Peppercorn or Marsala Sauce

3   tablespoons clarified unsalted
    butter
1-2 whole chicken breasts, skinned,
    boned, and split

Green Peppercorn Sauce or
Marsala Sauce

Melt butter in a heavy skillet over medium heat. Add chicken, and sauté until golden brown on both sides. Transfer to a serving platter, and keep warm. (Do not wipe skillet clean.)

Green Peppercorn Sauce

2   tablespoons minced onion
¼   cup dry white wine
½   cup whipping cream
1   teaspoon green peppercorns,
    rinsed, drained, and mashed

1   teaspoon whole green pepper-
    corns, rinsed and drained
1   teaspoon fresh tarragon leaves or
    ¼ teaspoon dried tarragon
    Salt and freshly ground black
    pepper to taste

Sauté onion in skillet with chicken drippings over medium-high heat until limp. Add wine; bring to a boil over high heat, and cook until reduced by half, scraping any browned bits loose. Stir in cream, mashed and whole peppercorns, and tarragon; boil until syrup consistency. Remove from heat, and add salt and pepper to taste. Pour mixture over chicken, and serve immediately.

Marsala Sauce

½   cup Marsala wine
½   cup chicken broth

    Salt and freshly ground black
    pepper to taste
2   tablespoons unsalted butter

Pour chicken drippings from skillet; add wine and broth to skillet, and boil over high heat until syrup consistency, scraping any browned bits loose. Season with salt and pepper to taste. Remove from heat, and whisk in butter, blending completely. Pour mixture over chicken, and serve immediately.

Makes 2 to 4 servings.

Chicken Breasts in Champagne

4	whole chicken breasts, halved	3	tablespoons all-purpose flour
	Salt and freshly ground pepper to taste	2	teaspoons dried tarragon
		3½	cups Champagne
5	tablespoons unsalted butter	½	cup whipping cream
½	cup Cognac		

Sprinkle chicken with salt and pepper to taste. Melt butter in a medium-size Dutch oven over medium-high heat; brown chicken on all sides, about 10 minutes, and remove from pan. Pour Cognac into pan to warm; light Cognac with a long match. When flames subside, stir in flour and tarragon. Cook mixture, stirring constantly, 2 minutes. Gradually whisk in 3 cups Champagne. Return chicken to pan; cover and simmer until chicken is tender, about 45 minutes. Remove chicken to a warm platter. Stir remaining ½ cup Champagne and cream into pan; cook sauce over high heat until reduced and slightly thickened. Pour over chicken, and serve immediately.

Makes 6 servings.

Chicken and Chiles

12	ounces boneless, skinless chicken breasts	1	(15-ounce) can black beans, rinsed and drained
¼	teaspoon salt	1	(4.5-ounce) can chopped mild green chiles
¼	teaspoon pepper		
2	teaspoons olive oil	1	teaspoon chile powder
1	medium-size onion, chopped	½	teaspoon ground cumin
2	garlic cloves, minced	1-2	teaspoons sugar (optional)
1	cup chicken broth	3	cups cooked rice
1	(8-ounce) can tomato sauce		

Sprinkle chicken with salt and pepper. Coat a large skillet with cooking spray. Add chicken to skillet, and cook over medium-high heat until browned, about 5 minutes; transfer to a bowl to cool. Cut cooled chicken into small strips. Combine oil, onion, garlic, and 2 tablespoons broth in skillet; cook, stirring often, until onion is tender, 5 to 6 minutes. Add tomato sauce, beans, and remaining broth to onion mixture, stirring to blend well. Add chiles, chile powder, cumin, and chicken strips. Bring mixture to a boil; reduce heat, and simmer until chicken is tender and liquid has thickened. Add sugar to sauce if too acidic. Serve over rice.

Makes 4 servings.

Chicken Breasts with Mushroom-Mustard Sauce

3	tablespoons butter	¾	cup dry white wine
6	boneless, skinless chicken breast halves	1	cup chicken broth
	Salt and freshly ground pepper to taste	¼	teaspoon salt
		1	tablespoon fresh rosemary or
6	green onions, sliced		¾ teaspoon dried rosemary, crumbled
2	teaspoons grated onion	2	tablespoons Dijon mustard
2	cups sliced fresh mushrooms	2	tablespoons chopped fresh parsley
			Garnish: fresh rosemary sprigs

Melt 2 tablespoons butter in a skillet over medium heat. Season chicken with salt and pepper to taste. Cook chicken in skillet until well browned and no longer pink in center, about 20 minutes; remove to a plate. Add remaining 1 tablespoon butter to skillet, and sauté green onions, onion, and mushrooms until soft, about 5 minutes. Add onion mixture to chicken. Add wine, broth, salt, and rosemary to skillet; increase heat to medium-high, and boil until liquid is reduced by half, about 8 minutes. Whisk in mustard and parsley. Return chicken and onion mixture to skillet, and simmer over low heat until heated through, 5 to 10 minutes. Garnish, if desired.

Makes 4 to 6 servings.

This can be made ahead and reheated at serving time.

Chicken Fiesta

1	cup Cheddar cheese cracker crumbs	2	cups whipping cream
2	tablespoons taco seasoning	1	cup shredded Monterey Jack cheese
8	chicken breast halves, skinned and boned	1	cup shredded Cheddar cheese
		1	(4½-ounce) can chopped green chiles, drained
4	green onions, chopped		
2	tablespoons butter, melted	½	teaspoon chicken bouillon granules

Preheat oven to 350°. Combine crumbs and taco seasoning. Dredge chicken in crumb mixture, and place in a greased 13- x 9- x 2-inch baking dish. Sauté onion in butter in a skillet over medium-high heat until tender. Stir in remaining ingredients, and pour over chicken. Bake, uncovered, for 45 minutes.

Makes 8 servings.

Chicken Chile Verde

3	pounds skinless, boneless chicken thighs, cut into ½-inch pieces	5	cups frozen corn kernels, thawed
	Salt and pepper to taste	6	cups chicken broth
5	tablespoons all-purpose flour	12	husked tomatillos, coarsely chopped
7	tablespoons olive oil	2	tablespoons chopped fresh oregano or 1 tablespoon dried oregano
3	cups chopped onion		
3	tablespoons chopped garlic	2	tablespoons chile powder
1¼	cups chopped fresh Anaheim chiles (or roasted, peeled, seeded New Mexico chiles)	1	tablespoon ground cumin
		1	teaspoon paprika
		2	cinnamon sticks
2	green bell peppers, cut lengthwise into ¼-inch-thick strips	1	cup chopped fresh cilantro
			Tortilla chips

Sprinkle chicken with salt and pepper to taste, and coat with flour. Sauté half of chicken in 1 tablespoon hot oil in a heavy skillet over medium-high heat until golden brown. Transfer from skillet to a Dutch oven. Repeat procedure with remaining chicken and 1 tablespoon oil. Heat 2 tablespoons oil in skillet; add onion and garlic, and sauté until tender. Remove to pan with chicken. Heat 1 tablespoon oil in skillet, and sauté chiles and bell pepper until tender. Remove to pan with chicken. Heat 1 tablespoon oil in skillet, and sauté half of corn until tender; repeat procedure with remaining 1 tablespoon oil and corn. Add broth and next 6 ingredients to pan with chicken; bring mixture to a boil. Reduce heat, and simmer, stirring occasionally, until mixture thickens and flavors blend, about 2 hours. Stir in cilantro, and transfer to a serving bowl; serve with tortilla chips.

Makes 12 servings.

Can be made 1 day ahead. Refrigerate until cool; store covered in refrigerator. Warm over medium heat before adding cilantro and serving.

Chicken Legs Paprika

3 pounds whole chicken legs, halved at joint (or use thighs)
   Salt and pepper to taste
3 tablespoons vegetable oil
1 onion, finely chopped
1½ tablespoons sweet paprika
1 (16-ounce) can tomatoes, drained and finely chopped

1 cup chicken broth
½ cup sour cream
2 tablespoons all-purpose flour
   Fresh lemon juice to taste
1 green bell pepper, thinly sliced
   Cooked noodles or boiled potatoes

Preheat oven to 325°. Brown chicken, seasoned with salt and pepper, in batches, in 2 tablespoons oil over medium-high heat in a Dutch oven. Transfer to a plate. Add onion to Dutch oven, and sauté over medium heat until tender. Add paprika to pan, and cook, stirring constantly, 10 seconds. Add tomatoes; cook mixture, stirring constantly, 2 minutes. Add broth, and return chicken, skin side up, to pan; bring to a boil. Cover pan, and cook in oven for 35 to 40 minutes or until tender. Transfer chicken to a plate. Bring liquid in pan to a boil over high heat; cook until reduced to about 2 cups. Whisk sour cream and flour in a small bowl until smooth; whisk in ½ cup cooking liquid. Whisk sour cream mixture into remaining cooking liquid in pan. Simmer sauce, stirring often, 2 to 3 minutes or until slightly thickened. Season with salt and pepper and lemon juice to taste. Return chicken to pan, and simmer until heated through. Heat remaining 1 tablespoon oil in a small skillet; sauté bell pepper 1 minute or until tender. Serve chicken with bell pepper arranged on top. Serve with noodles or potatoes.

Makes 6 servings.

Many generous Guild members provide "bed and breakfast" on concert weekends for out-of-town musicians. Some of the musicians have stayed with the same family for many years, have their own house key, and are considered "extended family".

Chicken Pot Pie with Cheese Crust

Cheese Pastry

1¼ cups all-purpose flour
1 teaspoon salt
¼ cup finely shredded sharp Cheddar cheese

2 tablespoons finely grated Parmesan cheese
½ cup shortening
6 tablespoons cold water

Combine flour, salt, and cheeses in a medium-size bowl; cut in shortening until mixture resembles coarse meal. Add water, and mix with fork just until mixture comes together. Shape into a ball, and wrap in plastic wrap; let rest 30 minutes.

Filling

4 (6-ounce) skinless, boneless chicken breast halves, cut in large dice
3 medium-size carrots, diced
4 potatoes, diced
2 teaspoons olive oil
1 large onion, diced
4 garlic cloves, chopped

3 celery ribs, diced
¾ cup white wine
½ cup dry sherry
2¼ cups heavy cream
1½ tablespoons chopped fresh tarragon
   Zest of 1 large lemon
1½ teaspoons Dijon mustard
   Salt and pepper to taste

Preheat oven to 425°. Combine first 3 ingredients in a large bowl. Heat oil in a skillet until very hot; sauté onion, garlic, and celery in oil until you can smell the aroma. Cool. Add onion mixture to chicken mixture, stirring well. Place in a 13- x 9- x 2-inch baking dish, and chill until sauce is ready. Bring wine and sherry to a boil in a saucepan over high heat until reduced to about ¾ cup, 3 to 4 minutes. Add cream, and reduce over high heat to 2¼ cups, 4 to 5 minutes. Add tarragon, lemon zest, and mustard to sauce; simmer over low heat 5 minutes. Season sauce with salt and pepper to taste; remove from heat. Pour cooled sauce over chicken mixture. Roll pastry to ¼-inch thickness large enough to cover baking dish; place over filling, and crimp edges. Bake for 15 minutes; reduce oven temperature to 350°, and bake for 45 to 50 minutes or until golden brown on top. Allow pie to cool 5 minutes before serving.

Makes 6 to 8 servings.

Chicken Rellenos

6 large chicken breasts, skinned and boned
2 cups shredded Monterey Jack cheese
3 eggs, lightly beaten

1 cup milk
2 cups all-purpose flour
2 cups yellow cornmeal
Vegetable oil
Green Chile Sauce

Preheat oven to 450°. Poach chicken in salted water until cooked through, about 10 minutes; drain and cool. Cut a horizontal slit in each chicken breast, and fill with cheese. Whisk eggs and milk together in a bowl. Coat chicken with flour, and dip into egg mixture; dredge in cornmeal. Heat about 1 inch oil in a large, heavy skillet. Cook chicken in hot oil until golden brown on both sides. Place chicken in a buttered 13- x 9- x 2-inch baking dish; cover with green chile sauce and remaining cheese. Bake about 5 minutes or until cheese melts.

Makes 6 servings.

Green Chile Sauce

5 (7-ounce) cans diced mild green chiles
2 (7-ounce) cans diced hot green chiles
1 garlic clove, minced

3-4 cups water
Salt to taste
½ cup vegetable oil
½ cup all-purpose flour

Combine chiles and their liquid, garlic, 3 cups water, and salt in a saucepan. Bring mixture to a boil; remove from heat. Heat oil in a separate pan; add flour, stirring to make a paste. Reheat chile mixture to simmer, and slowly add flour mixture, stirring constantly, until sauce consistency. Add water if needed for texture.

Chicken with Apple and Calvados

1 tablespoon vegetable oil
4 skinless, boneless chicken breast halves
3 tablespoons butter
2 tablespoons packed brown sugar
1 cup clear apple juice
½ cup chicken stock

1 tablespoon cornstarch
1 tablespoon cold water
½ cup heavy cream
1 tablespoon fresh chervil sprigs (or chives)
2 small apples, peeled and sliced
2 tablespoons Calvados or brandy

Heat oil in a large skillet. Add chicken, and cook until well browned and tender; remove and keep warm. Pour drippings from skillet. Heat butter and sugar in skillet; Add apples, and sauté until slightly browned. Remove from pan with a slotted spoon. Add apple juice, and simmer until reduced by one-third. Add stock and blended cornstarch and water to juice mixture; bring to a boil, stirring until thickened. Stir in cream, chervil, and apple. Heat Calvados gently in a small saucepan over low heat; light with a long match, and pour over sauce. Serve chicken with sauce immediately.

Makes 4 servings.

Chicken De Colores

1 whole chicken (3 to 3½ pounds), rinsed and dried
  Juice of ½ lemon
2 teaspoons ground cumin
1 teaspoon ground cardamom
2 teaspoons paprika
1 teaspoon chile powder

1 teaspoon salt
1 acorn squash, cut up
1 medium-size onion, cut up
1 red bell pepper, sliced
1 yellow bell pepper, sliced
1 cup white wine or water

Preheat oven to 350°. Remove skin from chicken, if desired. Rub chicken with lemon juice, and place on a rack in a baking dish. Combine spices, and sprinkle over chicken. Add vegetables to chicken, and pour wine into bottom of pan. Bake, covered, for 1 to 1½ hours or until juices run clear when chicken is pierced with a fork.

Makes 4 to 6 servings.

Crêpes with Curried Chicken

2 cups chopped cooked chicken
4 tablespoons butter
1 medium-size onion, chopped
1 celery rib, finely chopped
1 teaspoon chopped parsley
1 tablespoon curry powder
1 tomato, chopped
Salt and pepper to taste
1 cup chicken broth
1 tablespoon cornstarch
½ cup whipping cream
½ cup ground cashews
14-16 crêpes (see index)
Chopped cashews

Preheat oven to 375°. Heat butter in a large skillet, and sauté onion and celery 3 to 4 minutes. Add parsley, curry powder, and tomato; add salt and pepper to taste. Cover and cook 10 minutes. Add chicken broth, reserving 1 tablespoon; when mixture begins to boil, stir in reserved 1 tablespoon broth blended with cornstarch. Add chicken and cream to mixture, and cook until sauce is thickened, about 5 minutes. Stir in ground cashews, and remove from heat. Prepare crêpes. Place a spoonful of filling in center of each crêpe; fold over, and place, seam side down, in a buttered baking dish. Spread any remaining filling over crêpes. Top with chopped cashews, and bake 20 minutes.

Makes 6 to 8 servings.

This freezes well before baking. Thaw completely before baking.

Easy Orange Chicken

1 whole chicken (3 pounds), cut into serving pieces
½ cup all-purpose flour
1 teaspoon salt
½ teaspoon curry powder
½ teaspoon chile powder
½ teaspoon garlic powder
¼ teaspoon pepper
¼ cup butter or vegetable oil
3 oranges

Preheat oven to 350°. Combine flour and next 5 ingredients. Dredge chicken in flour mixture. Heat butter in a large skillet until hot. Brown chicken well on both sides. Place chicken in a greased baking dish just big enough to hold chicken in a single layer. Squeeze juice of oranges over chicken. Bake for 1 hour.

Makes 4 servings.

As it cooks, coating thickens orange juice to a wonderful sauce. This doesn't work well with orange juice from concentrate. Serve over rice and soak up the sauce!

Lighter Enchiladas Verde

2 whole chicken breasts (about ¼ pound each)
1 cup chicken stock
1 (8-ounce) package light cream cheese, softened
1 (12-ounce) can evaporated skimmed milk
1 large onion, chopped
1½ cups chopped New Mexico green chiles (or 6 Poblanos, roasted, peeled, seeded, and chopped)
1 (10-ounce) can green taco sauce
2 fresh serrano chiles, seeded and stemmed
½ cup chopped fresh cilantro
1 egg
1½ teaspoons salt
¼ teaspoon freshly ground black pepper
12 corn tortillas
½ cup freshly grated Parmesan cheese

Preheat oven to 350°. Cook chicken in stock in a large skillet until tender, about 20 minutes; reserve stock. Shred chicken. Beat cream cheese in a large bowl with a wooden spoon until smooth; beat in ½ cup milk, 3 tablespoons at a time, until mixture is blended. Stir onion into milk mixture; add chicken, and mix well. Set aside. Process green chiles, next 6 ingredients, ½ cup stock, and remaining milk in a blender 15 seconds. Pour puree into a bowl. Coat a nonstick skillet with cooking spray, and heat over medium-high heat. Heat tortillas, 1 at a time, about 10 seconds on each side, just until limp (recoat skillet as needed). Store warm tortillas between two heated plates. Dip 1 tortilla in puree; allow excess puree to drip off, and place tortilla in a 13- x 9- x 2-inch glass baking dish. Spread tortilla with ¼ cup chicken filling; fold 1 side of tortilla over filling, and roll up tightly. Place filled tortilla, seam side down, in baking dish. Repeat with remaining tortillas. Pour remaining puree over tortillas, and sprinkle top evenly with Parmesan. Bake on middle oven rack for 30 to 45 minutes. Serve immediately.

Makes 6 servings.

Southwest Orange-Chile Chicken with Black Beans

2	tablespoons olive oil	¾	cup chicken stock
1	whole chicken (3 to 4 pounds), skinned and cut into serving pieces	3	tablespoons hot chile sauce
		1¾	cups cooked black beans with 2 tablespoons liquid
1	large purple onion, halved and thinly sliced	1	red bell pepper, cut into strips
4	garlic cloves, minced	1	tablespoon dark rum
1½	cups freshly squeezed orange juice		Salt and pepper to taste
			Chopped fresh cilantro

Heat oil in a large skillet over medium heat. Brown chicken on all sides in oil; remove to a plate lined with paper towels. Sauté onion in pan drippings until limp and slightly browned, about 8 minutes. Add garlic, and sauté 1 minute. Return chicken to skillet, and add orange juice, stock, and chile sauce. Cover and simmer over low heat 30 minutes. Add black beans and liquid and bell pepper strips. Simmer, uncovered, 30 minutes. Add rum, salt, and pepper; simmer 15 minutes. Sprinkle with cilantro, and serve immediately.

Makes 4 to 6 servings.

Parmesan-Crumbed Drumsticks

½	cup freshly grated Parmesan cheese	1	teaspoon freshly ground black pepper
⅓	cup fine, dry breadcrumbs	¼	teaspoon cayenne pepper
1	garlic clove, pressed	2½	pounds drumsticks, patted dry
2	teaspoons grated lemon rind	7	tablespoons unsalted butter, melted
1½	teaspoons salt		
1	teaspoon crumbled dried rosemary (or 1 tablespoon fresh rosemary)		

Preheat oven to 425°. Combine first 8 ingredients in a large, shallow dish. Brush drumsticks, 1 at a time, with butter; dredge in crumb mixture, coating completely. Chill drumsticks, covered loosely on a jelly roll pan at least 1 hour or up to 24 hours. Arrange in a lightly buttered roasting pan, and drizzle with remaining butter. Bake for 30 to 35 minutes or until tender. Serve warm or at room temperature.

Makes 4 to 6 servings.

Pecan Chicken Paprika

1 cup all-purpose flour	1 cup buttermilk
1 cup ground pecans	8 (5-ounce) chicken breasts,
¼ cup sesame seeds (optional)	skinned and boned, or 2 broiler-
1 tablespoon paprika	fryers, cut into 8 pieces
1½ teaspoons salt	⅓ cup butter
⅛ teaspoon pepper	¼ cup coarsely chopped pecans
1 egg, beaten	

Preheat oven to 350°. Combine first 6 ingredients in a shallow dish. Whisk egg and buttermilk in a bowl. Dip chicken in egg mixture; dredge in flour mixture. Melt butter in a 13- x 9- x 2-inch baking dish; place chicken in dish, turning once to coat with butter. Sprinkle chicken with chopped pecans, and bake for 30 minutes.

Makes 8 servings.

Pecan Chicken Breasts

3 whole chicken breasts, skinned, boned, and halved	4 tablespoons butter
	1 tablespoon vegetable oil
Salt and pepper to taste	⅔ cup sour cream
6 tablespoons butter	1 tablespoon Dijon mustard
3 tablespoons Dijon mustard	Whole toasted pecans
8 ounces finely chopped pecans	

Preheat oven to 350°. Flatten chicken breast halves by pounding between 2 sheets of wax paper. Sprinkle chicken with salt and pepper to taste. Melt 6 tablespoons butter in a large saucepan over low heat; whisk in 3 tablespoons mustard. Dip each piece of chicken into butter mixture; coat with chopped pecans. Melt 3 tablespoons butter in a skillet over medium heat; add oil, and sauté half of chicken until lightly browned on both sides. Repeat procedure with remaining chicken. Transfer chicken to a baking dish; bake 15 to 20 minutes or until tender. Melt remaining 1 tablespoon butter in a saucepan; whisk in sour cream, remaining 1 tablespoon mustard, salt and pepper to taste; remove from heat. Place a spoonful of sauce on each serving plate, topped with a piece of chicken. Top with toasted pecans.

Makes 6 servings.

Very rich, but worth every bite!

Rolled Chicken Capitan

½ cup chopped fresh mushrooms
2 tablespoons butter
2 tablespoons all-purpose flour
½ cup half-and-half
¼ teaspoon salt
⅛ teaspoon cayenne pepper
1¼ cups shredded sharp Cheddar cheese

6 whole chicken breasts, skinned and boned
Salt to taste
All-purpose flour
2 eggs, lightly beaten
¾ cup fine, dry breadcrumbs

Preheat oven to 325°. Sauté mushrooms in butter 5 minutes. Stir in 2 tablespoons flour; stir in half-and-half. Add salt and cayenne; cook, stirring constantly, until mixture is very thick. Stir in cheese, and cook over low heat, stirring constantly, until cheese is melted. Turn mixture into a pie plate; cover and chill 1 hour or until firm. Cut chilled cheese mixture into 6 equal portions; shape each into a short stick. Place chicken between two layers of plastic wrap; pound chicken, working from center out with a meat mallet, to ¼-inch thickness. Sprinkle chicken with salt to taste, and place a cheese stick on each piece. Fold sides in, and roll jelly roll fashion. Press to seal well. Dust chicken rolls with flour, and dip into beaten egg; roll in breadcrumbs. Cover and chill at least 1 hour. About 1 hour before serving, fry chicken rolls in hot oil (375°) in a large skillet 5 minutes or until crisp and golden brown. Drain on paper towels. Place rolls in a shallow baking dish, and bake for 30 to 45 minutes.

Makes 6 servings.

 In these days of UFO's (Under Funded Orchestras) we are so fortunate in Roswell to have a symphony which has operated debt-free since its inception in 1959. This would not have been possible without the backing of the community and the Roswell Symphony Guild, who supports and contributes volunteer services to this cultural organization.

Sagebrush Chicken Cobbler

2 tablespoons olive oil	½ teaspoon ground cumin
1 small onion, chopped	½ teaspoon finely grated lime zest
1 small red bell pepper, diced	2 cups diced cooked chicken
1 jalapeño, seeded and minced	½ cup cooked corn kernels
1 garlic clove, minced	½ cup cooked black beans, rinsed
¼ cup all-purpose flour	and drained
1 (14½-ounce) can chicken broth	2 tablespoons chopped fresh cilantro
¼ cup lime juice	Garnish: fresh cilantro sprigs

Heat oil in a 10-inch ovenproof skillet over medium-low heat. Add onion, bell pepper, jalapeño, and garlic to skillet; sauté 1 minute. Stir in flour, and cook 2 minutes. Add broth, lime juice, cumin, and lime zest to onion mixture; cook, stirring constantly, over medium heat until thickened and smooth, about 8 minutes. Stir in chicken, corn, black beans, and chopped cilantro.

Topping

½ cup all-purpose flour	2 tablespoons sliced black olives
½ cup yellow cornmeal	1 egg, lightly beaten
¼ cup shredded Cheddar cheese	1 tablespoon olive oil
½ teaspoon chile powder	½ cup milk

Preheat oven to 400°. Combine all ingredients in a bowl until well blended. Drop batter by tablespoonfuls over chicken mixture. Bake for 30 to 35 minutes or until topping is golden brown. Garnish, if desired.

Makes 4 servings.

Spinach-Stuffed Chicken with Tarragon Sauce

2   tablespoons butter
½   cup diced onion
½   cup diced red bell pepper
1   (10-ounce) package frozen chopped spinach, thawed and squeezed dry
½   teaspoon salt
⅛   teaspoon freshly ground pepper

¼   teaspoon dried tarragon, crumbled
⅛   teaspoon ground nutmeg
6-8 chicken breast halves, skinned and boned
½   cup shredded Swiss cheese
⅓   cup dry white wine
    Paprika
    Tarragon Sauce

Preheat oven to 375°. Melt butter in a skillet over medium heat; add onion and bell pepper, and sauté 5 minutes. Add spinach to onion mixture; stir in salt, pepper, tarragon, and nutmeg. Remove mixture from heat. Rinse chicken, and pat dry. Place chicken between 2 sheets of plastic wrap, and pound, from center out using a meat mallet, to ¼-inch thickness. Divide spinach mixture among chicken breasts, and sprinkle each with cheese. Roll up, jelly roll fashion, and secure with wooden picks. Place rolls, seam sides down, in an oiled 11¾- x 7½-inch baking dish. Pour wine over rolls, and sprinkle with paprika. Bake 35 minutes or until chicken is tender. Transfer rolls to a serving platter, and remove picks. Add pan drippings to Tarragon Sauce, and spoon over each chicken roll.

Makes 6 to 8 servings.

Tarragon Sauce

2   tablespoons butter
2   tablespoons all-purpose flour
¼   teaspoon salt
⅛   teaspoon ground white pepper

¼   teaspoon dried tarragon, crumbled
1   cup chicken broth
¼   cup shredded Swiss cheese
2   tablespoons dry white wine

Melt butter in a saucepan over medium heat. Add flour, salt, pepper, and tarragon to butter; stir until blended. Add broth slowly, and cook, stirring constantly, until bubbly and thickened, about 3 minutes. Reduce heat, and stir in cheese, wine, and pan drippings from chicken rolls. Cook until cheese melts, about 1 minute.

Makes 1½ cups.

Tequila-Lime-Grilled Chicken

⅔ cup olive oil
½ cup fresh lime juice
1 jalapeño, seeded and minced
¼ cup tequila
2 tablespoons Triple Sec
¼ cup minced fresh cilantro

6 skinned and boned chicken breast halves
Green Chile Salsa, Pumpkin Seed Salsa, or Red Pepper Sauce (see index)

Combine first 6 ingredients; pour into a shallow pan. Add chicken, and turn to coat. Cover and chill chicken 4 hours, turning several times. Prepare grill, or preheat broiler. Remove chicken from refrigerator 30 minutes before cooking, discarding marinade. Cook chicken 4 minutes per side on grill, or 4 inches from broiler. Serve with desired salsa.

Makes 6 servings.

Turkey Thighs Baked in Red Wine

2 turkey thighs, skinned and boned
2 garlic cloves, sliced
4 small sprigs fresh rosemary or 1½ teaspoons dried rosemary
1 cup dry red wine

2 tablespoons olive oil
Salt and freshly ground pepper to taste
Garnish: fresh parsley sprigs

Preheat oven to 350°. Spread turkey thighs out flat, and sprinkle with garlic and rosemary; fold back over, and place in a small baking dish. Pour wine over turkey, and chill 4 to 5 hours, turning once. Remove turkey from marinade, reserving enough marinade for basting. Bring reserved marinade to a boil in a small saucepan over medium-high heat. Remove from heat. Brush turkey with oil, and sprinkle with salt and pepper. Bake 50 minutes, basting often with reserved marinade. Slice meat into neat slices, and serve fanned on a platter. Garnish, if desired.

Makes 4 servings.

Turkey Tacos

2 tablespoons vegetable oil
1 cup chopped onion
1 garlic clove, minced
1 pound ground turkey
1 teaspoon ground cumin
1 (8-ounce) can tomato sauce
¼ cup water
¼ teaspoon dried red pepper flakes
¼ cup chopped fresh cilantro

Salt to taste
8-12 taco shells
2 cups shredded Monterey Jack cheese
2 cups shredded lettuce
½ cup thinly sliced scallions, including green tops
½ cup sliced black olives
Taco sauce or fresh salsa (see index)

Preheat oven to 350°. Heat oil in a large skillet over medium-high heat. Sauté onion and garlic in hot oil 3 minutes. Add turkey, and cook, breaking up clumps, until no longer pink, about 5 minutes. Stir in cumin, and cook 1 minute. Add tomato sauce and water, and simmer, partially covered, over low heat 10 minutes. Increase heat to medium, uncover, and simmer 5 minutes or until mixture is thick but not dry. Stir in pepper flakes, cilantro, and salt. Heat taco shells on a baking sheet in oven until crisp, 6 to 8 minutes. Place cheese, lettuce, scallions, and olives into serving bowls. Spoon meat into taco shells, and top with desired toppings. Drizzle with taco sauce or salsa.

Makes 4 servings.

You may use leftover cooked turkey or chicken instead of ground turkey. Simply sauté meat 1 minute before adding cumin and tomato sauce.

Fish, Game, & Ostrich

Ostrich

Ostrich is one of the Roswell area's newest agricultural industries. The ostrich, largest member of the ratite family, comes originally from South Africa and has been commercially raised there for over 100 years. Ostrich is a very "showy" bird and comes in shades of black, blue, and red. They grow from 8 to 12 feet tall and can live for 75 years. Ostrich hens survive longer in New Mexico than anywhere else in the nation.

After reaching maturity, ostrich hens lay between 50 and 100 2- to 3-pound eggs per season. The ostrich egg, equal to 2 dozen chicken eggs, has a 42-day incubation period. The ostrich is the largest bird in existence, lays the largest eggs, the only bird that has two toes, and the only bird that does not fly.

Ostrich yields an excellent red meat that is low in fat and cholesterol, a leather considered one of the finest available, feathers for dusters and costumes, and an oil for fine cosmetics.

Featured on page 139 "Ostrich Chorus Line"

New Mexico Baked Shrimp

½ cup flat beer
1 tablespoon olive oil
2 garlic cloves, minced
2 teaspoons chile powder
1 teaspoon ground cumin
2 drops Tabasco

¼ teaspoon salt or to taste
   Freshly ground black pepper to
   taste
1 pound large, fresh shrimp, peeled
   and deveined
¼ cup chopped fresh parsley
   Hot cooked rice

Preheat oven to 425°. Combine first 8 ingredients in a 13- x 9- x 2-inch baking dish. Add shrimp, stirring to coat. Marinate shrimp at room temperature 1 hour, turning occasionally. Bake shrimp in marinade 10 minutes or until shrimp turn pink. Serve shrimp and sauce over rice as a main dish, or serve shrimp alone as an appetizer, sprinkled with parsley.

Makes 4 main dish servings.

Marinated Trout

4 whole trout (about 1 pound each)
½ cup vegetable oil
¼ cup lemon juice
3 tablespoons fresh lime juice
½ cup dry white wine
1 tablespoon minced fresh cilantro

½ teaspoon dried hot red pepper
   flakes
½ teaspoon dry mustard
1 teaspoon freshly ground black
   pepper
1 garlic clove, minced

Wash trout in cold water, and drain on paper towels. Combine remaining ingredients in a large, shallow dish; add trout, and marinate 1 hour at room temperature, turning occasionally. Prepare grill. Remove trout from marinade. Bring marinade to a boil in a saucepan over medium-high heat; remove from heat. Grill trout over medium-hot coals 7 to 10 minutes per side, basting with marinade. Or broil about 3 inches from heat 7 to 10 minutes per side. Serve immediately.

Makes 4 servings.

Pecan Trout

8	bacon slices		All-purpose flour
4	whole boneless trout	6	tablespoons unsalted butter
	Salt and freshly ground pepper to taste	1	cup chopped toasted pecans
		2	tablespoons lemon juice
8	green onions	2	tablespoons chopped fresh sage

Cook bacon in a large skillet over medium heat until crisp. Transfer bacon to paper towels to drain, reserving drippings in skillet. Sprinkle trout cavities with salt and pepper; lay 2 green onions inside each trout. Dredge trout in flour, shaking off excess. Cook trout in reserved drippings over medium heat until opaque throughout, about 12 minutes, turning once. Transfer to platters, and keep warm. Chop bacon. Melt butter in a small saucepan; stir in pecans, lemon juice, sage, and bacon. Pour over trout, and serve immediately.

Makes 4 servings.

Salmon with Sauce Verde

1	tablespoon olive oil	1	sprig fresh parsley
4	salmon steaks	1	small onion, sliced
2	tablespoons lemon juice		Sauce Verde
6	peppercorns		

Oil a skillet or flat baking dish. Place salmon in skillet. Add lemon juice, next 3 ingredients, and water to cover salmon. Cover and poach until salmon is just cooked through, 15 to 20 minutes. Let cool in liquid. Drain well. Arrange salmon on plates, and top with Sauce Verde.

Sauce Verde

½	cup chopped green bell pepper	1	tablespoon lemon juice
¼	cup chopped fresh parsley	1	cup mayonnaise
¼	cup chopped spinach		Garnish: green onion tops or chives, chopped

Process first 4 ingredients in a food processor until smooth. Add mayonnaise, and chill. Garnish, if desired.

Makes 2 cups.

Braised Quail

4	bacon slices, diced	1	teaspoon finely chopped garlic
8	quail, split	½	cup dry red wine
	Salt and freshly ground pepper to taste	½	cup beef bouillon
		1	tablespoon tomato paste
½	cup all-purpose flour	½	cup whipping cream
¼	cup finely chopped onion		Hot cooked wild rice

Cook bacon in a Dutch oven over medium-high heat until crisp; remove from pan, reserving drippings in pan. Drain bacon on paper towels. Sprinkle quail with salt and pepper to taste; dredge in flour. Brown quail, skin side down, in reserved drippings over medium-high heat; transfer quail to a warm platter. Reduce heat to medium, and add onion and garlic to pan; sauté until onion is translucent. Add wine, bouillon, and tomato paste to onion mixture. Return quail to pan, and simmer, covered, 15 to 20 minutes. Add cream and bacon, and cook until heated through. Serve over wild rice.

Makes 4 servings.

Most game birds can be interchanged with chicken in recipes.

Glazed Charbroiled Quail

1	tablespoon pure ground New Mexico red chile	8	partially boned quail
			Vegetable oil
1	cup honey		

Cook chile and honey in a saucepan over medium-low heat 10 minutes to combine flavors. Brush quail with oil, and charbroil over a slow grill 5 to 8 minutes per side. Brush both sides of quail with chile mixture when nearly cooked. Avoid glazing too soon, or honey will burn and quail will char. Transfer quail to a platter, and brush once more with glaze.

Makes 4 servings.

If quail are not partially boned, allow them a longer cooking time.

Gussie Du Jardin

"I was born in 1918 in San Francisco and spent my childhood between summers at the family ranch in Colorado and winters in Honolulu, T.H., where I attended Punahou Academy. I returned to the United States to attend the University of Colorado and continued to spend summers at the ranch. However, upon graduation I returned to Honolulu. At that time, the people of Hawaii were well aware of the danger of invasion, but as a Territory, could get no assistance. The men that could afford to do so sent their families back to the mainland to wait out the impending war, so I returned to the United States in January of 1941.

Elmer Schooley and I were married in September of 1941 and immediately left for the University of Iowa where we both got our masters degrees. Elmer enlisted in the air force and was stationed various places, and it was during this time our sons David and Edwin were born. Our son Teddy was born in 1955.

After Elmer's tour of duty in New Guinea, the Philippines, Okinawa and Japan, he left the air force and got a position at the New Mexico State Teacher's college, where he taught for two years. I only got one painting done during all that time.

In the fall of 1976, I started painting seriously and had a gallery in Sante Fe, New Mexico until we came to Roswell in 1977 on a double grant with the Artist-in-Residence program. We liked Roswell, so we bought a house, built studios and have lived here since. Some of each summer is still spent at the family ranch which I have managed for many years. Elmer and I have been married for 56 years."

Honeysuckle Rose
Artist – Gussie Dujardin
60″ × 72″   1987
oil on canvas
Collection of the artist
Photograph by Jose Rivera.

Ostrich-and-Vegetable Kabobs

2½ pounds ostrich steak
1 large red bell pepper, cut into squares
1 large green bell pepper, cut into squares
1 ear fresh corn
2 medium-size zucchini (about ½ pound)
8 baby pattypan squash (about ¼ pound)

6 cups fresh cilantro sprigs
1 cup olive oil
½ cup fruity red wine
12 garlic cloves
1½ tablespoons salt
1½ tablespoons ground cumin
1 cup apricot jam
½ cup fresh lemon juice
16 (12-inch) bamboo skewers

Pat ostrich steak dry with paper towels, and cut into 1-inch cubes; place in a large bowl. Place bell pepper in another large bowl. Shuck corn, and halve lengthwise. Cut each half crosswise into 8 pieces; add to bell pepper. Halve zucchini lengthwise, and cut halves crosswise into ¾-inch-thick slices; add to bell pepper mixture. Cut pattypans in half, and add to other vegetables. Process cilantro and next 5 ingredients in a food processor until smooth; Divide mixture into 2 bowls, and add jam to 1 bowl, and lemon juice to the other, stirring well. Stir ostrich into jam marinade and vegetables into lemon marinade. Cover and chill separately at least 12 hours or up to 24 hours. Soak skewers in warm water to cover 1 hour. Prepare grill. Thread ostrich alternately with vegetables onto skewers; grill kabobs on an oiled food rack 5 to 6 inches from glowing coals, brushing with vegetable marinade and turning every 5 minutes, 15 minutes for medium-rare. Or broil kabobs 3 inches from heat in oven. Discard any remaining marinade.

Makes 8 servings.

Pheasant with Onion Sauce

2 plump pheasants
4 thin slices salt pork or thick bacon slices
½ pound lean bacon, diced
6 tablespoons butter
2 large sweet onions, finely chopped
2 cups half-and-half

½ cup condensed chicken stock, undiluted
Salt and freshly ground pepper to taste
Grated nutmeg
Juice of ½ lemon (optional)

Truss pheasants, and cover breasts with salt pork slices. Cook diced bacon in butter in a flameproof pan over medium-high heat until golden. Remove bacon, and sauté onion in drippings until translucent. Remove onion, and sauté pheasants in drippings until they are a soft golden brown on all sides. Return onion and diced bacon to pan, and add half-and-half and stock. Season with salt, pepper, and nutmeg. Cover pan, and simmer gently over very low heat until pheasants are tender. Transfer pheasants and bacon bits to a hot serving dish. Process cream mixture and onion in a blender until pureed, and pour over pheasants. Adjust seasonings, and add lemon juice, if desired.

Makes 6 to 8 servings.

Quail and Artichokes

6-8 whole quail
6 tablespoons butter, divided
Salt, pepper, and paprika to taste
½ pound sliced fresh mushrooms

1 (16-ounce) can artichoke hearts, drained
2 tablespoons all-purpose flour
⅔ cup chicken broth
3 tablespoons sherry

Preheat oven to 350°. Sprinkle quail with salt. Melt 4 tablespoons butter in a large skillet over medium heat; add quail, and brown on all sides. Sprinkle quail with paprika, and transfer from skillet to a deep baking dish. Place artichoke hearts between quail. Melt remaining butter in skillet; add mushrooms, and sauté until browned. Stir flour into mushrooms. Stir broth into mushroom mixture, and cook, stirring constantly, 5 minutes. Stir in sherry. Adjust salt and pepper, and pour gravy over quail. Bake, covered, 1 hour or until quail are done.

Makes 6 to 8 servings.

You may substitute doves or combine them with quail.

Ostrich Marsala

3 pounds ostrich meat
2 tablespoons olive oil
2 yellow onions, peeled and chopped
3 garlic cloves, chopped
½ teaspoon dried rosemary
½ teaspoon dried oregano

½ teaspoon dried basil
   Salt and pepper to taste
1 cup Marsala
½ pound sliced fresh mushrooms
½ cup Chablis
½ cup beef broth

Brown ostrich in hot oil in a skillet over high heat; remove from pan. Sauté onion and garlic in skillet until tender. Add remaining ingredients, and return ostrich to pan. Simmer, covered, 1½ to 2 hours or until meat is tender, adding more broth, if needed.

Makes 6 to 8 servings.

Picante Pan-Fried Quail

8 whole or split quail (6 to 7 ounces each)
3 cups milk
1 cup all-purpose flour
2 garlic cloves, minced
1 tablespoon ground dried red chile (New Mexico or ancho)

½ teaspoon cumin seed, toasted and ground
½ teaspoon salt
¼ teaspoon freshly ground black pepper
⅛ teaspoon ground cinnamon
   Vegetable oil
3 cups unsalted chicken stock

Soak quail in milk at least 1 hour, preferably 2 to 3 hours. Pat quail lightly with paper towels, discarding milk. Combine flour and next 6 ingredients in a shallow dish; dredge quail in flour mixture. Reserve ¼ cup flour mixture. Add enough oil to a cast-iron skillet to measure 1 inch. Heat oil to 350°. Fry quail in hot oil over medium-high heat until golden and crispy outside and juicy inside, 3 to 4 minutes per side. Transfer quail to a serving platter, and keep warm. Pour off all but ¼ cup oil through a wire-mesh strainer, and return cracklings from strainer to skillet. Warm reserved ¼ cup drippings and cracklings over medium heat, adding reserved flour mixture and stirring to avoid lumps. Pour stock into drippings mixture, and simmer, stirring often, until thickened to a rich, brown gravy. Adjust seasonings, and serve with quail.

Makes 8 servings.

Beer-Braised Venison Roast

2½ pounds boneless venison roast
2 garlic cloves, slivered
1 cup beer
1 (8-ounce) can tomato sauce
1 tablespoon beef bouillon granules
2 ounces salt pork

3 tablespoons chopped fresh parsley
4 small potatoes, peeled and quartered
2 large onions, quartered
¼ cup all-purpose flour
Salt and pepper to taste

Preheat oven to 450°. Cut small slits in roast; insert garlic into slits. Combine beer, tomato sauce, and bouillon in a large glass bowl; add roast. Cover bowl with plastic wrap, and chill 2 hours, turning once. Line a 13- x 9- x 2-inch pan with heavy-duty foil, leaving a 1½-inch foil collar. Remove roast from marinade, reserving marinade. Place roast in pan. Cut salt pork into 6 (4- x ½-inch) strips. Roll pork strips in parsley, and place in a crisscross pattern over roast. Bake for 15 minutes; reduce temperature to 325°, and add vegetables to pan. Dissolve flour in reserved marinade, and pour over roast and vegetables. Sprinkle with salt and pepper. Seal pan with heavy-duty foil, and insert a meat thermometer into thickest part of roast through foil. Bake 1½ to 2 hours or until thermometer registers 180°.

Makes 6 servings.

Hot and Tasty
If ever the phrase "good manners spoil good food" applies, it is when venison is on the table. Serve steaks and chops right from the grill and insist no one waits until all are served. If your meal is a roasted leg or haunch, do not "rest" the meat as you would beef or pork. Bring it from the oven hot on a platter and serve it on hot plates. Enlist help to serve the vegetables and pour the wine, for your job is to carve and serve with the greatest dispatch to seated guests.

The sauce or gravy should be skimmed of as much fat as possible and hurried to the table. When venison fat is cooled, it is rigid ice on an autumn pond and just about as appetizing.

Easy Venison Pot Roast

1 envelope dry onion soup mix
½ cup water
4 pounds venison roast or any big game meat

6 potatoes, quartered
3 tablespoons all-purpose flour
1½ cups water

Preheat oven to 300°. Place onion soup mix in a Dutch oven; add ½ cup water, and stir until blended. Place roast in pan, turning to coat. Place potatoes into pan, and stir to coat. Bake, covered, for 2½ hours or until meat is done. Remove roast and potatoes to a warm platter. Combine flour and 1½ cups water, and stir into pan juices.

Makes 8 servings.

Elk Medallions with Cranberry Sauce

2 teaspoons salt
1 teaspoon pepper
2 tablespoons butter
12 (2-ounce) elk medallions (can use venison or beef tenderloin)

½ cup cranberry chutney
⅓ cup Cointreau
⅓ cup chicken broth
¾ cup whipping cream
Hot cooked rice or pilaf

Heat a cast-iron skillet over medium-high heat. Rub salt and pepper into both sides of meat. Melt butter in skillet, and add 4 to 6 medallions, without crowding. Sear meat on both sides to medium-rare, and set aside. Repeat procedure with remaining medallions. Add chutney, Cointreau, and broth to skillet, scraping skillet to loosen browned bits. Simmer chutney mixture until reduced slightly, about 3 minutes; add cream, and simmer 5 minutes to create a medium thick sauce that will cling to meat. Return all medallions and any accumulated juices to skillet, and cook until heated through. Serve with rice or pilaf.

Makes 4 servings.

If cranberry chutney isn't available, use another chutney. You can use ½ cup cranberry relish combined with 1 tablespoon grated fresh ginger, 1 chopped serrano chile, and 2 tablespoons finely chopped green onions.

Hearty Venison Stew

2 tablespoons vegetable oil
2 pounds venison stew meat, cut into 1½-inch chunks
2 medium-size onions, quartered
1 teaspoon salt
6 whole allspice
1 bay leaf
⅛ teaspoon pepper

1 beef bouillon cube
2½ cups water
3 carrots, thinly sliced
1 pound zucchini, thinly sliced
1 cup dried apricots
½ teaspoon sugar
1 tablespoon all-purpose flour
¼ cup water
Hot cooked noodles or rice

Heat oil in a Dutch oven over medium heat; add venison, and brown well on all sides. Add onion and next 6 ingredients to pan, and bring to a boil. Reduce heat, cover, and simmer until meat is tender, 1½ hours. Add carrot to meat mixture, and cook 5 minutes. Add zucchini, apricot, and sugar, and cook until vegetables are tender, about 10 minutes. Remove and discard bay leaf. Blend flour and ¼ cup water until smooth; slowly stir into stew liquid. Cook, stirring constantly, until sauce thickens. Serve over noodles or rice.

Makes 4 to 6 servings.

Pecos Venison

2 pounds venison steak, cut 1-inch thick
¼ cup all-purpose flour
1 teaspoon salt
Freshly ground pepper to taste
3 tablespoons bacon drippings
1 celery rib, cut up

3 medium-size onions, sliced
2 New Mexico green chiles, roasted, peeled, seeded, and chopped
1 tablespoon Worcestershire sauce
2 cups chopped tomato
Hot cooked noodles or rice

Cut steak into serving-size pieces. Combine flour, salt, and pepper, and rub over steaks. Heat drippings in a skillet over medium heat; add steaks, and brown on all sides. Add celery and onion to skillet, and cook until browned. Add chiles, Worcestershire sauce, and tomato, and cook, covered, until steaks are tender, 1 to 2 hours. Serve over noodles or rice.

Makes 6 to 8 servings.

Hunters' Chile

¼ cup pork lard
3 pounds venison (flank, neck, or trimmings), cubed
4 tablespoons chile powder
3 dried red chile peppers, crushed
1 tablespoon dried oregano

1 teaspoon dried cumin seed, bruised
2 garlic cloves, chopped
2 teaspoons salt
  Ground black pepper to taste
3 onions, chopped
  Garnish: fresh lime wedges

Melt lard in a large Dutch oven over medium heat; add venison, and brown in batches, adding lard, if needed. Pour off any excess fat. Add chile powder and next 6 ingredients to venison in pan, stirring to coat meat with spices. Reduce heat to low, and cook 10 minutes. Add enough water to cover meat; bring mixture to a boil. Cover, reduce heat, and simmer, stirring occasionally, 1 hour. Add onion to meat mixture, and simmer 1 hour, add more water, if needed, until onion dissolves. Remove mixture from heat, and let stand 10 minutes before serving, skimming off any fat that rises to top. Garnish and serve with biscuits, if desired.

Makes 6 servings.

Chile can be made with almost any meat - the leaner the better. Elk or antelope works just as well.

Six-Layer Venison

2 cups sliced potato
2 cups thinly sliced celery
2 cups ground venison or thin slices of a tender cut
1 cup thinly sliced onion
1 cup chopped New Mexico green chiles, roasted, peeled, and seeded

2 cups canned tomatoes
1-2 cups shredded sharp Cheddar cheese
2 teaspoons salt
½ teaspoon pepper
1 teaspoon garlic powder
1 teaspoon crushed dried oregano

Preheat oven to 350°. Butter a 2-quart baking dish, and add layers of potato, celery, venison, onion, chiles, and tomatoes, each layer sprinkled with mixture of salt, pepper, garlic powder, and oregano. Bake, covered, for 1 hour and 45 minutes. Uncover and sprinkle casserole with cheese; bake 15 more minutes.

Makes 4 to 6 servings.

Marinated Antelope Rolled Roast

1	quart buttermilk	4	shallots, chopped
2	onions, chopped	2	tablespoons all-purpose flour
1	garlic clove, smashed	2	bay leaves
3	pounds antelope roast	½	teaspoon rosemary, crumbled
2	tablespoons capers, with liquid	1½	cups beef broth
1	garlic clove, sliced	½	cup white wine
¼	pound salt pork, sliced	¾	cup sour cream
4	tablespoons butter	1	tablespoon paprika

Preheat oven to 400°. Combine first 3 ingredients in a large, shallow dish. Add meat, and chill 48 hours. Remove roast from marinade, discarding marinade. Crush capers, and rub, with liquid, into roast's inside side. Scatter garlic slices over same side. Roll roast, and tie with string at 8 intervals to ensure a neat roll. Lay salt pork in a roasting pan, and cover with roast; bake for 15 minutes. Melt butter in a skillet over medium heat; add shallot, and sauté 3 to 4 minutes. Stir flour into shallot mixture, and cook 2 minutes; add bay leaves, rosemary, broth, and wine, and cook over low heat, stirring constantly, until thickened. Stir in sour cream and paprika. Pour half of sour cream sauce over roast; reduce oven temperature to 300°. Cook 20 minutes per pound. When roast is done, add remaining sour cream sauce, place over burner just until heated through.

Makes 6 servings.

 *The Roswell Symphony Guild is extremely proud that four of their programs have received American Symphony Orchestra Leagues National Conference Awards; "Denim & Diamonds", "**Savoring The Southwest** Cookbook," "The Story of Babar the Elephant," and "Music In the Classroom."*

Tawny Roasted Pheasants

2 pheasants (about 2½ pounds each)
2 oranges, halved
¼ cup olive oil
Salt and pepper to taste
8 fresh flat-leaf parsley sprigs
4 garlic cloves, peeled and bruised
2 bay leaves
12 bacon slices
½ cup defatted chicken broth
¼ cup tawny port
Autumn Pear Salsa

Preheat oven to 350°. Rinse pheasants, cleaning cavities well; remove excess fat, and pat dry with paper towels. Squeeze oranges all over pheasants and inside cavities. Brush pheasant with oil, and sprinkle inside and out with salt and pepper. Place 4 parsley sprigs, 2 garlic cloves, and a bay leaf inside each pheasant. Place birds in a shallow roasting pan; arrange 6 bacon slices over each. Add broth and port to pan. Bake for 1 hour and 45 minutes (removing bacon after 1 hour), basting with pan juices 2 to 3 times, until juice from thickest portion of thighs runs clear when pricked with a knife. Let birds rest 10 minutes. Carve and serve with Autumn Pear Salsa

Makes 4 servings.

Autumn Pear Salsa
1 large grapefruit, preferably pink
2 medium-size ripe pears
½ cup dried cherries or cranberries
2 tablespoons finely chopped purple onion
½ teaspoon finely chopped garlic
½ teaspoon finely chopped jalapeño
½ teaspoon grated lime zest
2 tablespoons fresh lime juice

Peel grapefruit, removing all white pith. Section it, and cut each section crosswise into thirds. Place sections into a bowl with any accumulated juice. Peel and core pear; cut into ¼-inch dice. Add at once to grapefruit to prevent discoloration. Add remaining ingredients to grapefruit mixture, tossing to blend.

Makes 3 cups.

Venison Empanadas

1 recipe Basic Pastry	¼ cup sherry
1 tablespoon butter	2 teaspoons ground cinnamon
1 pound ground venison	1 teaspoon salt
1 garlic clove, minced	½ teaspoon ground cloves
½ onion, finely chopped	2 tablespoons vinegar
¼ cup minced green bell pepper	1 tablespoon sugar
½ cup tomato puree	¾ cup slivered almonds
½ cup raisins	Vegetable oil

Melt butter in a large skillet over medium heat; add venison, and cook until browned. Add garlic and next 10 ingredients, and cook, uncovered, 20 minutes. Add almonds to skillet, and cool mixture. (Add water if mixture seems too thick.) Roll pastry to ⅛-inch thickness, and cut into 4- to 5-inch rounds. Spoon venison mixture onto 1 side of each round; moisten edges of pastry, fold over, and pinch seams to seal. Make slits in tops of packets to vent. Heat 1 inch of oil to 370° in a deep skillet. Fry empanadas until lightly browned, and drain on paper towels. Or bake on baking sheets in a 400° oven for 15 to 20 minutes.

Makes 4 to 6 servings, about 15 empanadas.

Basic Pastry

2 cups all-purpose flour	⅔ cup vegetable shortening
1 teaspoon salt	4 tablespoons water

Combine flour and salt; cut in shortening with a pastry blender until mixture resembles coarse meal. Sprinkle dough with water, a little at a time, until dough can be formed into a ball. Roll out as directed above.

Makes enough pastry for a 2-crust pie.

Pasta

El Capitan and Smokey Bear

El Capitan rises majestically to a height of 10,083 feet from the foothills of the Capitan Mountain Range near Arabella, New Mexico. This range is one of the few ranges in the country that extend east and west rather than north and south. Also, it is one of the few mountain ranges without a major stream.

The "blue triangle" of El Capitan that fascinated artist Peter Hurd from a very young age appears in many of his southwestern landscapes. The mountain has also inspired at least one symphonic offering.

In May of 1950, near the small crossroads village of Capitan, a forest fire had raged for five days and burned more than 17,000 acres. In the midst of the charred remains, firefighters found a small bear cub and named him "Hot Foot Teddy." Flown to Santa Fe for medical care, he was rechristened "Smokey Bear" when fully recovered. Smokey then moved to Washington, D.C.'s National Zoo and became a national icon as part of the Forest Service's advertising effort to dissuade campers from creating dangerous fires.

Without any government assistance, the citizens of Capitan constructed a log museum to tell the story of the cub's beginnings. Over the years, millions came to Capitan to pay their respects to Smokey, and he was even assigned his own ZIP code.

Smokey Bear died during the Bicentennial year and was taken home to the Capital Mountains and buried in the Smokey Bear Historical State Park. A tree planted next to the spot where he was buried is nourished by the great bear himself.

Featured on page 155 "El Capitan"

Baked Ziti with Beef and Mushrooms

1½ tablespoons olive oil	1 pound fresh mushrooms, sliced
1 large onion, coarsely chopped	1½ cups dry white wine
2 garlic cloves, minced	1 (6-ounce) can tomato paste
2 teaspoons dried basil, crumbled	1½ teaspoons salt
1 teaspoon dried oregano, crumbled	½ teaspoon pepper
1 pound lean ground beef	

Sauce

¼ cup olive oil	1 cup shredded Monterey Jack cheese
4 tablespoons butter	1 cup shredded sharp Cheddar cheese
1 garlic clove, minced	¾ cup freshly grated Parmesan
1 cup all-purpose flour	cheese
5½ cups milk	1½ teaspoons salt
½ teaspoon grated nutmeg	¼ teaspoon ground black pepper
½ cup dry white wine	1 pound ziti or rigatoni pasta

Preheat oven to 350°. Heat 1½ tablespoons oil in a skillet over medium-high heat; sauté onion in oil until soft, about 5 minutes. Add garlic, basil, and oregano; sauté 1 minute. Push onion mixture to 1 side of skillet, and crumble beef into skillet. Brown beef well, about 5 minutes. Add mushrooms to beef, and cook 2 minutes. Stir in wine, tomato paste, salt, and pepper. Reduce heat, and simmer, stirring occasionally, about 20 minutes. Oil a lasagna dish or 4-quart baking dish. Combine ¼ cup olive oil, butter, and garlic in a large, heavy Dutch oven; cook over medium heat, stirring until butter melts. Add flour to mixture, and cook, stirring constantly, 2 minutes; add half of milk, and whisk until blended. Add remaining milk and nutmeg, whisking until mixture boils. Add wine; reduce heat, and simmer, stirring constantly, until sauce thickens, 3 to 4 minutes. Remove sauce from heat, and stir in Monterey Jack, Cheddar, and ½ cup Parmesan until melted. Add salt and pepper. Set aside 1½ cups sauce for top of casserole. Cook pasta in boiling water until al dente; drain. Place half of pasta and sauce into oiled baking dish; spoon half of beef mixture over top. Repeat layers, and spoon reserved 1½ cups sauce over top. Sprinkle with remaining Parmesan. Place dish on a baking sheet, and bake for 30 to 35 minutes or until bubbly and slightly browned.

Makes 8 servings.

Chicken-Zucchini-Mushroom Lasagna

1½ pounds leeks, washed, drained, and thinly sliced
5 tablespoons unsalted butter
1 pound skinless, boneless chicken breast halves
1 pound mushrooms, thinly sliced
1¼ pounds zucchini, cut lengthwise into thin strips
2 tablespoons all-purpose flour
2½ cups milk
1 cup cottage cheese
1 pound lasagna noodles
⅓ cup freshly grated Parmesan cheese
½ cup whipping cream, well chilled
Salt and pepper to taste

Preheat oven to 375°. Cook leeks in 3 tablespoons butter in a large saucepan over medium-low heat, stirring occasionally, 30 minutes or until soft. Heat remaining 2 tablespoons butter in a skillet over medium-high heat until foam subsides. Pat chicken dry, and season with salt and pepper; cook in butter 5 minutes on each side or just until firm to touch. Transfer with a slotted spatula to a plate. Add mushrooms to skillet, and sauté over medium heat, adding any chicken juices accumulated on plate, and cooking until all liquid evaporates. Blanch zucchini in a large saucepan of boiling water, stirring constantly, 30 seconds; drain well. Stir flour into leeks, and cook over medium-low heat, whisking constantly, 3 minutes; whisk in milk, and bring mixture to a boil. Reduce heat, and simmer, whisking, 5 minutes. Coarsely chop chicken. Stir cottage cheese, chicken, salt, and pepper into leek mixture. Remove from heat. Cook lasagna in a pan of boiling water until al dente, 8 to 10 minutes; drain and rinse under cold water, draining well. Butter a 13- x 9- x 2½-inch baking dish. Arrange a single layer of noodle strips in bottom of dish; sprinkle with ¼ cup Parmesan. Top with half of zucchini. Sprinkle half of mushrooms over zucchini, and spread half of chicken mixture on top. Repeat layers, and add top layer of noodle strips. Beat cream at high speed with an electric mixer until soft peaks form; add salt and pepper to taste, and spread over noodle layer. Sprinkle top of lasagna with remaining Parmesan, and bake for 30 minutes or until top is golden brown. Cool 15 minutes before serving.

Makes 8 servings.

Curried Linguine with Vegetables

½   cup vegetable oil
2   teaspoons curry powder
6   tablespoons unsalted butter,
    softened and cut into 6 pieces
2   tablespoons water
2   small carrots, peeled and julienned
2   small zucchini, julienned

1   medium-size leek, washed,
    trimmed of all but 1 inch of green,
    and julienned
    Salt and freshly ground pepper to
    taste
½   pound linguine
½   cup whipping cream

Combine oil and curry powder in a small glass jar; cover tightly, and shake vigorously. Let stand 3 hours or overnight, shaking jar occasionally. Melt 2 tablespoons butter in a large skillet over medium heat; add water and vegetables. Season with salt and pepper, and cook, covered, just until tender, about 5 minutes. Keep warm. Bring cream to a simmer; whisk in remaining butter, piece by piece. Cover and keep warm. Cook pasta in a pan of boiling salted water until al dente, about 8 minutes. Add cold water to pasta to stop cooking process; drain well, and return to pan. Shake oil mixture, and add 3 tablespoons to pasta, tossing well. Add vegetables and cream, tossing over medium-low heat until pasta is just heated through and coated with cream, about 1 minute. Season to taste with salt and pepper.

Makes 6 servings.

Fettuccine with Pecans

¾   pound fresh or dried fettuccine or
    other flat pasta
2   tablespoons butter
¼   cup finely chopped pecans
⅛   teaspoon Tabasco

⅛   teaspoon freshly ground nutmeg
¼   cup whipping cream
½   cup finely chopped fresh basil
½   cup freshly grated Parmesan
    cheese

Cook pasta in a pan of boiling water until al dente; drain, reserving ¼ cup cooking liquid. Return pasta to pan, and add butter; toss, adding reserved liquid and next 5 ingredients. Serve with Parmesan cheese.

Makes 4 servings.

———Fettuccine, Smoked Chicken, and Ricotta———

3   tablespoons unsalted butter
¼   cup finely diced onion
3   tablespoons finely diced red bell pepper
2   teaspoons minced garlic
1   cup whipping cream
½   cup chopped toasted pecans

¼   pound smoked chicken or turkey, julienned
¼   cup ricotta cheese
2   tablespoons minced fresh cilantro
10 ounces fettuccine
    Salt and freshly ground pepper to taste

Melt butter in a large, heavy skillet over medium heat; add onion, bell pepper, and garlic, and sauté until soft, about 5 minutes. Add cream and next 4 ingredients, and bring to a boil, stirring constantly. Cook pasta in a pan of boiling salted water until al dente; drain and add to sauce. Cook over medium heat until heated through, stirring occasionally. Add salt and pepper to taste.

Makes 4 servings.

——————— Pasta with Asparagus———————

12 ounces penne pasta
2   cups (1-inch) fresh asparagus pieces
1   tablespoon olive oil
½   cup diced purple onion
2   garlic cloves, minced
½   cup chicken broth
2   teaspoons balsamic vinegar

½   cup diced roasted red pepper
2   tablespoons freshly grated Parmesan cheese
½   teaspoon freshly ground black pepper
2   tablespoons chopped fresh basil (optional)

Cook pasta in a pan of boiling water until al dente; add asparagus, and cook 3 to 4 minutes or until pasta is tender and asparagus is bright green. Heat oil in a large, nonstick skillet over medium heat; add onion and garlic, and sauté until tender, 2 to 3 minutes. Stir broth and vinegar into onion mixture, and bring to a boil. Reduce heat to low, and stir in red pepper, Parmesan, and black pepper. Cook until heated through, 1 to 2 minutes. Drain pasta and asparagus, and place in a large serving bowl; add onion mixture, tossing well. Sprinkle with basil, if desired.

Makes 4 servings.

Glenn's Pasta

1½ pounds lean ground beef
1 large onion, chopped
8 ounces fresh mushrooms, sliced
2 (15-ounce) cans tomato sauce
1 teaspoon garlic powder

1 teaspoon salt
4 tablespoons hot curry powder
½ teaspoon pepper
8 ounces pasta
Freshly grated Parmesan cheese

Brown beef in a large skillet over medium-high heat; drain. Add onion and mushrooms to beef, and sauté until soft. Add tomato sauce and next 4 ingredients; bring to a boil. Reduce heat, and simmer, covered, 30 minutes. Cook pasta in a pan of boiling water according to package directions; drain. Serve sauce over pasta, and top with Parmesan.

Makes 6 to 8 servings.

Curry adds an exciting flavor to this unusual sauce.

Linguine with Chicken and Spicy Pesto Sauce

2 tablespoons olive oil
1 pound skinless, boneless chicken breasts, cut into ⅓-inch-wide strips
Salt and pepper to taste
3 green onions, thinly sliced
⅓ cup chopped fresh cilantro
⅓ cup chopped pecans, toasted

1 tablespoon minced garlic
2 teaspoons minced, seeded jalapeño
¼ teaspoon dried crushed red pepper
½ cup pesto (purchased or see index)
12 ounces linguine
Chopped fresh cilantro
Freshly grated Parmesan cheese

Heat oil in a large, heavy skillet over medium-high heat. Season chicken with salt and pepper, and add to skillet; sauté until cooked through and lightly browned. Transfer chicken with a slotted spoon into a bowl. Add green onions and next 5 ingredients to skillet; sauté until green onions wilt, about 2 minutes. Add pesto, chicken, and any accumulated chicken juices to onion mixture, stirring to blend. Remove from heat. Cook linguine in a pan of boiling water until al dente; drain, reserving ¼ cup cooking liquid. Bring sauce mixture to simmer; add pasta and reserved liquid, tossing to coat. Season with salt and pepper to taste. Transfer to a large bowl, and sprinkle with additional cilantro. Serve with Parmesan.

Makes 4 servings.

Mucho Gusto Pasta

1   tablespoon olive oil
½   red bell pepper, seeded and cut
    into ⅜-inch strips, halved
6   green onions, sliced
¼   pound fresh mushrooms, sliced
1   zucchini, sliced lengthwise and cut
    into ⅜-inch pieces
3   garlic cloves
1   (14½-ounce) can diced tomatoes
    in puree or juice

Salt and freshly ground pepper to
taste
5   fresh basil leaves, chopped, or
    ¾ teaspoon dried basil
8   ounces mostaccioli, penne, or ziti
    pasta, cooked and drained
⅓   cup freshly grated Parmesan
    cheese
1   tablespoon olive oil or butter
¼   cup chopped fresh parsley
    Parmesan cheese

Heat oil in a large skillet over medium heat; add bell pepper and next 4 ingredients, and sauté until crisp-tender, about 8 minutes. Add tomatoes, salt, pepper, and basil to bell pepper mixture; cook, stirring occasionally, until flavors are blended, about 20 minutes. Toss sauce with pasta, cheese, oil, and parsley. Top with additional Parmesan, if desired.

Makes 4 main dish servings or 6 side dish servings.

Vegetables can be prepared ahead and chilled in a bowl to help flavors blend.

Linguine with Broccoli and Pecans

1½ pounds broccoli, cut into bite-size
    florets
8   ounces linguine
2   tablespoons olive oil
2   garlic cloves, minced
⅛   teaspoon ground cayenne pepper

2   tablespoons fresh lemon juice
⅔   cup grated Parmesan cheese
½   cup large pecan halves, toasted
    Salt and freshly ground pepper to
    taste

Blanch broccoli in boiling water 3 minutes; rinse in a bowl of ice water, and drain. Cook pasta in a pan of boiling water until al dente; drain, reserving ¼ cup cooking liquid. Heat oil in a large skillet over medium-high heat; add garlic and cayenne pepper. Cook, stirring constantly, until garlic is tender but not browned. Add broccoli, and stir until heated through. Add pasta, stirring to coat with oil (moisten with reserved cooking liquid, if needed). Add lemon juice; toss to coat. Stir in cheese and pecans. Season with salt and pepper to taste, and toss.

Makes 4 servings.

Mushroom Lasagna

1 pound farmer's cheese or cottage cheese with excess moisture drained
½ pound low-fat ricotta
2 egg whites
2 tablespoons grated Parmesan cheese
1 tablespoon minced fresh chives
1 tablespoon minced fresh parsley
¼ teaspoon pepper
8 ounces lasagna noodles
1 large onion, minced
¼ cup dry red wine
1½ pounds fresh mushrooms, sliced
4 cups Red Sauce

Preheat oven to 375°. Process farmer's cheese, ricotta, egg whites, and Parmesan in a food processor until pureed; stir in chives, parsley, and pepper. Cook lasagna in a pan of boiling salted water until al dente, about 10 minutes; dip in cold water, and lay flat on kitchen towels (not paper). Simmer onion and wine in a skillet over medium heat, keeping skillet covered between stirrings, until onion is very soft, about 5 minutes. Add mushrooms, and cook until soft, about 5 minutes; drain vegetables. Combine cheese mixture and all but ¼ cup mushroom mixture. Spread 2 cups Red Sauce in bottom of a 13- x 9- x 2½-inch baking dish; alternate layers of noodles and cheese mixture, ending with noodles. Cover noodles with remaining Red Sauce. Sprinkle with reserved ¼ cup mushroom mixture. Bake, covered, for 1 hour. Uncover and bake 5 minutes. Let stand 10 minutes before cutting.

Makes 9 servings.

Red Sauce

1 celery rib, minced
¼ purple onion or 1 small onion, minced
3 garlic cloves, minced
⅓ cup dry red wine
1 (28-ounce) can tomato puree
1½ cups canned peeled tomatoes, undrained and coarsely chopped
1 whole carrot, peeled
1 tablespoon minced fresh parsley
1 tablespoon dried basil
1 bay leaf
2 teaspoons dried oregano
¼ teaspoon dried rosemary
⅛ teaspoon salt

Sauté first 3 ingredients in 1 tablespoon wine in a skillet over medium heat; add remaining wine, and simmer 10 minutes (use tomato liquid if too dry). Add tomato puree and tomatoes, carrot, and spices; simmer, uncovered, 30 to 45 minutes or until sauce thickens. Discard bay leaf and carrot before serving.

Makes 5 cups.

Sauce is best after being stored in refrigerator overnight.

Mexican Chicken Pasta

¼ cup olive oil
¼ cup pine nuts
1 large onion, chopped
2 garlic cloves, minced
1½ teaspoons dried basil
1½ teaspoons dried oregano
½ teaspoon crushed dried hot chiles
2 small zucchini, sliced ⅛-inch thick

8 ounces fresh mushrooms, sliced
2 medium-size tomatoes, cored and chopped
1 cup shredded cooked chicken or turkey
10 ounces fresh or dried fettuccine
¾ cup grated Parmesan cheese
Salt and pepper to taste

Heat 2 tablespoons oil in a large skillet over medium-high heat. Add nuts, and cook, stirring constantly, until lightly toasted, about 1 minute. Remove nuts from skillet. Add onion and next 4 ingredients to skillet; sauté until onion is limp, about 4 minutes (add remaining oil, if needed). Add zucchini, mushrooms, and tomato; cook 3 minutes. Add chicken, and stir just until heated through, about 1 minute. Cook pasta in a pan of boiling water until al dente; drain and pour onto a rimmed platter. Spoon chicken mixture over pasta, and toss with forks. Season with salt and pepper to taste. Sprinkle with nuts and ¼ cup cheese. Serve with remaining cheese.

Makes 4 to 6 servings.

Penne with Olive-and-Tomato Sauce

½ tablespoon olive oil
2 garlic cloves, chopped
1 small chile pepper, chopped, or ½ teaspoon dried chile flakes
1 (28-ounce) can plum tomatoes, undrained

7 ounces large black olives, chopped
Salt and pepper to taste
1 pound penne or other short pasta
Garnish: chopped fresh parsley

Heat oil in a large skillet over medium heat; add garlic and chile, and sauté until garlic turns golden, about 3 minutes. Add tomatoes with juice, breaking up tomatoes with a spoon; simmer 20 minutes. Add olives and salt and pepper to taste; keep sauce warm. Cook pasta in a pan of boiling water until al dente; drain. Serve sauce over pasta, and garnish, if desired.

Makes 4 to 6 servings.

Pasta Baked with Two Cheeses and Ham

1 recipe Garlic Béchamel
10 ounces medium-sharp Cheddar cheese, shredded
10 ounces mild, rindless goat cheese, crumbled
1 tablespoon salt
1 pound short pasta, such as fusilli or rotelle
12 ounces smoked ham, trimmed and cut into ½-inch cubes (2½ cups)
2 teaspoons freshly ground pepper
2 tablespoons fine breadcrumbs
2 tablespoons freshly grated Parmesan cheese

Warm béchamel sauce in a heavy saucepan over low heat; whisk in Cheddar and goat cheeses until smooth. Bring a large stockpot of water to a boil; stir in 1 tablespoon salt. Add pasta, and cook just until tender, about 7 minutes. Drain immediately, and rinse well under cold water. (Recipe may be made to this point several hours ahead. Cover béchamel sauce with plastic wrap, pressing it onto surface of sauce. Toss pasta with 2 tablespoons olive oil, and cover.) Preheat oven to 400°. Combine warm béchamel mixture and pasta in a large bowl. Add ham and ground pepper to pasta mixture, and stir thoroughly. Spoon pasta mixture into a buttered 3-quart baking dish. Combine breadcrumbs and Parmesan, and sprinkle over pasta. Bake for 30 to 40 minutes or until top is slightly browned and pasta mixture is bubbly. Let stand 5 minutes before serving.

Makes 6 servings.

Garlic Béchamel

3 tablespoons unsalted butter
2 garlic cloves, minced
3 tablespoons all-purpose flour
2½ cups milk
½ teaspoon salt
Freshly grated nutmeg
Cayenne pepper to taste

Melt butter in a skillet over medium heat; add garlic, and sauté, without browning, 2 to 3 minutes. Whisk in flour, and cook, stirring often, 2 to 3 minutes without browning flour. Remove skillet from heat, and slowly add milk, whisking vigorously to avoid clumping. Place skillet over low heat; stir in salt, nutmeg, and cayenne pepper, and bring to a simmer. Cook, partially covered, stirring often, until sauce is thick enough to coat a spoon, about 15 minutes. (Sauce may be made up to 1 day ahead. Cool, cover, and chill.)

Makes about 3 cups.

Pasta with Sun-Dried Tomatoes, Mushrooms, and Artichokes

¼ cup butter
1 (14½-ounce) can diced tomatoes, undrained
¾ cup half-and-half
½ cup vodka
¼ teaspoon dried crushed red pepper
2 tablespoons olive oil
6 ounces shiitake mushrooms, sliced and stems removed
¾ cup sliced, drained oil-packed sun-dried tomatoes
1 (14-ounce) can artichoke hearts, drained and quartered
1 tablespoon chopped shallot
½ cup plus 2 tablespoons chopped fresh basil
1 pound penne pasta
Salt and pepper to taste
Freshly grated Parmesan cheese

Melt butter in a large, heavy skillet over medium heat; add diced tomatoes with juice, half-and-half, vodka, and dried red pepper. Simmer until mixture thickens to sauce consistency, about 8 minutes. Season to taste with salt and pepper. Heat oil in a separate skillet over medium-high heat; add mushrooms, and sauté 4 minutes. Add dried tomatoes, artichoke hearts, and shallot; sauté 2 minutes. Add tomato mixture to mushroom mixture, and cook 5 minutes. Season with salt and pepper. Stir in ½ cup basil. Cook pasta in a pan of boiling water until al dente; drain, reserving ½ cup cooking liquid. Return pasta to pan, and pour sauce and reserved liquid over top. Toss to coat. Transfer to a bowl, and sprinkle with remaining 2 tablespoons basil and Parmesan.

Makes 4 servings.

Pistachio Pasta

1 garlic clove, minced
¼ cup minced onion
2 tablespoons olive oil
½ cup coarsely chopped pistachios
¼ cup chopped ripe olives
¼ cup minced parsley
1 teaspoon lemon juice or ½ teaspoon grated lemon rind
⅛ teaspoon pepper
¼ teaspoon crushed basil leaves
8 ounces pasta, cooked and drained
⅓ cup grated Parmesan cheese

Sauté garlic and onion in hot oil in a skillet over medium heat until onion is tender. Add nuts and next 6 ingredients; cook over medium heat 2 to 3 minutes. Add Parmesan, and toss.

Makes 6 servings.

Peppers with Pasta Stuffing

6 large green bell peppers	1 garlic clove, minced
Salt and pepper to taste	4 anchovy fillets, chopped
1 tablespoon olive oil	1 teaspoon capers, drained
7 ounces black olives, chopped	8 ounces small pasta
2 tablespoons chopped fresh parsley	½ pound mozzarella cheese, cubed

Preheat oven to 400°. Cut tops off peppers, and remove seeds; sprinkle insides with salt and pepper and a little oil. Combine olives and next 4 ingredients in a bowl. Cook pasta in a pan of boiling water for half of cooking time on package; drain and toss with olive mixture and mozzarella. Stuff peppers with olive mixture. Place peppers on greased baking sheets, and bake for 35 minutes, shielding with foil to prevent excessive browning, if needed.

Makes 6 servings.

Spaghetti with Green Peppercorn-and-Mushroom Sauce

2 tablespoons drained green peppercorns, minced	1 cup Crème Fraîche
	Salt to taste
¼ cup unsalted butter	½ pound spaghetti
2 cups sliced fresh mushrooms	Freshly grated Parmesan cheese

Sauté peppercorns in butter in a skillet over medium heat 10 seconds. Add mushrooms, and sauté 5 minutes. Stir in Crème Fraîche, and cook until mixture is heated through; add salt to taste. Cook spaghetti in a pan of boiling water until al dente; drain. Spoon sauce over spaghetti, and serve with Parmesan.

Makes 2 servings.

Crème Fraîche

1 cup whipping cream	1 tablespoon buttermilk

Combine ingredients in a jar; cover tightly, and shake vigorously at least 1 minute. Let stand at room temperature at least 8 hours or until thick. Keeps chilled 4 to 6 weeks.

Makes 1 cup.

Jalapeño Fettuccine with Mexican Cream

2 medium-size red bell peppers
2 ounces Parmesan cheese, cubed
½ cup loosely packed fresh cilantro
   leaves
1 medium-size zucchini, trimmed
½ pound jalapeño fettuccine
2 tablespoons unsalted butter
¾ cup Mexican Cream

Roast bell peppers under broiler; peel and remove stems and veins. Cut peppers into 2- x ¼-inch slices; set aside on paper towels to drain. With food processor running, drop Parmesan cubes through chute, and process until finely chopped, about 1 minute; set aside. Pulse cilantro in processor 6 to 8 times or until coarsely chopped; set aside. Using shredding disc, put zucchini vertically through food chute; set aside on paper towels to drain. Bring 2 quarts salted water to a boil; add fettuccine, and cook just until al dente; drain and set aside. Heat butter in large skillet over medium heat; stir in roasted peppers, and cook 1 minute. Add cilantro, fettuccine, and Mexican Cream, tossing to coat pasta. Cook mixture, stirring constantly, just until pasta is heated through; remove from heat, and stir in zucchini. Transfer to a serving dish, and sprinkle with Parmesan.

Makes 4 servings.

Mexican Cream

½ cup whipping cream
½ cup sour cream
1 teaspoon fresh lime juice

Combine cream, sour cream, and juice in a small bowl; cover with plastic wrap, and chill at least 2 hours before serving. Store up to 1 week in refrigerator.

Summer Pasta

3 garlic cloves, minced
4 plum tomatoes, diced
8 ounces mozzarella cheese, diced
¼ cup olive oil
1 teaspoon salt
1 teaspoon pepper
1 tablespoon minced basil
1 pound ziti or rigatoni, cooked and
   drained
   Italian-style breadcrumbs

Combine first 7 ingredients in a large bowl; add pasta, and toss. Cover mixture, and let stand 5 minutes. Sprinkle breadcrumbs over top before serving.

Makes 4 servings.

Spaghetti with Swordfish

12 ounces spaghetti	2 tablespoons salted capers, rinsed
¼ cup olive oil	20 Greek cured olives, pitted
2 garlic cloves, minced	16 cherry tomatoes, halved
1 fresh thyme sprig	Salt and pepper to taste
1 pound swordfish, cubed	½ cup fresh basil, minced

Cook spaghetti in a stockpot of boiling water until just tender; drain, reserving ½ cup cooking liquid. Rinse spaghetti. Heat oil in a large skillet over medium heat; add garlic and thyme, and cook until garlic is golden. Discard garlic, and add swordfish; cook over high heat 3 to 4 minutes. Add capers, olives, tomatoes, salt and pepper, and reserved liquid to swordfish mixture; cook 1 minute. Add spaghetti and basil, stirring to blend.

Makes 4 servings.

Thai Pasta with Turkey

¼ cup chicken broth	½ pound cooked turkey, cut into thin strips
¼ cup rice vinegar	
2 tablespoons soy sauce	⅓ cup fresh cilantro, minced
1 tablespoon minced fresh ginger	2 tablespoons lime juice
1 tablespoon minced garlic	2 tablespoons chopped roasted peanuts
¼ teaspoon hot chile pepper flakes	
¼ pound linguine, cooked and drained	

Combine first 6 ingredients in a 2- to 3-quart saucepan; cover and bring to a simmer over medium-high heat. Toss pasta and next 3 ingredients with broth mixture; transfer to a serving bowl, and sprinkle with peanuts.

Makes 2 to 4 servings.

Three-Cheese Pasta

6 tablespoons unsalted butter
6 tablespoons all-purpose flour
4 cups milk
1½ cups shredded Fontina cheese
½ pound Gorgonzola cheese, cut up

1 cup freshly grated Parmesan cheese
Salt and pepper to taste
¾ pound penne, ziti, fusilli, or macaroni pasta
½ cup fresh breadcrumbs

Preheat oven to 375°. Melt butter in a large saucepan over medium heat. Whisk flour into butter, and cook, stirring constantly, 2 minutes. Gradually whisk in milk, and cook, stirring constantly, until smooth and thickened, about 5 minutes. Add cheeses, and stir until melted. Season with salt and pepper; set aside. Cook pasta in a pan of boiling water until al dente; drain. Add pasta to sauce, and turn out into a buttered shallow baking dish; sprinkle with breadcrumbs. Bake for 25 to 30 minutes or until sauce is bubbly and browned on top.

Makes 6 servings.

Tortellini and Black Beans

1 (15-ounce) can refried black beans with lime juice
8-10 ounces fresh spinach tortellini stuffed with cheese, cooked
¾ cup diced green onions
1 (4-ounce) can diced green chiles
1 cup sour cream

¼ cup fresh lime juice
2 ripe tomatoes, seeded and diced
½ cup sliced black olives
2 cups shredded Monterey Jack cheese
Garnish: ¼ cup chopped fresh cilantro

Preheat oven to 350°. Lightly grease a 9-inch square pan. Spread black beans in bottom of pan. Layer tortellini over beans. Sprinkle with green onions and chiles. Combine lime juice and sour cream in a bowl; spread over onions and chiles. Top with diced tomato and olives. Cover with cheese. Cover pan with foil, and bake for 30 minutes. Remove foil, and bake 30 minutes or until cheese is lightly browned. Let stand, covered, about 10 minutes before serving; garnish, if desired.

Makes 6 servings.

Salads

Bitter Lakes National Wildlife Refuge

Bitter Lakes National Wildlife Refuge built in the early 1940's, near Roswell, New Mexico, provides a protected winter resting and feeding area for thousands of migratory waterfowl, sandhill cranes, and birds. They leave their northern breeding grounds each fall, and many of them travel south through New Mexico along the two major river corridors, the Rio Grande and Pecos Rivers.

Bitter Lake, a shallow playa lake named by early cattlemen, is fed year round by small springs. However, the lake often goes dry during the hot summer months, leaving nothing but a white alkaline lakebed. The water from the springs is very brackish creating a lake with water too "bitter" to drink, but is a favored roosting site for cranes, snow geese and other waterfowl.

The Refuge's main body of open water consists of six man-made lakes formed within the ancient riverbed of the Pecos River. These lakes receive no water from the river, but rely upon springs that flow when the water table is high enough. Therefore, when the first migrants arrive in the fall, the lakes may have very little water, but steadily fill during their winter stay. The lake water is of high salt content also, but does not deter their use by carp, certain small fish of the desert communities, several species of turtles and of course, waterfowl, cranes and many species of shore and wading birds.

Besides the lakes, nearby marshland, mudflats and the Pecos River provide other wetlands. Growing of agricultural crops on some of the Refuge land helps to meet the needs of the migratory birds, but most geese and cranes feed extensively off-Refuge on the fertile croplands of the Pecos Valley.

Featured on page 171 "Bitter Lakes Wildlife Refuge"

Almond-Orange Chicken Salad

1	cup orange juice	6	poached chicken breast halves
¼	cup fresh cilantro or parsley	3	celery ribs, cut into strips
¼	cup vegetable oil	2	cups shredded romaine or iceberg
1	tablespoon red wine vinegar		lettuce
1	tablespoon Dijon mustard	3	green onions, including tops
1	teaspoon grated orange rind	1	large red bell pepper, cut into strips
1	teaspoon sugar	¾	cup salted cashews
1	teaspoon salt	1	(11-ounce) can mandarin oranges
	Freshly ground black pepper		Chopped cashews

Bring orange juice to boil in a saucepan, and reduce to ½ cup; let cool. Process orange juice and next 8 ingredients in a food processor or blender 20 seconds. Cut chicken into ½-inch slices; transfer to a large bowl. Add celery, lettuce, green onions, bell pepper, and cashews to chicken; pour dressing over, and toss gently. Mound salad on glass plates, and surround with mandarin orange slices. Sprinkle with additional chopped cashews (optional).

Makes 4 servings.

Avocados with Jícama

1	jícama, peeled and cut into 2-inch julienne		Dressing
3	large avocados, peeled and cut into medium chunks	6	large romaine lettuce leaves, in chiffonade
		1	pimiento, diced small

Plunge jícama into ice water 10 minutes. Drain, then toss avocado and jícama with dressing, and pile onto beds of romaine chiffonade. Sprinkle with pimiento.

Makes 4 servings.

Dressing

2	teaspoons dry mustard		Juice and grated zest of 1 lemon
⅓	cup white vinegar	1	cup extra-virgin olive oil
2	canned chipotle peppers and their sauce	½	teaspoon salt
		½	teaspoon pepper

Process first 4 ingredients in a food processor 30 seconds; add olive oil in a slow, steady stream. Stir in salt and pepper.

Makes 2 cups.

_____Avocados with Pistachios_____

½ cup shelled pistachios
½ cup olive oil
2-3 tablespoons lime juice
1 tablespoon rum
1 garlic clove, slightly flattened and peeled

Salt and freshly ground pepper to taste
2 ripe avocados
4 Boston lettuce leaves

Rub pistachios between layers of paper towels to remove most of papery coating; coarsely chop pistachios. Set aside. Combine oil and next 4 ingredients in a jar. Halve, pit, and peel avocados; cut each half lengthwise into ½-inch-thick slices, and lay in a fan over lettuce leaves. Sprinkle with chopped nuts. Shake dressing well, remove garlic, and drizzle over salad.

Makes 4 servings.

_____Black Bean Chicken Salad_____

2 tablespoons olive oil
1 whole chicken breast, skinned, boned, and cut in 2-inch strips
1 garlic clove, minced
½ jalapeño pepper, finely chopped
¾ teaspoon salt
1 cup peeled, seeded cucumber cubes

1 cup red bell pepper strips
1 cup chopped fresh tomato
½ cup chopped purple onion
4 cups chopped romaine lettuce
1 (15-ounce) can black beans, rinsed and drained

Dressing
½ cup chopped toasted pecans
⅓ cup tomato vegetable juice
2 tablespoons fresh lime juice

2 tablespoons olive oil
½ teaspoon ground cumin
½ teaspoon salt

Heat olive oil in a skillet over medium heat; add chicken, and stir-fry until fork tender, about 2 minutes. Add garlic, jalapeño, and salt; stir-fry 30 seconds. Remove chicken mixture, and place in a large salad bowl. Add cucumber and next 5 ingredients to chicken. Combine all dressing ingredients, and add to frying pan; heat until slightly warm. Pour warm dressing over salad, tossing to coat. Sprinkle with pecans, and garnish with tomato roses and parsley sprigs.

Makes 4 servings.

Blooming Desert Slaw

3   cups shredded cabbage
½   cup shredded peeled carrot
1   small yellow bell pepper, thinly
    sliced
1   small red bell pepper, thinly sliced
1   small green bell pepper, thinly
    sliced
½   cup thinly sliced purple onion

1   chile de arbol
2   tablespoons cider vinegar
1   tablespoon fresh lime juice
2   teaspoons honey
⅓   cup vegetable oil
    Salt and freshly ground pepper to
    taste

Combine first 6 ingredients in a large bowl. Toast chile in a dry skillet, turning once, 1 to 2 minutes. Remove seeds, and puree to powder. Put chile in a medium-size bowl, and whisk in vinegar and next 4 ingredients. Toss cabbage mixture with dressing.

Makes 6 servings.

Chickpea-and-Sun-Dried Tomato Salad

1½ cups dried garbanzos, sorted and
    soaked overnight, or 2 (15-ounce)
    cans garbanzos
1   bay leaf (omit if using canned
    garbanzos)
1   fresh sage leaf (¼ teaspoon dried
    sage if using canned peas)
2   fresh marjoram or oregano sprigs
    (¼ teaspoon dried if using canned
    peas)

½   cup diced purple onion
1   tablespoon champagne vinegar
¼   cup red wine vinegar
1   garlic clove, finely chopped
¾   teaspoon salt
⅛   teaspoon pepper
2   tablespoons olive oil
2   sun-dried tomatoes packed in oil,
    drained and diced
2   tablespoons chopped flat leaf
    parsley

Drain and rinse garbanzos, and place in a large saucepan with water to cover; add bay leaf and sage. Boil gently until very tender, 50 to 60 minutes. (Omit this phase if using canned garbanzos.) Bring water to a boil in a small saucepan; add onion, and cook 15 seconds. Drain and toss with champagne vinegar. Combine red wine vinegar, garlic, salt, and pepper in a small bowl. (If using canned garbanzos, add sage and marjoram.) Gradually whisk in olive oil; add garbanzos, onion mixture, and sun-dried tomatoes Marinate at least 1 hour; add parsley, and serve at room temperature.

Makes 4 to 6 servings.

Elmer Schooley

Elmer Schooley has lived and worked in Roswell, NM, since 1977. He was born in Lawrence, Kansas, and passed his youth in Illinois, Missouri, Oklahoma, and Colorado. As he matured, he traveled and studied European painting. Some of the artists that influenced him were Pierre Bonnard, Piero della Francesca, Edouard Vuillard, and Jan Van Eyck. As a young man, the American Regionalists-Grant Wood, John Steuart Curry, and Thomas Hart Benton also stimulated him, since they were actively working at that time.

In 1938, Schooley received his B.F.A. from the University of Colorado, and in 1942, his M.F.A. from the University of Iowa. He married artist Gussie DuJardin in 1941, and they are still partners in art and in life. From 1942 to 1946, he served in the Army Air Corps in the South Pacific. In 1946 and 47, he taught at New Mexico Western University, and then settled in to New Mexico Highlands University for thirty years. At Highlands, he established the art library, the art gallery, and the graphics department, before printmaking was significant in New Mexico.

Elmer Schooley's art is collected nationally by private and public patrons including the Museum of Modern Art and the Metropolitan Museum in New York. His work is also included in the collections of the Albuquerque Museum of Fine Arts, the Museum of New Mexico in Santa Fe, The Dallas Museum of Fine Arts, The Brooklyn Museum of Art, and the Library of Congress, Washington, D.C.

In 1986 Schooley was awarded the New Mexico Governor's Award for Excellence in Art.

Between Here and Santa Fe
Artist – Elmer Schooley
60″ × 72″   1974-75
oil on canvas
Permanent collection, Roswell
Museum and Art Center. Gift of the
artist in honor of Patricia Luben
Bassett. Photograph by Jose Rivera.

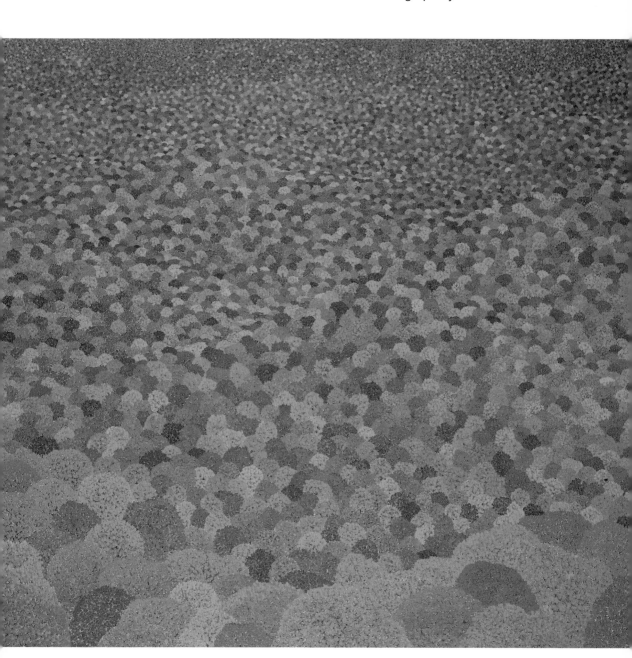

Caesar Salad with _____.
_____Spicy Polenta Croutons

Croutons

2¾ cups milk
4   serrano chiles, seeded and minced
2   teaspoons salt

½   teaspoon cayenne pepper
1½ cups yellow cornmeal
    Vegetable oil for frying

Dressing

1   shallot, coarsely chopped
4   anchovy fillets
4   roasted garlic cloves
3   egg yolks
¼   cup lemon juice
4   teaspoons Dijon mustard
1   tablespoon balsamic vinegar

2   teaspoons chopped chipotle in
    adobo
¼   teaspoon ground cumin
1   cup extra virgin olive oil
4-6 hearts romaine lettuce, washed,
    dried, and torn
1½ cups shaved Parmesan cheese

Croutons

Bring milk, serranos, 1½ teaspoons salt, and ¼ teaspoon cayenne pepper to a boil in a medium saucepan. Slowly add 1 cup cornmeal, stirring constantly; reduce heat to medium, and cook 3 minutes or until mixture pulls away from side of pan and forms a ball. Press mixture into a 9-inch pie plate lined with plastic wrap; chill, uncovered, until cooled. Remove from pie plate, and cut into ½-inch cubes. Heat 1 inch oil in a large heavy skillet to 350°. Dredge polenta cubes in remaining ½ cup cornmeal, and fry in oil until crisp and golden brown, about 2 minutes. Remove from oil, and drain on a paper towel-lined baking sheet. Keep warm until ready to serve.

Dressing

Process shallot, anchovies, and garlic in a food processor until finely chopped. Add egg yolks, next 5 ingredients, remaining ½ teaspoon salt, and ¼ teaspoon cayenne pepper; blend until smooth. With machine running, slowly pour olive oil through feed tube, and process until emulsified and thoroughly incorporated. Set aside. In a large salad bowl, toss lettuce with dressing, croutons, and ¾ cup cheese. Divide among 8 plates, and top with remaining ¾ cup cheese. Serve immediately.

Makes 8 servings.

Celery with Tarragon Mayonnaise

4 cups chopped celery	½ teaspoon pepper
2 cups chopped, seeded cucumber, well drained	½ teaspoon dry mustard
	1 cup Tarragon Mayonnaise
1 small onion, grated	Lettuce leaves
1 teaspoon salt	Garnish: fresh tarragon sprigs

Blanch celery 30 seconds in rapidly boiling water; drain and cool. Toss cucumber with onion and salt, and let stand 10 minutes in a sieve over a bowl. Toss celery with cucumber, onion, pepper, and mustard. Stir in mayonnaise. Serve on a bed of lettuce, and garnish, if desired.

Makes 8 servings.

Basic Homemade Mayonnaise

2 large egg yolks	1½ cups olive oil
1 teaspoon dry mustard	Juice of ½ lemon
1 teaspoon salt	

Have all ingredients at room temperature. Beat egg yolks until thick and sticky; add mustard and salt. Beating constantly, add oil 1 drop at a time, increasing volume of oil as mixture thickens. When all oil has been absorbed and mayonnaise is thick and cream colored, add lemon juice.

Lemon Mayonnaise: add juice of 1 lemon.

Curry Mayonnaise: stir in 1 tablespoon mild curry powder per cup of Basic Mayonnaise.

Tarragon Mayonnaise: add 2 teaspoons chopped fresh tarragon per cup of Basic Mayonnaise.

Chicken-and-Chile Salad

4 whole chicken breasts, skinned, boned, and cut into bite-size pieces
1 large purple onion

1 medium-size jícama, peeled and cubed
5 mild green chiles (Anaheim or poblano)

Dressing
1 tablespoon lime juice
1 tablespoon white wine vinegar
2 teaspoons dry mustard
1-1½ teaspoons salt
¼ teaspoon ground white pepper

⅛ teaspoon cayenne pepper
½ cup mayonnaise
3½ ounces cream cheese, softened
3-4 tablespoons milk or cream
Garnish: papaya or melon slices

Place chicken in a large bowl. Peel, slice, and blanch onion. Roast, peel, and thinly slice green chiles. Add onion, jícama, and green chiles to chicken; toss to mix. Process all dressing ingredients in a blender or food processor until blended. Pour half of dressing over chicken mixture; cover and chill until ready to assemble salad. Arrange seasonal greens on each of 6 plates; divide chicken mixture among plates, and drizzle with remaining dressing. Garnish with slices of papaya or honeydew, cantaloupe or Cranshaw melon.

Makes 6 servings.

Cinco De Mayo Salad

1   cup sliced young green beans,
    steamed
    3 minutes
1   cup cooked garbanzos, rinsed
1   cup cooked pinto beans, rinsed
1   cup cooked lima beans
1   cup cooked black beans, rinsed
1   medium-size onion, sliced into
    rings
3   serrano or jalapeño chiles, seeded
    and stemmed and cut into rings

2   tablespoons sugar
½   cup red wine vinegar
½   cup olive oil
½   teaspoon salt
½   teaspoon dry mustard
½   teaspoon basil
1   tablespoon freshly chopped
    cilantro
1   teaspoon finely minced habanero
    chile

Combine all beans, onion, and chiles in a bowl. Refrigerate. Combine sugar and remaining ingredients in a jar; cover tightly, and shake vigorously until sugar dissolves.
Let stand at room temperature 30 minutes. Shake dressing again, and pour over bean
mixture; cover and allow salad to marinate in refrigerator several hours or overnight.

Makes 6 servings.

Cucumber Salad with Dill Dressing

2   large cucumbers, peeled
½   purple onion, sliced and separated
    into rings

1   small red bell pepper, seeded and
    chopped
    Dill Dressing

Halve cucumbers lengthwise, and scrape out seeds; cut crosswise into ¼-inch-thick
slices. Combine cucumber, onion, and bell pepper in a bowl; toss with dressing. Cover
and chill several hours or overnight.

Dill Dressing

½   cup light sour cream
¼   cup plain nonfat yogurt
1   tablespoon white wine vinegar
1   tablespoon fresh lemon juice
1   teaspoon sugar

1   tablespoon fresh dill or 1 teaspoon
    dried dill weed
½   teaspoon salt
    Freshly ground pepper to taste

Whisk all ingredients together.

Makes 1 cup.

Colorful Rice-and-Vegetable Salad

8	cups hot cooked rice	2	shallots, finely diced
1½-2	cups Vinaigrette	1	(10-ounce) package frozen peas, thawed and blanched in boiling salted water 3 minutes
1	red bell pepper, cut into thin julienne		
1	green pepper, cut into thin julienne	½	cup black olives, finely chopped
		¼	cup chopped parsley
1	medium-size purple onion, diced	½	cup chopped fresh dill
6	scallions, finely sliced		Salt and freshly ground black pepper to taste
1	cup dried currants		

Combine rice and 1½ cups Vinaigrette in a bowl; toss thoroughly, and cool to room temperature. Add remaining ingredients, and toss thoroughly. Taste, correct seasoning, and add additional Vinaigrette if needed. Serve immediately, or cover and chill up to 4 hours. Serve at room temperature.

Makes 8 to 10 servings.

Vinaigrette

1	tablespoon Dijon mustard	½	teaspoon freshly ground black pepper
4	tablespoons red wine vinegar		Minced parsley and/or snipped fresh chives to taste
1	teaspoon granulated sugar		
½	teaspoon salt	½	cup olive oil

Place mustard in a bowl; whisk in vinegar, sugar, salt, pepper and herbs to taste. Continue to whisk mixture while slowly dribbling in oil until mixture thickens. Adjust seasonings to taste. Cover until ready to use. (This vinaigrette is best if made just before it is to be used.) If necessary, whisk again before serving.

Makes 1 cup.

"Music on Main Street," a ticket sales promotion, received National Bravos for providing musicians to local downtown businesses to entertain patrons. One could feel the vibrations of sound and merriment as the singers and musicians (with music for almost any taste) took over the downtown streets. The mayor proclaimed it "Music On Main Street Day."

_____Corn Salad with Southwestern Dressing_____

2   teaspoons vegetable or olive oil
2½ cups fresh corn kernels
1   small purple onion, diced

2   red bell peppers, roasted, peeled, seeded, and julienned
3   large tomatoes, seeded and diced
    Salt and black pepper to taste

Heat oil in a large skillet over medium-high heat until very hot; add corn, and sauté about 2 minutes. Add onion, bell pepper, and tomato; lightly sauté 2 minutes. Season with salt and pepper. Pour into a bowl to cool, and toss with Southwestern Dressing.

Makes 6 servings.

Southwestern Dressing
2   shallots, chopped
3   garlic cloves, chopped
    Juice of 1 lemon
    Juice of 1 lime
1   jalapeño, diced
2   tablespoons Cayenne Sauce or 2 teaspoons Tabasco

½   cup olive oil
¼   cup sour cream
½   teaspoon chile powder
1   teaspoon ground cumin
1   teaspoon chopped cilantro
    Salt and pepper to taste

Whisk together first 6 ingredients in a medium-size bowl. Slowly whisk in oil until well blended and smooth. Add sour cream, and whisk again. Add chile powder, cumin, and cilantro, and season with salt and pepper.

_____ Jícama Coleslaw_____

2   cups shredded radicchio or red cabbage
½   cup grated carrot
1   medium-size jícama, peeled and julienned
1   red bell pepper, julienned
1   yellow bell pepper, julienned

1   small onion, grated
1   jalapeño, seeded and minced
½   cup mayonnaise
1   tablespoon honey
1   tablespoon raspberry vinegar
1   tablespoon fresh lemon juice
    Salt and pepper to taste

Combine all ingredients in a large bowl; refrigerate until serving time.

Great with barbecue brisket or ribs!

Makes 4 servings.

Fiesta Chicken Salad

Dressing

½ cup fresh cilantro leaves
1 garlic clove
1 jalapeño pepper, seeded
1 large tomatillo, husked and halved
1 (2- x ½-inch) piece purple onion
½ cup fresh lime juice

½ cup olive oil
1 tablespoon mayonnaise
2 teaspoons sugar
2 teaspoons Dijon mustard
¾ teaspoon salt

Place cilantro in bowl of food processor. With machine running, drop garlic and jalapeño through feed tube, and mince. Scrape down sides of bowl. Add tomatillo and onion; process until chopped, 10 to 15 seconds. Scrape down sides of bowl. Add lime juice, olive oil, mayonnaise, sugar, mustard, and salt; process until well mixed. Transfer to large bowl.

Salad

1 cup chicken stock
4 large chicken breast halves, boned and skinned
½ large red bell pepper, diced
½ large yellow bell pepper, diced
1½ cups peeled and diced jícama

¼ small red cabbage, diced
1 firm ripe avocado, peeled and cut into ½-inch pieces
6 large green onions, sliced
1 pound cherry tomatoes, halved
Garnish: fresh cilantro sprigs

Bring chicken broth to a boil in a large, heavy skillet. Add chicken, reduce heat, and simmer until cooked through, turning occasionally, about 8 minutes. Remove from heat, and let stand until just cool enough to handle. Reserve broth. Cut chicken into ¾-inch pieces; toss with dressing in a large bowl. Add peppers, jícama, cabbage, avocado, green onions, and tomatoes; toss gently. Garnish, if desired.

Makes 4 to 6 servings.

You can microwave chicken by wrapping each breast in plastic wrap and arranging breasts around outer edge of a paper plate. Cook on MEDIUM-HIGH until cooked through, about 5 minutes, turning once. Let stand 5 minutes. Pierce meat to make sure juices run clear.

Fillet-of-Beef Salad with Peppercorn Dressing

1 (2-pound) beef tenderloin, tied
1 tablespoon olive oil
3 bunches salad greens, such as spinach and endive, washed, dried, and cut into ribbons

2 red bell peppers, roasted and peeled
Garnish: fresh parsley sprigs
Peppercorn Dressing

Preheat oven to 400°. Fry tenderloin in oil over medium-high heat until browned on all sides. Transfer to a roasting pan, and place in oven; cook for 30 minutes for rare. Allow to go cold, and slice thinly. Pile greens to 1 side of 8 plates. Arrange 3 to 4 slices beef on each plate. Cut peppers, and place on salad greens. Spoon a little dressing over edge of each piece of beef, and garnish, if desired.

Makes 4 to 6 servings.

Peppercorn Dressing

3 tablespoons green peppercorns
2 tablespoons Dijon mustard
8 tablespoons sunflower oil

3 tablespoons red wine vinegar
2 teaspoons lemon juice
2 teaspoons warm water

Crush peppercorns with a mortar and pestle until roughly broken; stir in mustard, and gradually beat in oil, adding a little at a time with vinegar and lemon juice to form an emulsion. Stir in warm water, and store in a sealed jar.

Gazpacho Salad

1 ripe avocado, peeled, pitted, and diced
1 tablespoon fresh lemon juice
1 large cucumber, peeled, seeded, quartered, and sliced
1 green bell pepper, cored, seeded, and julienned

1 red bell pepper, cored, seeded, and julienned
1 yellow bell pepper, cored, seeded, and julienned
3 ripe tomatoes, seeded and diced
1½ cups shredded Monterey Jack cheese
¼ cup sliced ripe olives

Dressing
2 tablespoons fresh lime juice
1 garlic clove, minced
1 tablespoon minced onion
2 teaspoons minced fresh cilantro
¼ teaspoon cayenne pepper
¼ teaspoon ground cumin

1 jalapeño pepper, seeded and minced
½ cup olive oil
Salt and freshly ground black pepper to taste
Garnish: tortilla chips

For salad, toss together avocado and lemon juice in a large bowl. Add remaining salad ingredients, tossing gently. For dressing, whisk together lime juice and next 7 ingredients; gradually whisk in oil, and season with salt and pepper. Toss dressing into salad just before serving. Garnish, if desired.

Makes 6 to 8 servings.

To reduce the jalapeño's effect on the eyes, hold pepper under cold water while seeding and removing its skin.

"Denim and Diamonds" was a successful fundraiser that was selected as one of only eight events to receive an Award of Merit in Canada at the American Symphony Orchestra Leagues National Conference. There were 320 competitors in this symphony guild season ticket campaign. Hard work paid off— what an honor!

Green Chile Aspic

3   tablespoons unflavored gelatin
4   cups tomato juice
3   tablespoons lemon juice
3   (4-ounce) cans chopped green
    chiles, undrained
½   cup minced celery
2   medium avocados, peeled, pitted,
    and cubed
½   teaspoon garlic salt

½   teaspoon Beau Monde seasoning
½   teaspoon onion salt
    Freshly ground black pepper to
    taste
⅛   teaspoon Tabasco
    Mayonnaise
    Toppings: 1 cup sour cream,
    2 tablespoons mayonnaise, curly
    endive, seedless green grapes

Soften gelatin in 1 cup tomato juice in a small bowl. Bring remaining 3 cups tomato juice to a boil in a saucepan; remove from heat. Add gelatin mixture to hot tomato juice, and stir until gelatin is dissolved. Cool. Add lemon juice and next 8 ingredients to tomato mixture, stirring well. Spread a film of mayonnaise on inside of a mold; pour tomato mixture into mold, and chill 4 hours or overnight. Stir together sour cream and mayonnaise in a small bowl. Unmold aspic onto a chilled platter; top with endive and grapes. Serve with sour cream mixture.

Makes 8 to 10 servings.

Green Pea, Cashew, and Jícama Salad

2   (10-ounce) packages frozen tiny
    English peas, thawed
1   cup bean sprouts
1   large jícama, peeled and chopped
    into
    1½-inch pieces
1   cup chopped celery

1   bunch green onions, chopped
    (about ¾ cup), including tops
1   cup sour cream
    Salt and freshly ground pepper to
    taste
1   cup cashews
8-10 ounces bacon, cooked and
    crumbled

Thoroughly drain peas on paper towels. (If peas are not well drained, salad dressing will be thin and watery.) Combine peas and next 6 ingredients in a bowl; mix well. Refrigerate 4 hours or overnight. Just before serving, add cashews and bacon. Mix gently but thoroughly.

Makes 8 servings.

_____Grilled Chicken-Spinach Salad_____

Dressing

1 cup sun-dried tomato halves, snipped into thin strips
3 bacon slices, cut into ½-inch pieces
3 tablespoons olive oil

3 tablespoons minced onion
3 tablespoons balsamic vinegar
Garlic salt and black pepper to taste

Salad

4 skinned and boned chicken breast halves
1½ teaspoons olive oil
Garlic salt and black pepper to taste

8 cups trimmed spinach leaves, lightly packed
2 medium-size ripe tomatoes, cut into wedges
2 cups sliced fresh mushrooms

For Dressing, place dried tomato strips in a bowl of hot water to cover; let stand 10 minutes. Cook bacon in a nonstick skillet over medium heat 5 minutes; add oil and onion to skillet, and cook until onion is translucent. Add vinegar to onion mixture, and cook 1 minute; add dried tomato strips with 3 tablespoons soaking liquid. Season mixture with garlic salt and pepper to taste; set aside. For Salad, rub chicken with oil, and season with garlic salt and pepper to taste. Grill or sauté over medium heat about 10 minutes or until chicken juices run clear, turning once. Slice chicken across the grain. Toss spinach and chicken with dressing in a large bowl; top with tomato wedges and mushrooms.

Makes 4 servings.

_____Orange-Jícama Salad_____

1 small jícama, peeled and cut into thin slices
¾ cup fresh orange juice
2 tablespoons rice wine vinegar
¼ teaspoon salt, divided

¼ teaspoon cayenne pepper, divided
3 navel oranges, peeled, cut in half, and sliced
3 large radishes, thinly sliced
Garnish: fresh cilantro sprigs

Place jícama slices into a small bowl, and toss with orange juice; add vinegar, ⅛ teaspoon salt, and ⅛ teaspoon cayenne pepper. Add oranges to jícama; toss to mix. Add remaining salt and pepper. Allow salad to sit for a while before serving. Place on serving plates; top with radishes and cilantro, if desired.

Makes 4 to 6 servings.

Mexican Avocado Salad

2	tomatoes, seeded, diced, and drained	2	tablespoons chopped fresh parsley or cilantro
1	cucumber, seeded and sliced		Lime-Cumin Dressing
¼	cup chopped green bell pepper	3	ripe avocados
½	cup chopped purple onion	2	tablespoons lemon juice
¾	cup garbanzos, rinsed and drained		Lettuce leaves

Combine first 6 ingredients in a large bowl; add dressing, and mix well. Cover and chill several hours. Just before serving, peel avocados, cut in half, and remove pits. Brush avocados with lemon juice. Place lettuce leaves on a platter or individual plates; add avocados. Using a slotted spoon, fill each avocado half with dressing mixture.

Makes 6 servings.

Lime-Cumin Dressing

	Juice of 1 lime	¼	teaspoon ground cumin
1	tablespoon white wine vinegar	¼	teaspoon dry mustard
3	tablespoons olive oil	¼	teaspoon salt
1	tablespoon honey	¼	teaspoon white pepper
¼	teaspoon dried oregano, crumbled		

Whisk all ingredients together in a bowl until blended.

Pinto Bean Salad

4	cups cooked pinto beans (canned, drained and rinsed or dried, cooked and seasoned)	2	garlic cloves, minced
		1¼	cups plus 1 tablespoon olive oil
		2-3	tablespoons red wine vinegar
1	large purple onion, diced	¼	cup chopped fresh parsley
1	large green bell pepper, diced	1	cup cooked corn kernels
1	large yellow bell pepper, diced	1	teaspoon chile powder
5	green onions, minced	½	teaspoon ground cumin

Combine all ingredients; toss well, and chill overnight or at least 6 hours to allow flavors to meld. Toss again when ready to serve. Serve chilled.

Makes 8 cups.

Perfect for picnics!

Mexican Turkey Salad

2	tablespoons fresh lime juice	1	(12-ounce) can whole kernel corn, well drained
2	teaspoons Dijon mustard		
¼	teaspoon salt	6	green onions, thinly sliced
¼-½	teaspoon chile powder	1	small red bell pepper, finely chopped
5	tablespoons vegetable oil		
1	cup cilantro, coarsely chopped	1	small avocado, peeled, pitted, and diced
2	cups cubed white or dark turkey		
			Lettuce leaves

Combine first 4 ingredients in a small bowl; add oil in a slow, thin stream, whisking constantly until slightly thickened. Stir in cilantro. Stir together turkey and next 4 ingredients in a large bowl; add dressing, and toss until well blended. Spoon salad onto lettuce-lined plates.

Makes 4 servings.

Mixed-Grain Salad with Dried Fruit

¼	cup vegetable oil	½	cup chopped dried apricots
½	cup chopped shallots	½	cup dried currants
1	cup brown rice	½	cup sherry wine vinegar
1	cup wild rice	2	tablespoons walnut oil or olive oil
1	cup wheat berries	2	tablespoons chopped fresh sage or 2 teaspoons dried rubbed sage
2	cups water		
2	cups chicken stock		Salt and pepper to taste
¾	cup dried cranberries	1	cup coarsely chopped pecans

Heat oil in a large saucepan over medium heat; add shallot, and sauté until translucent, about 5 minutes. Add brown rice, wild rice, and wheat berries; stir to coat. Add water and stock; bring to boil. Reduce heat to low. Cover and cook until grains are tender and liquid is absorbed, about 40 minutes. Remove mixture from heat, and stir in cranberries, apricots, and currants. Cool to room temperature. Whisk vinegar, walnut oil, and sage in a small bowl to blend; pour over salad, and toss to coat. Season generously with salt and pepper. Stir pecans into salad, and serve.

Makes 8 servings.

New Mexican Salad

Dressing

⅓ cup orange juice
2   tablespoons fresh lime juice
2   teaspoons grated lemon rind
½   tablespoons white wine vinegar

2   tablespoons tequila
¼   teaspoon salt
⅛   teaspoon pepper
¼   cup olive oil

Salad

4   cups lettuce, torn into 2-inch
    pieces
1   large jícama, julienned
2   cups diced tomato

½   cup thinly sliced purple onion
½   cup chopped fresh mint
¼   cup chopped fresh parsley
2   cups crushed tortilla chips

Whisk together all dressing ingredients. Toss lettuce with ¼ cup dressing. Arrange lettuce on serving plates. Combine remaining salad ingredients with remaining dressing. Spoon over lettuce.

Makes 6 servings.

Rio Hondo Pasta Salad

1   (8-ounce) jar marinated artichoke
    hearts, undrained
1   (12-ounce) package vegetable
    corkscrew pasta, cooked and
    drained
1   mild purple onion, chopped
1   green bell pepper, chopped
1   red bell pepper, chopped
4   plum tomatoes, sliced thinly

1   (6-ounce) can sliced black olives,
    drained
1   (14-ounce) can garbanzos, well
    drained
6   ounces feta cheese, crumbled
½   cup Italian low-fat dressing or
    homemade vinaigrette dressing
    Salt and pepper to taste

Drain marinade from artichoke hearts into a bowl containing cooled cooked pasta. Toss. Chop artichoke hearts, and combine with onion, bell pepper, tomato, and olives; add to pasta mixture. Toss garbanzos into mixture, and top with feta cheese. Chill in a covered bowl 1 to 3 hours. Just before serving, toss with additional dressing and season with salt and pepper to taste.

Makes 6 to 8 servings.

Salpicon (Cold Roast Beef Salad)

1	pound shredded roast beef	1	avocado, diced
1	large tomato, chopped	3	tablespoons white wine vinegar
1	small onion, chopped	⅔	cup olive oil
1	medium-size potato, cooked and diced	1	teaspoon dried oregano
			Salt and pepper to taste

Combine beef and next 4 ingredients in a bowl. Blend remaining ingredients in a separate bowl, and stir into beef mixture. Cover and chill at least 2 hours before serving.

Makes 6 servings.

Sant's Spinach Salad

Salad

2	bunches fresh spinach, washed, drained, and torn into bite-size pieces	1	can sliced water chestnuts
		2	hard-cooked eggs, cooled and chopped
1	cup fresh bean sprouts	4	bacon slices, cooked and crumbled

Toss all ingredients together.

Dressing

½	cup olive oil	1	teaspoon bottled steak sauce
⅓	cup sugar	1	tablespoon brandy
⅓	cup catsup	1	small onion, grated
¼	cup white wine vinegar		Salt and freshly ground black pepper to taste
1	teaspoon paprika		

Whisk together all ingredients; toss with salad.

Makes 4 to 6 servings.

_____Santa Fe Potato Salad_____

½ cup olive oil
6 tablespoons fresh lime juice
3 garlic cloves, peeled
2 tablespoons chopped jalapeño with seeds
3½ teaspoons ground cumin
1 teaspoon dried oregano
Salt and pepper to taste

1 (15-ounce) can golden hominy, drained
¾ cup chopped fresh cilantro
⅔ cup diced peeled jícama
½ cup chopped white onion
2 pounds medium-large Yukon Gold potatoes (about 5), unpeeled

Process first 6 ingredients in a blender until almost smooth. Season generously with salt. Pour dressing into a medium-size bowl, and stir in hominy, ½ cup cilantro, jícama, and onion. Let stand 30 minutes. Steam potatoes until tender, about 30 minutes. Cool 15 minutes; peel and cut lengthwise in half, then crosswise into ½-inch-thick slices. Place potato in a large bowl; add hominy mixture, and toss to blend. Season to taste with salt and pepper. Sprinkle with ¼ cup cilantro. Serve at room temperature.

Makes 6 servings.

_____Spicy Egg Salad_____

12 hard-cooked eggs, cooled and chopped
4 celery ribs, chopped
5 green onions (white part and 2 inches green tops), sliced
2 jalapeños, minced
1 red bell pepper, diced
1 garlic clove, minced
1½ cups shredded Cheddar cheese

1 cup mayonnaise (or as needed)
Juice of 1 lime
1 tablespoon ground cumin
1 tablespoon chile powder
Salt and freshly ground black pepper to taste
Garnish: avocado slices sprinkled lightly with lime juice, and fresh cilantro sprigs

Combine first 7 ingredients in a large bowl, tossing to blend. Combine mayonnaise and next 3 ingredients in a small bowl; fold gently into egg mixture, adding mayonnaise, if needed. Season with salt and pepper to taste. Transfer to a serving bowl; chill several hours. Garnish, if desired.

Makes 10 to 12 servings.

Tomatoes and Black Beans
with Fresh Basil Dressing

Black Beans
Fresh Basil Dressing

6 red or green garden lettuce leaves
3 large ripe tomatoes

Black Beans

2 cups black beans
1 teaspoon ground cumin
1 tablespoon brown sugar
4 cups chicken stock

Salt and freshly ground pepper to taste
½ cup olive oil
½ cup chopped fresh parsley

Fresh Basil Dressing

1 cup mayonnaise
1 garlic clove, minced
1 teaspoon Worcestershire sauce
1 tablespoon finely sliced green onion

½ teaspoon dry mustard
½ teaspoon sugar
3 tablespoons freshly chopped basil
¾ cup beef broth or bouillon
Salt and pepper to taste

Soak beans overnight. Drain, place in kettle, and add cumin, sugar, and chicken stock. Bring bean mixture to boil; reduce heat, and simmer until beans are tender yet firm, about 2 hours. (Add more stock or water if necessary.) Drain beans, and rinse under cold water. Place in a bowl, and toss with salt and pepper to taste, olive oil, and chopped parsley. (Beans can be prepared 1 day ahead and kept covered and chilled.) Process mayonnaise and next 6 ingredients in a food processor until smooth. Add beef broth a little at a time until of dressing consistency. Add salt and pepper to taste. (Dressing can be prepared 1 day ahead, covered, and chilled.) Line each plate with a lettuce leaf, and top with tomato slices. Spoon dressing mixture over top, and sprinkle generously with black beans.

Makes 6 servings.

Wagon Wheel Pasta Salad

Dressing

3 ounces reduced-fat cream cheese
4 tablespoons lemon juice
3 tablespoons skim milk
1 tablespoon olive oil
1 teaspoon freshly grated lemon rind
½ teaspoon ground cumin
¼ teaspoon salt
¼ teaspoon garlic powder
2 tablespoons water
2 tablespoons grated Parmesan cheese

Combine first 8 ingredients in a 2-cup glass measuring cup; microwave on HIGH 1 minute or until cream cheese is soft. Stir to blend. Add water to cream cheese mixture to thin; add Parmesan, and set aside.

Salad

2 cups cooked wagon wheel or other small pasta
1 (15-ounce) can black beans, rinsed and drained
1 (15¼-ounce) can whole kernel corn
1 (4-ounce) can roasted, peeled, and chopped green chiles
¼ cup chopped fresh tomato
¼ cup chopped fresh cilantro, parsley, or oregano
1 green onion, chopped

Toss pasta and dressing in a large bowl; add remaining ingredients, and serve warm or at room temperature.

Makes 6 servings.

Strawberry-Spinach Salad

⅓ cup sugar
2 green onions
½ teaspoon Worcestershire sauce
¼ teaspoon paprika
¼ cup apple cider vinegar
⅛ teaspoon Tabasco
½ cup vegetable oil
1 package fresh spinach, washed and torn into pieces
1 pint fresh strawberries, sliced
2-3 fresh kiwifruit, peeled and sliced

Process first 6 ingredients in a food processor 20 seconds or until well blended. With processor running, add oil through feed tube in a slow, steady stream. Store dressing, covered, in refrigerator until ready to use. Toss spinach, berries, and kiwifruit together. Drizzle with dressing just before serving.

Makes 8 to 10 servings.

Wild Rice Salad

4   cups water
1   teaspoon salt
1   cup wild rice
½   cup finely chopped dried
    Calimyrna figs
⅓   cup chopped toasted pecans
⅓   cup chopped toasted unsalted
    cashews
¼   cup finely chopped green onion
    tops, including tops
2   tablespoons finely chopped celery

2   tablespoons finely chopped purple
    onion
2   tablespoons raspberry vinegar or
    red wine vinegar
1   tablespoon fresh lemon juice
1   garlic clove, minced
1   teaspoon Dijon mustard
1   teaspoon sugar
¼   cup vegetable oil
¼   cup olive oil
    Salt and pepper to taste

Bring water and salt to boil in a large saucepan; add rice. Reduce heat to medium-low; cover and simmer until rice is tender, about 45 minutes. Drain well. Cool. Transfer rice to a large bowl, and stir in figs and next 5 ingredients. (Can be prepared 1 day ahead and chilled.) Process vinegar and next 4 ingredients in a blender until combined. With blender running, gradually add both oils. Pour dressing over rice mixture, and toss. Season salad with salt and pepper.

Makes 6 servings.

Spinach, Bacon, and Jícama Salad

1   large bunch fresh spinach
2   tablespoons vegetable oil
2   tablespoons olive oil
3   tablespoons white wine vinegar
1   teaspoon sugar
½   teaspoon Dijon mustard
⅛   teaspoon salt

    Freshly ground pepper to taste
6   ounces (4 or 5 slices) thick bacon
6   ounces jícama, cut in 1-inch-long
    julienne
2   ounces Swiss cheese, shredded
1   cup thinly sliced red cabbage

Wash spinach, and chill until ready to use. Combine vegetable oil and next 6 ingredients; mix well. Chill until ready to use. Slice bacon into ¼-inch pieces, and cook until crisp but not overly brown. Drain on paper towels, and set aside. Tear washed spinach into a serving bowl; add bacon, jícama, Swiss cheese, and red cabbage. Toss to combine. Stir dressing, and toss with salad. Arrange on serving plates, and serve immediately.

Makes 6 to 8 servings.

Winter Salad

¾ cup dried red kidney beans, sorted and rinsed well (or a 16-ounce can red kidney beans, rinsed and drained)

½ cup dried or 1 cup frozen black-eyed peas, thawed

½ cup pearl barley
Salt

1½ cups fresh or frozen corn kernels

⅓ cup finely chopped fresh Italian parsley

2 tablespoons finely chopped fresh cilantro

2 tablespoons finely chopped purple onion

½-1 teaspoon crushed red pepper

3 tablespoons olive oil
Rind and juice of 2 large limes

½ teaspoon ground cumin

If using dried beans and black-eyed peas, soak separately overnight; drain and rinse. In 2 separate saucepans, cover beans and peas with 2 to 3 inches of water. Cover and simmer until tender. Cool beans and peas completely in their liquid, then drain and transfer to a serving bowl. (If using canned beans and frozen peas, combine them in a bowl, omitting soaking.) Simmer barley in 2 cups water and ½ teaspoon salt until tender but chewy, about 40 minutes. Drain well, and add to bean mixture. Cook corn in a little water until crisp-tender, about 5 minutes for fresh corn and 2 minutes for frozen. Drain well, and add to bean mixture. Stir in parsley, cilantro, onion, and red pepper. Whisk together oil, ½ teaspoon salt, lime rind, juice, and cumin. Pour over salad, and toss gently.

Makes 6 servings.

Vegetables

New Mexico Military Institute

Proudly commanding a hill just outside Roswell's downtown, the New Mexico Military Institute has played an important role in the growth and development of southeastern New Mexico. Founded in 1891, the Institute is a land grant school with permanent land funds dedicated to its support. With a Corps of around 900 cadets, it offers a 4-year high school and 2-year college program. The Institute is a public institution and is governed by a Board of Regents appointed by the Governor of New Mexico.

The New Mexico Military Institute is known for academic excellence within a military orientation. Its mission is to develop the whole cadet through academics, physical training, leadership, and spiritual growth, and the centerpiece of this program is the Honor Code. The Institute's early commissioning program is unique for a Junior College. Once a cadet has completed the baccalaureate, he or she can enter the Army on active duty as an officer.

In 1997, the Institute celebrated 20 years of women's presence in the Corps, having admitted women just one year after the service academies opened their doors. Currently, women comprise 23% of the Corps and are fully and successfully integrated into every phase of campus, classroom, and military life.

Alumni of New Mexico Military Institute have made important contributions in the military, government, business, academia, and the arts; they include artist Peter Hurd, journalist Sam Donaldson, hotelier Conrad Hilton, star quarterback Roger Staubach, cable TV pioneer Bill Daniels, and Desert Storm leader Brig. Gen. Joe Frazier III, among others. Although for a long time the student body came primarily from southern New Mexico and west Texas, today the Institute has cadets from 43 states and 13 countries.

For more than 25 years, the Institute's Pearson Hall has provided the setting for the Roswell Symphony Orchestra. NMMI's support of the Symphony, however, is just one of the many ways that the Institute enhances the civic and cultural life of the Roswell community.

Featured on page 197 "Clock Tower at New Mexico Military Institute"

Baked Corn Pudding

2 (10-ounce) packages frozen corn kernels, thawed and drained
3 large eggs, beaten
1 teaspoon grated onion
¼ cup all-purpose four
2 teaspoons salt
¼ teaspoon ground white pepper
1 tablespoon sugar
¼ teaspoon ground nutmeg
2 tablespoons butter, melted
2 cups half-and-half
1 (4-ounce) jar pimientos, drained and coarsely chopped

Preheat oven to 325°. Lightly grease a 1½-quart shallow baking dish. Combine first 3 ingredients in a large bowl, blending well. Combine flour, salt, pepper, sugar, and nutmeg in a separate bowl; stir into corn mixture. Add butter, cream, and pimientos; blend well. Pour mixture into prepared dish. Place dish in a larger pan; add 1 inch hot water to larger pan. Bake, uncovered, for 1 hour or until a knife inserted in center comes out clean. Cut into squares, and serve hot.

Green chile can be substituted for pimientos. If substituting, omit nutmeg.

Makes 8 servings.

Billy The Kid Potatoes

8 bacon slices, diced
3 pounds baking potatoes, peeled and cut into ¼-inch slices
6 tomatoes, peeled, quartered, and seeded
3 garlic cloves, crushed
2 teaspoons minced fresh thyme or ¾ teaspoon dried thyme
2 cups sliced fresh mushrooms
1½ cups black olives, quartered
Salt and freshly ground pepper to taste
½ cup medium-dry sherry
½ cup butter, melted
3 garlic cloves, minced

Preheat oven to 350°. Cook bacon until almost crisp; drain. Arrange potato and tomato in a 15- x 10-inch baking dish; sprinkle with bacon, crushed garlic, and thyme. Add mushrooms and olives to dish. Season with salt and pepper to taste. Pour sherry over mixture, and cover with foil. Bake for 30 minutes. Combine butter and minced garlic; pour over mixture. Bake, uncovered, until potato is tender, 40 to 45 minutes. Serve immediately.

Makes 6 servings.

Baked Vegetables Fiesta

1¼ pounds small eggplants
 Salt to taste
½ cup mild olive oil
1 pound russet potatoes, peeled and thinly sliced
 Freshly ground black pepper to taste
1 pound onions, peeled and thinly sliced

2 medium-size green bell peppers, cored, seeded, and cut into ⅜-inch rings
1 pound ripe tomatoes, cored and cut into ⅛-inch slices
1 (5-ounce) can black olives, rinsed and drained and halved

Preheat oven to 450°. Using a vegetable peeler, make ½-inch-wide stripes down sides of eggplants. Cut eggplants crosswise into ¼-inch-thick slices; spread slices on a large platter, and sprinkle with ½ teaspoon salt. Set aside 15 minutes, then rinse and pat dry with paper towels. Coat the bottom of a 15- x 10-inch baking dish with 2 tablespoons oil. Adjust oven rack to lowest position. Spread potato in an even layer in bottom of pan; sprinkle with salt and pepper. Spread onion over potato in an even layer, sprinkling with salt and pepper. Arrange bell pepper over onion, followed by even layer of eggplant; sprinkle with salt and pepper. Layer tomato over eggplant, followed by olives, salt, and pepper. Drizzle remaining oil over vegetables. Cover pan loosely with foil, and bake for 25 minutes. Reduce temperature to 325°, and bake 45 minutes or until a knife inserted meets no resistance. Uncover and cool. Serve warm or at room temperature.

Makes 6 to 8 servings.

Chopped fresh herbs can be added to each layer, and any oil left over can be strained and used on salads.

Broccoli with Green Chile Butter

6 tablespoons unsalted butter
¼ teaspoon ground cumin
2 ripe tomatoes, seeded and finely chopped

3 New Mexico green chiles, roasted, peeled, seeded, and finely chopped
4½-5 pounds broccoli, cut into florets, steamed, and kept warm
 Salt and pepper to taste

Melt butter in a heavy saucepan over medium heat; stir in cumin, and add tomato and chiles. Reduce heat, and cook mixture until hot. Add broccoli, tossing quickly; season with salt and pepper. Serve immediately.

Makes 6 servings.

Cabbage Supreme with Pecans

¼ cup water
1 beef-flavored bouillon cube
5 cups shredded cabbage
1 cup peeled, thinly sliced carrot
½ cup chopped onion
½ teaspoon salt

½ teaspoon pepper
¼ cup butter
⅓ cup chopped pecans
1 teaspoon prepared mustard
 Paprika

Combine water and bouillon in a large saucepan; bring to a boil, stirring until bouillon cube is dissolved. Add cabbage, carrot, onion, salt, and pepper; stir well, cover, and reduce heat to simmer, stirring occasionally, 5 minutes. Melt butter in a small saucepan; stir in pecans and mustard. Cook pecan mixture over medium heat, stirring constantly, 2 minutes. Pour pecan mixture over cabbage mixture, stirring well. Sprinkle with paprika.

Makes 6 to 8 servings.

Calabacitas

1½ tablespoons olive oil
4½ cups cubed zucchini
1 green onion, chopped
3 garlic cloves, minced
1 teaspoon ground cumin
¼ teaspoon salt
⅛ teaspoon pepper
½ teaspoon dried oregano

1 (7-ounce) can whole kernel corn
1 (4-ounce) can roasted diced green chiles
3 tablespoons fresh lime juice (juice of 1 lime)
½ teaspoon sugar
½ cup chopped fresh cilantro

Heat oil in a large skillet over medium-low heat; add zucchini, green onion, and garlic, and sauté 4 to 5 minutes. Stir in cumin and remaining ingredients. Reduce heat to low, and cook, stirring occasionally, 5 to 6 minutes. Cover skillet, and let dish rest 5 to 10 minutes before serving.

Makes 6 servings.

Carrots with Pistachios

2 tablespoons butter
½ cup shelled, skinned pistachios
¼ cup Cointreau, Triple Sec, or Grand Marnier
1 pound carrots, peeled and cut into ¼-inch diagonal slices

3 tablespoons butter
3 tablespoons water
1 teaspoon salt

Melt 2 tablespoons butter in a medium skillet over medium heat; add nuts, and sauté 1 minute. Stir in Cointreau; remove from heat, and set aside. Bring carrot, 3 tablespoons butter, water, and salt to a boil in a saucepan. Reduce heat to medium-low, and simmer until carrot is barely tender, 5 minutes. Transfer carrot with a slotted spoon to a heated serving bowl. Bring carrot liquid to a boil, and reduce to 2 tablespoons. Pour over carrot; add nut glaze, and toss.

Makes 6 servings.

Celery with Almonds

3 tablespoons butter
4 cups (3-inch) celery strips
2 tablespoons minced chives

½ cup finely chopped green onions (tops included)
1 garlic clove, minced
½ cup slivered almonds, toasted

Melt butter in a heavy skillet; add celery, and cook over low heat, stirring constantly, 3 minutes. Add chives, green onions, and garlic; cook, stirring constantly, until crisp-tender. Just before serving, stir in almonds, sprinkling a few on top of each serving.

Makes 6 servings.

Clyde's Eggplant Casserole

1	pound eggplant, cut into 8 slices	½	teaspoon poultry seasoning
	Salt	¼	teaspoon ground red chile pepper
2	tablespoons canola oil	1	teaspoon orange peel
2	green onions, chopped	1	cup sliced fresh mushrooms
2	garlic cloves, minced	1	cup chopped cooked chicken
4	teaspoons cornstarch		breast
½	cup orange juice	2	cups cooked white rice
½	cup chicken broth	2	ripe tomatoes, each cut into
½	cup evaporated skimmed milk		4 thick slices

Preheat oven to 350°. Sprinkle eggplant with salt, and set aside 30 minutes. Pat eggplant dry with paper towels and brush with 1 tablespoon oil. Place eggplant on a baking sheet. Broil eggplant 5 minutes per side. Heat remaining oil in a small skillet over medium heat; add onion and garlic, and sauté until tender. Dissolve cornstarch in orange juice; stir into onion mixture with broth, milk, poultry seasoning, pepper, and orange peel. Cook mixture until thickened; add mushrooms and chicken, stirring well. Spoon rice into a 13- x 9-inch baking dish; top with eggplant in a single layer. Top each eggplant slice with a tomato slice. Pour chicken mixture over all. Bake, covered with foil, for 30 minutes.

Makes 8 servings.

Corn Acapulco

3	tablespoons butter	1	cup shredded Monterey Jack cheese
3	medium-size onions, finely	1	(4.5-ounce) can diced green chiles
	chopped	1	teaspoon salt
3	large ears corn, cut from cob	¼	teaspoon ground white pepper
¼	cup water		Garnish: diced pimientos
1	cup sour cream		

Melt butter in a skillet over medium heat; add onion, and sauté until soft. Add corn and water; cover and cook 5 minutes. Uncover and cook over high heat, boiling away liquid. Add sour cream, cheese, chiles, salt, and pepper; cook until heated through. Do not boil again. Garnish, if desired.

Makes 6 servings.

Dijon Potatoes

3   pounds potatoes (about 6 large)
2   tablespoons unsalted butter
1   large yellow onion, thinly sliced
    Salt and freshly ground pepper to
    taste
2   tablespoons chopped fresh chervil
    or 2 teaspoons dried chervil

½   cup chopped fresh parsley
2   cups crème fraîche
3   heaping tablespoons Dijon
    mustard
¼   cup fresh lemon juice
4   ounces grated Gruyère or
    Emmenthaler cheese

Preheat oven to 400°. Bring potatoes and water to cover to a boil in a large stockpot; cook until just tender. Drain and let stand until cool enough to handle. Peel potatoes, and cut into ⅓-inch-thick slices. Melt butter in a skillet over medium heat; add onion, and sauté until golden brown, about 15 minutes. Remove from heat. Butter a shallow 12-inch gratin dish; set aside. Combine potato and onion in a large bowl; add salt, pepper, chervil, and parsley. Whisk crème fraîche, mustard, and lemon juice in a small bowl until smooth. Gently stir mustard mixture into potato mixture. Turn mixture into gratin dish, and arrange evenly. Sprinkle cheese over top. Bake for 30 minutes or until bubbly and lightly browned.

Makes 8 to 10 servings.

Green Beans with Piñons

1   pound green beans
⅓   cup piñon nuts, toasted
¼   cup olive oil
¼   cup red wine vinegar
1   teaspoon fresh oregano or
    ½ teaspoon dried oregano

1   teaspoon chopped fresh cilantro
1   garlic clove, minced
    Salt and freshly ground pepper to
    taste
¼   cup grated Parmesan cheese

Cook beans in boiling water until just tender; drain and rinse with cold water. Combine nuts and next 5 ingredients in a large skillet over medium heat. Add beans, and cook, stirring constantly, until all ingredients are heated through. Season with salt and pepper to taste. Sprinkle with cheese.

Makes 6 servings.

Green Chile-Spinach Enchiladas

2 tablespoons olive oil
1 tablespoon butter
½ large onion, chopped
2 garlic cloves, minced
1½ pounds trimmed fresh spinach
(or 2 packages frozen)

Salt to taste
¾ pound Swiss or Monterey Jack
cheese, shredded
10 fresh corn tortillas

Sauce
1 tablespoon butter
1 tablespoon all-purpose flour
1 cup milk, heated
1 cup low-fat sour cream

¾ cup chopped green chile
¼ cup shredded Swiss or Monterey
Jack cheese

Preheat oven to 350°. Heat oil and 1 tablespoon butter in a skillet over medium heat; sauté onion and garlic until golden. Add spinach, stirring until liquid is evaporated. Spread a heaping tablespoon shredded cheese in a line down center of each tortilla; add a heaping tablespoon spinach mixture. Roll up tortillas, and place, seam side down, in a baking dish. Melt 1 tablespoon butter in a saucepan; add flour, whisking to form a roux. Add heated milk slowly, stirring with whisk until sauce is creamy and thickens. Stir in sour cream and chile; remove from heat. Season sauce with salt to taste. Pour sauce over enchiladas, and sprinkle with remaining shredded cheese. Bake, covered, for 25 to 30 minutes. Just before serving, place dish under broiler to brown top.

Makes 4 to 5 servings.

Green Chile-Sweet Potato Puree

4 large sweet potatoes, peeled
⅔ cup roasted, peeled, seeded green
chiles
1 teaspoon fresh thyme

4 tablespoons unsalted butter,
softened
½ cup brown sugar
Salt and pepper to taste

Place potatoes in a large saucepan with water to cover by 1 inch. Bring to a boil, and cook until potatoes are tender but not mushy; drain. Pass potatoes through a food mill, and fold in remaining ingredients.

Makes 6 to 8 servings.

Herbed Vegetable Casserole

4   medium-size red potatoes,
    unpeeled and thinly sliced
    Salt and freshly ground pepper to
    taste
3   medium tomatoes, peeled and
    sliced
1   large onion, sliced and separated
    into rings

3   garlic cloves, minced
½   teaspoon dried thyme, crumbled
1   tablespoon chopped fresh basil or
    1 teaspoon dried basil, crumbled
2   tablespoons chopped fresh parsley
½   cup chicken broth
1   tablespoon butter
1   cup shredded Cheddar cheese

Preheat oven to 350°. Place half of potato into an oiled 11- x 7½-inch baking dish; sprinkle with salt and pepper. Add half each of tomatoes and next 5 ingredients; repeat layers. Pour broth over vegetables; dot with butter. Bake, covered, for 1¼ hours; sprinkle cheese over top, and bake, uncovered, for 15 to 20 minutes or until vegetables are tender and cheese is melted.

Makes 6 servings.

Julienned Pepper Medley

3   tablespoons lemon juice
2   tablespoons chopped fresh cilantro
    or parsley
½   teaspoon ground cumin
1   teaspoon sugar
⅓   cup olive oil

2   red or purple bell peppers, seeded,
    deveined, and sliced into thin strips
2   green or yellow bell peppers,
    seeded, deveined, and sliced into
    thin strips
    Salt and freshly ground pepper to
    taste

Combine first 4 ingredients in a large bowl. Gradually whisk in oil until thoroughly blended. Place pepper strips into a serving bowl, and pour oil mixture over top; toss until coated. Add salt and pepper to taste. Cover and chill at least 1 hour before serving.

Makes 4 servings.

Lima Beans Au Gratin

1½ cups minced onion
½ cup chopped mushrooms
1 tablespoon vegetable oil
3 cups fresh or frozen baby lima bean, cooked and drained

1 cup whipping cream
1 cup walnuts
1½ cups shredded Muenster cheese
2 tablespoons Tabasco
½ teaspoon salt

Preheat oven to 350°. Sauté onion and mushrooms in hot oil over medium heat 4 minutes. Add lima beans, tossing to combine. Transfer mixture to a well-buttered 10-inch gratin dish. Pour cream over beans. Process walnuts in a blender until a paste forms. Combine paste with cheese, Tabasco, and salt. Sprinkle cheese mixture over bean mixture. Bake for 20 to 25 minutes or until top is golden.

Makes 4 to 6 servings.

New Mexico Potato Pancakes

4 medium potatoes, peeled and shredded
3 eggs
1 teaspoon minced garlic
4 green chiles, roasted, seeded, and chopped

1 small onion, finely chopped
½ teaspoon salt
3 tablespoons all-purpose flour
Vegetable oil

Press potato in a colander to drain excess liquid. Combine potato and next 6 ingredients in a bowl; cover and chill 30 minutes. Coat a skillet with oil; place over medium-high heat. Stir batter, and spoon onto pan, ¼ cup at a time. Cook pancakes about 3 minutes on each side or until golden. Drain on paper towels, and serve immediately.

Makes 4 to 6 servings.

"The Roswell Symphony Virtuoso Parties" are one of the very successful and popular fundraisers for the Roswell Symphony. RSVP parties range from black-tie gourmet dinners to informal chuck wagon campfire suppers. These parties are proposed, planned, and paid for by symphony patrons. All proceeds from ticket sales directly benefit the orchestra.

Martha Zelt

Martha "Martie" Zelt is most known in Roswell for her 10-foot by 30-foot mosaic mural that adorns the interior entrance to the Roswell Civic and Convention Center. The brightly colored and educational mural was commissioned in 1996 by New Mexico Arts for the state's One Percent for Art Program. The mosaic highlights Roswell's geological foundation, its historical and/or notable landmarks, and its wildlife inhabitants.

Zelt first came to Roswell in 1982 when she was awarded a residency at the Roswell Artist-in-Residence Program. She subsequently returned to the residency in 1989 and has resided in Roswell ever since. In 1998 she was honored with a retrospective of her work at the Roswell Museum and Art Center.

Other exhibitions include solo shows at the Brooklyn Museum, Carnegie Institute, Humboldt State University and the North Dakota Museum of Art. She is included in collections at the Anderson Museum of Contemporary Art in Roswell, Brooklyn Museum, Carnegie Institute, Philadelphia Museum, Yale University and the University of New Mexico. Zelt has held teaching positions at the Philadelphia College of Art, the University of North Carolina and the University of Delaware, among others, and she has given numerous lectures and workshops at universities throughout the United States. Her work is included in such publications as *Printmaking in New Mexico-1880-1990,* published by the University of New Mexico Press in 1991; *The Complete Printmaker,* published by Ross, Romano, MacMillan Co.; and *Prints-History of an Art,* published by Beguin, Field, Skira-Rissoli.

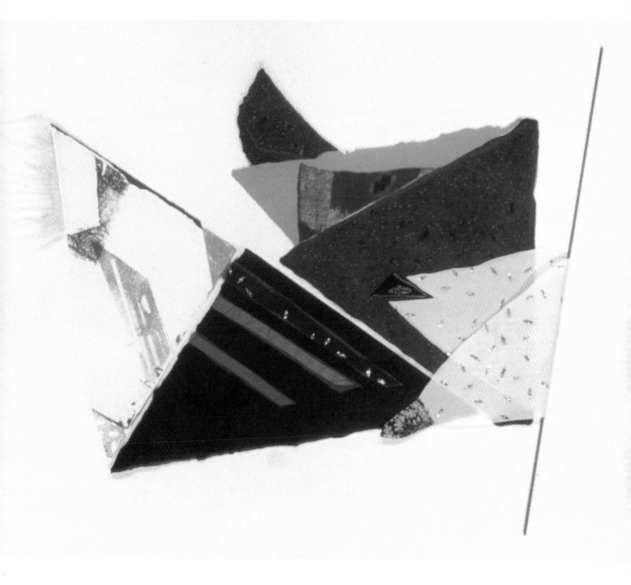

Grey Cat
Artist – Martha (Martie) Zelt
38″ × 30″   1986
lithograph, screenprint on paper, fabric, stick
Printed at the Tamarind Institute, ed. 22,
assembled by artist. Permanent collection,
Anderson Museum of Contemporary Art,
Roswell, NM.

Potatoes with Green Chiles

¼ cup vegetable oil
4 unpeeled russet potatoes, thinly sliced
2 cups diced purple onion
1 red bell pepper, cored, seeded, and diced

1 Anaheim chile, cored, seeded, and diced
Salt and freshly ground pepper to taste

Heat oil in a large, heavy skillet; add potato, and sauté until tender, about 10 minutes. Add onion and bell pepper, and sauté 3 minutes. Stir in Anaheim chile, salt, and pepper, and sauté 5 minutes.

Makes 6 servings.

If red bell pepper is not available, use green.

Sautéed Green Beans with Chile Crumbs

2 tablespoons unsalted butter
½ teaspoon dried oregano, crumbled
1½ teaspoons chile powder
⅛ teaspoon cayenne pepper
1 cup coarse, fresh whole-grain or rye breadcrumbs, lightly toasted

2 tablespoons vegetable oil
1 pound green beans, trimmed and cut into ½-inch pieces
Fresh lemon juice to taste

Melt butter in a skillet over medium heat; add oregano and next 3 ingredients. Cook mixture, stirring occasionally, until crumbs are lightly toasted. Transfer mixture to a bowl. Wipe skillet clean, and heat oil over medium-high heat until almost smoking. Sauté beans in oil until crisp-tender, 6 to 8 minutes. Stir lemon juice, salt, and pepper into beans; add crumb mixture, and toss.

Makes 4 servings.

_____Sherried Sweet Potatoes with Lime_____

2   pounds sweet potatoes, peeled and
    cut into ¼-inch slices
3   tablespoons butter
    Salt and freshly ground pepper to
    taste

2   tablespoons fresh lime juice
2   tablespoons dry sherry
    Sour cream

Drop potato slices into a pan of boiling salted water; cook until soft, about 8 minutes. Drain well. Place a paper towel over pan; cover with lid, and let steam several minutes. Put potatoes through a food mill into a bowl; mash with butter, and add salt and pepper, lime juice, and sherry. To serve, heat well, and dollop with sour cream.

Makes 4 servings.

If made ahead, reheat in top of a double boiler.

_____Sonora Casserole_____

3   cups sliced zucchini, steamed until
    soft
1   cup frozen or canned corn kernels,
    drained
2   cups tomato sauce
½   tablespoon chile powder
¼   teaspoon cayenne pepper
¼   teaspoon ground cumin

1   teaspoon vinegar
6   corn tortillas, quartered and fried
    in oil
1   (4.5-ounce) can diced green chiles
1½ cups shredded Cheddar cheese
¾   cup sour cream
    Chopped green onions

Preheat oven to 350°. Combine first 9 ingredients; place in a greased ovenproof baking dish. Top mixture with cheese. Bake for 12 minutes or until well heated and cheese melts. Top with sour cream, and sprinkle with green onions before serving.

Makes 6 to 8 servings.

Can be used as a light lunch meal or as a spicy side dish to add interest to a simple supper.

Roasted Asparagus

1 tablespoon olive oil	Salt and freshly ground pepper to
1½ pounds very slender asparagus	taste
spears, ends removed	¼ cup grated Parmesan cheese
3 tablespoons balsamic vinegar	

Preheat oven to 500°. Place a 10-inch ovenproof skillet in oven for 5 minutes. Remove from oven. Swirl oil in pan; using tongs, roll asparagus in hot oil. Bake until crisp-tender, 5 to 7 minutes. Drizzle cooked asparagus with vinegar. Season with salt and pepper to taste. Sprinkle with cheese.

Makes 4 servings.

Sophisticated Succotash

1 large bunch broccoli, cut into florets	2 medium-size yellow squash, scrubbed and cut into ¼-inch-thick slices
Salt to taste	
10 tablespoons unsalted butter	1 (10-ounce) package frozen baby lima beans, thawed and drained
1 pound carrots, peeled and cut diagonally into ¼-inch slices	1 cup corn kernels (optional)
2 medium-size red bell peppers, cut into ¼-inch-thick strips	Freshly ground pepper to taste

Bring a large pan of salted water to a boil; add broccoli, and cook just until crisp-tender, 3 to 4 minutes. Drain and rinse in ice water. Pat dry. Melt butter in a large, heavy skillet over medium-low heat; add carrot, and cook until crisp-tender, about 15 minutes. Increase heat to medium-high, and add bell pepper; cook, stirring constantly, 5 minutes. Add squash to skillet, and cook 1 minute. Add lima beans, corn, and broccoli; season with salt and pepper to taste. Cover and cook just until heated through, stirring twice, about 4 minutes.

Makes 10 servings.

_____ Southwestern Onion Rings _____

4 cups buttermilk	3 cups all-purpose flour
2 large sweet onions, cut into ¼-inch-thick slices and separated into rings	3 tablespoons ground cumin
	1 tablespoon salt
Vegetable oil	3 tablespoons chile powder
	1 tablespoon cayenne pepper

Pour buttermilk into a large bowl. Add onion rings, and toss to coat. Let stand at room temperature 20 minutes, turning occasionally. Pour 3 inches oil into a large heavy saucepan; heat to 350°. Combine flour and next 4 ingredients in a large bowl. Toss 1 handful onion rings with flour mixture. Fry coated onion rings in oil until crisp, about 2 minutes. Use tongs to remove and transfer to paper towels to drain. Repeat procedure with remaining onion rings. Mound in a bowl, and serve immediately.

Makes 6 to 8 servings.

_____ Spinach-Stuffed Tomatoes _____

2 large tomatoes, halved	¼ teaspoon dried basil or 3 teaspoons chopped fresh basil
½ small onion, chopped	
1 garlic clove, minced	4 teaspoons whole wheat breadcrumbs
2 tablespoons vegetable stock	
1½ teaspoons minced fresh parsley	2 tablespoons freshly grated Parmesan cheese
¼ teaspoon dried thyme or 1 teaspoon minced fresh thyme	
	½ cup cooked, well-drained spinach
¼ teaspoon dried oregano or 1 teaspoon minced fresh oregano	Parmesan cheese

Preheat oven to 350°. Remove pulp from tomatoes, and chop pulp; invert shells to drain. Sauté onion and garlic in hot broth in a skillet over medium heat until translucent. Add tomato pulp and herbs to onion mixture. Combine crumbs and 2 tablespoons cheese; stir into onion mixture. Add spinach to filling; stuff shells with filling, and top with additional Parmesan cheese. Bake for 20 minutes or until tender.

Makes 4 servings.

Spinach-Cheese Burritos

2	tablespoons butter	6	medium-size flour tortillas
4	cups sliced fresh mushrooms	2	cups Green Chile Sauce (see index)
	Salt and pepper to taste	2	cups shredded Monterey Jack
3	bunches fresh spinach, washed, dried, trimmed, and chopped		cheese

Preheat oven to 450°. Melt butter in a large skillet over medium heat; add mushrooms, and sauté 2 to 3 minutes. Season mushrooms with salt and pepper to taste. Add spinach to mushrooms, and sauté until leaves are hot. Divide spinach mixture among tortillas, and roll up tightly. Place burritos, seam side down, in a shallow baking dish. Pour green chile sauce over top, and sprinkle with Monterey Jack cheese. Bake for 5 minutes or until cheese is bubbly.

Makes 6 servings.

Summer Squash-Pecan Sauté

¼	pound butter	¼	cup diced smoked ham
½	cup chopped pecans	¼	cup diced tomato
10	yellow squash, diced		Salt and cayenne pepper to taste
½	cup chopped onion	¼	cup seasoned breadcrumbs
½	cup chopped celery	¼	cup grated Parmesan cheese
½	cup diced red bell pepper		
¼	cup diced garlic		

Melt butter in a 10-inch skillet over medium-high heat; add pecans, and sauté until golden brown and pecan flavor spices butter. Remove pecans from skillet, and set aside. Add squash and next 5 ingredients to skillet; sauté until squash is tender, 5 to 7 minutes. Add tomato to squash mixture, and season with salt and cayenne pepper. Cook until tomato is heated through; remove from heat. Stir breadcrumbs, Parmesan, and pecans into squash mixture. Serve immediately.

Makes 6 servings.

A combination of yellow squash and zucchini squash is attractive. Consider dicing any garden vegetable and adding to skillet with squash.

_____Sweet Potato Gratin_____

2	cups whipping cream	3	medium-size sweet potatoes, peeled and thinly sliced
½	canned chipotle pepper		Salt and freshly ground pepper to taste

Preheat oven to 350°. Process cream and chipotle in a blender until pureed, being careful not to overprocess or cream will turn to butter. Arrange one-fourth of sweet potato slices in an 8-inch pan. Season with salt and pepper, and cover with one-fourth of cream. Repeat procedure until all the potatoes and cream are layered. Bake for 1 hour or until cream has been absorbed and potatoes are browned.

Makes 4 to 5 servings.

The gratin may be prepared a day ahead, covered tightly, and chilled. Reheat at 350° for 15 minutes or until hot.

_____Sweet Potatoes Margarita_____

¾	cup butter	2	tablespoons tequila
2	pounds sweet potatoes, peeled and shredded in food processor	1	tablespoon fresh lime juice
			Salt and pepper to taste
2	tablespoons sugar		Garnish: lime wedges

Place a 12- to 14-inch frying pan over medium heat; add butter, and stir until melted. Stir sweet potato into butter, and sprinkle with sugar. Cook mixture over medium heat, turning occasionally with a spatula, until potato begins to caramelize and look slightly translucent, about 15 minutes. Stir in tequila and lime juice; cook, stirring constantly, 3 minutes. Season with salt and pepper to taste. Pour mixture into a serving bowl, and garnish, if desired.

Makes 6 to 8 servings.

Two-Potato Gratin

2	large russet potatoes (about 1¼ pounds), peeled and thinly sliced Salt and freshly ground pepper to taste	2	sweet potatoes (about 1 pound), peeled and thinly sliced
1	tablespoon minced fresh rosemary or 2 teaspoons dried crumbled rosemary	1½	cups whipping cream
		1	cup shredded Swiss cheese
		⅓	cup grated Parmesan cheese

Arrange half of russet potato in an 8-inch square microwavable baking dish; season with salt and pepper. Sprinkle one-fourth of rosemary over potato in dish. Top with half of sweet potato; season with salt and pepper, and sprinkle with one-fourth of rosemary. Repeat layers with remaining potato slices, salt and pepper, and rosemary. Pour cream over potato mixture. Cover tightly with plastic wrap, and microwave on HIGH for 18 minutes or until potato slices are tender. Sprinkle both cheeses over top, and microwave, uncovered, on HIGH for 3 minutes or until cheeses melt. Cool 10 minutes before serving.

Makes 4 servings.

 Receiving a favorite cake never fails to bring a smile to the face of a New Mexico Military Institute Cadet. "Symphony Guild Moms" give families the opportunity to order any-occasion cakes for their cadet. These special order cakes are baked and delivered to the cadet by Guild members. To date, there have been no complaints from the cadets about this program! All proceeds support the symphony.

Torta De Calabacitas

5 tablespoons butter	Salt to taste
1 large onion, chopped	3 tablespoons minced, seeded
2 teaspoons ground cumin	jalapeño
3 large zucchini, trimmed and	3 (11-inch) flour tortillas
shredded	4 cups shredded Monterey Jack
3 garlic cloves, minced	cheese

Melt 3 tablespoons butter in a heavy skillet over medium heat; add onion and cumin, and sauté until tender, about 9 minutes. Add zucchini and garlic to onion mixture; sauté until mixture is dry and zucchini is tender, about 14 minutes. Season mixture with salt, and add jalapeño; cook 2 minutes. Transfer mixture to a bowl to cool. Place 1 tortilla on an oiled, flat plate; sprinkle one-fourth of cheese over tortilla. Spread half of zucchini mixture over cheese; sprinkle one-fourth of cheese over top. Top cheese with second tortilla, and repeat layers, ending with third tortilla. Press stack firmly to compact. Heat 1 tablespoon butter in a heavy 12-inch skillet over medium heat; slide torta into skillet. Cover and cook until bottom is golden brown, about 4 minutes. Using spatula, slide torta onto plate. Add remaining 1 tablespoon butter to skillet. Invert torta into skillet, and cook until bottom is golden brown, about 4 minutes. Transfer to a serving platter. Let stand 5 minutes, and cut into wedges.

Makes 6 servings.

Salsa, Sauces, & Pesto's

The State Question: Red or Green?

Few cuisines of the world could hold their own without the wonderful chile pepper. Chile use by humans began as early as 7500 B.C. in Bolivia and Peru. Although chiles have been grown in New Mexico for at least four centuries, they have been a significant cash crop only in the past two decades.

Versatile in taste as well as appearance, chiles can be hot to mild, green to deep violet, and, when used in cooking, juicy fresh or wrinkled and dried. Chile is considered the New Mexico State Vegetable, along with frijoles, but the chile pod is actually a fruit. The magical, addictive source of the chile's heat is the chemical capsaicin, found in the pepper's heart and membrane. The seeds themselves are not hot, but they absorb capsaicin from their contact with the heart and membrane.

Chile is a dieter's delight: not only low in fat, it is also high in vitamins A, C, and betacarotene. Chile may protect against blood clots and prevent heart attacks, and it is known to hinder cholesterol absorption.

Medicinal uses of chile extend from pre-history into modern medicine. The heat-producing chemical capsaicin is known to trigger the brain's production of endorphins, the body's natural painkiller. According to chile authority Jean Andrews, chile "protects against colds and malaria, aids digestion, clarifies the blood, develops robustness and resistance to the elements; it even acts as a stimulant to the romantically inclined." Dried red chiles ristras are not only decorative, but also serve the cook as convenient storage for the chile pod, which could well be the world's oldest and best-provisioned medicine chest.

Featured on page 217 "Ristra"

Avocado Salsa

2   avocados, peeled, pitted, and cut into chunks
4   plum tomatoes, peeled, seeded, and cut into ½-inch chunks
1   teaspoon finely minced fresh jalapeño
1   teaspoon finely minced garlic

¼   cup finely minced green bell pepper
3   tablespoons finely minced purple onion
2   tablespoons red wine vinegar
2   tablespoons minced fresh cilantro
½   cup olive oil
     Salt and pepper to taste

Combine all ingredients; serve with grilled meat.

Makes about 2 cups.

Black Bean Salsa

1   (15-ounce) can black beans, rinsed and drained
1   teaspoon vegetable oil
¾   cup chopped onion
2   garlic cloves, minced
½   cup diced fresh tomato (canned may be used)

½   cup picante sauce or green chile sauce (see index)
½   teaspoon ground cumin
½   teaspoon chile powder
½   cup shredded reduced-fat Monterey Jack cheese
¼   cup chopped fresh cilantro
3   tablespoons fresh lime juice

Mash beans in a bowl until chunky. Heat oil in a medium-size nonstick skillet over medium heat. Add onion and garlic, and sauté in hot oil until tender, about 4 minutes. Add beans, tomato, picante sauce, cumin, and chile powder to skillet; cook, stirring constantly, 5 minutes or until thick. Remove from heat. Add cheese, cilantro, and lime juice to mixture, stirring well. This can be served warm or at room temperature. Use as a dip, or serve with desired meat.

Makes about 3 cups.

Basic Pico De Gallo

1 tomato, chopped (or 1 cup canned diced tomato)	1 jalapeño, chopped
1 small onion, chopped	1 lemon
5 fresh cilantro sprigs, chopped	Salt and black pepper to taste

Combine first 4 ingredients in a bowl. Squeeze lemon juice over mixture, and add salt and pepper to taste. Let stand several hours before using.

Makes about 1½ cups.

Corn Salsa

3 cups fresh corn kernels, blanched 3 minutes	⅓ cup rice wine vinegar
	1 tablespoon Dijon mustard
1 (15-ounce) can black beans, rinsed and drained	1 tablespoon olive oil
	⅔ cup finely chopped fresh cilantro
5 scallions, thinly sliced	⅛ teaspoon Tabasco
1 medium-size red bell pepper, cored, seeded, and diced	⅛ teaspoon cayenne pepper
	Salt and freshly ground black
1 medium-size jalapeño, cored, seeded, and finely diced	pepper to taste

Combine first 5 ingredients in a large bowl. Whisk vinegar and mustard in a small bowl; add oil, 1 drop at a time,, whisking constantly. Add cilantro to vinegar mixture, along with Tabasco, cayenne, and salt and black pepper. Whisk well. Drizzle vinegar mixture over corn mixture, and toss until well combined. Chill at least 2 hours before serving.

Makes 6 servings.

SOS! SOS! This is another popular program for the cadets at NMMI. "Symphony of Snacks" boxes are offered during holidays and exam week and include fruit, chips, cookies, crackers and other "goodies". Parents pre-order these SOS boxes and then they are packed, labeled, and delivered to the lucky cadet at the proper time. Some cadets who do not get a box have been known to tell their parents "everyone gets one but me". Sometimes this even works! All profits are for the benefit of the symphony.

Chipotle Pico De Gallo

¼ cup fresh lime juice
2 teaspoons minced chipotle chiles in adobo sauce
4 garlic cloves, minced

2 cups chopped, seeded tomato
1 cup chopped onion
½ cup chopped fresh cilantro
Salt and black pepper to taste

Combine first 3 ingredients in a large bowl. Add remaining ingredients, and season with salt and pepper. Let stand 1 hour at room temperature before serving.

Makes about 3 cups.

Green Chile Salsa

¼ cup chopped nopalitos
4 New Mexico green or Anaheim chiles, roasted, peeled, seeded, and diced
1 poblano chile, roasted, peeled, seeded, and diced
1 green bell pepper, cored, seeded, and diced

1 red or yellow bell pepper, cored, seeded, and diced
1 serrano chile, seeded and diced
¼ cup chopped purple onion
½ cup chopped husked tomatillo
½ cup chopped tomato
2 tablespoons fresh lime juice
1 tablespoon chopped fresh cilantro
Salt to taste

Combine all ingredients in a non-aluminum bowl, and let stand at room temperature at least 30 minutes. Salsa can be kept covered in refrigerator up to 1 week.

Makes about 2 cups.

Nopales
Nopales are the fleshy, oval pads, or leaves, of the prickly pear cactus. The smaller, deep-green pads are the most tender, and their flavor is similar to a green bean. Fresh nopales are available fresh in produce departments. They keep up to a week in the refrigerator if they are well wrapped. With a vegetable peeler, scrape the thorns away before using. Cut the pads into dice or slices to be used in salads, salsas, vegetable and egg dishes. If fresh nopales are unavailable, substitute nopalitos, which are canned or pickled nopales.

Salsa Picante

16 large tomatoes, chopped
2 fresh green chiles, chopped
2 fresh red chiles, chopped
4 onions, chopped
2 hot peppers, chopped

2 tablespoons salt
1 cup vinegar
½ teaspoon celery salt
½ teaspoon mustard seed

Place all ingredients in a large Dutch oven, and simmer over low heat until sauce consistency, about 2 hours. Freezes well.

Makes about 3 quarts.

Pumpkin Seed Salsa

1 cup cooked corn kernels
1½ cups chopped tomato
1 New Mexico green or Anaheim chile, roasted, peeled, seeded, and chopped
1 red serrano chile, seeded and diced

2 tablespoons fresh lime juice
¼ teaspoon ground cumin
1 cup unsalted green pumpkin seeds (pepitas), toasted
Salt and freshly ground black pepper to taste

Combine first 6 ingredients in a non-aluminum bowl. Stir in pumpkin seeds. Season with salt and pepper.

Serve with poultry or fish.

Makes 3½ cups.

Strawberry Salsa

1 pint fresh strawberries, diced
4 plum tomatoes, seeded and diced
1 small purple onion, diced
1-2 medium-size jalapeños, diced

Juice of 1 lime
2 garlic cloves, minced
1 tablespoon olive or vegetable oil
Salt and pepper to taste

Combine strawberries, tomato, onion, and peppers in a bowl. Stir in remaining ingredients. Cover and chill 2 hours. Serve with poultry or pork. Can be a dip with tortilla chips.

Makes 4 cups.

Spicy Nut Salsa with Blue Cheese

3	tablespoons hazelnut or olive oil	1	cup chopped celery
4	teaspoons dry mustard	1	cup crumbled Gorgonzola or blue
2	teaspoons ground allspice		cheese (about 5½ ounces)
½	cup hazelnuts, coarsely chopped	2	tablespoons honey
½	cup pecan pieces		Salt and pepper to taste
½	cup slivered almonds, coarsely chopped		

Heat oil, mustard, and allspice in a large skillet over medium heat. Add nuts, and sauté until golden, about 7 minutes. Transfer to a large bowl. Stir in celery, cheese, and honey. Season with salt and pepper. Can be prepared 2 days ahead. Cover and chill. Serve at room temperature.

Makes 4 cups.

Terrific with leg of lamb, or use in endive spears or celery sticks for appetizers.

Zia Salsa

4	plum tomatoes	¾	cup fresh orange juice
2	husked tomatillos	1	tablespoon fresh lime juice
½	avocado	1	tablespoon olive oil
¼	purple onion		Salt to taste
1	fresh jalapeño		Freshly chopped cilantro to taste

Cut first 5 ingredients into ¼-inch pieces. Stir in remaining ingredients. Use immediately, as avocado will darken.

Makes 2 cups.

Pineapple Salsa

10	ounces unsweetened pineapple, chopped	½	bunch fresh cilantro, chopped
3	green onions, chopped	1	teaspoon salt
1	red bell pepper, chopped	3	kiwifruit, peeled and chopped

Combine first 5 ingredients; chill overnight. Add kiwifruit just before serving at room temperature. Serve with fish, pork, or chicken.

Makes about 2 cups.

Tomatillo Sauce

1 pound tomatillos, husked, rinsed, and cut into ⅛-inch pieces	1 jalapeño, stemmed and finely chopped
¼ medium-size onion, cut into ⅛-inch pieces	½ cup fresh cilantro, finely chopped
½ cup water	¼ teaspoon salt

Place tomatillos, onion, and water in a medium-size microwave-safe bowl; microwave, uncovered, on HIGH 5 minutes. Stir mixture, and microwave until onion is quite soft, about 5 minutes. Remove from microwave, and let stand 15 minutes or until completely cooled. Process mixture in a blender until smooth; stir in jalapeño, cilantro, and salt. Serve immediately. Can be stored in refrigerator up to 2 weeks.

Caper Sauce

1 cup chopped fresh parsley	1 tablespoon finely minced, drained anchovy fillets in oil
⅓ cup drained capers, coarsely ground	2 small sour pickles, finely minced
½ cup finely minced white onion	½ cup fine, dry breadcrumbs (optional)
⅓ cup white vinegar	Salt and pepper to taste
1¼ cups olive oil	

Combine all ingredients until well blended.

Makes 2½ cups.

Cold Horseradish Cream

½ cup thinly sliced, peeled horseradish	1 teaspoon salt
4 tablespoons white wine vinegar	½ teaspoon freshly ground pepper
1½ cups sour cream	3 tablespoons chopped fresh dill (optional)
½ cup whipping cream	

Process horseradish and vinegar in a food processor until smooth. Transfer to a bowl. Stir in remaining ingredients until well mixed. Add additional vinegar, if tartness is desired. Chill at least 2 hours.

Makes 2 cups.

Creamy Mustard Sauce

2 tablespoons unsalted butter	2 tablespoons chopped fresh tarragon or 2 teaspoons dried tarragon
2 tablespoons all-purpose flour	
1 cup chicken stock, heated	2 tablespoons chopped fresh chives
6 tablespoons Dijon mustard	Salt and pepper to taste
1 cup whipping cream	

Melt butter in a saucepan over medium heat; add flour, and cook, whisking constantly, until smooth. Gradually add stock, whisking constantly. Whisk in mustard and cream, and simmer until slightly thickened, about 5 minutes. Stir in tarragon, chives, salt, and pepper.

Makes 2 cups.

Avocado Butter

½ cup unsalted butter, room temperature	2 garlic cloves, minced
	⅛ teaspoon red hot pepper sauce
½ cup mashed ripe avocado	Salt and pepper to taste
¼ cup fresh lemon juice	
2 tablespoons minced fresh flat-leaf parsley	

Process all ingredients in a food processor until blended. Taste and adjust seasoning. Place in a decorative bowl or butter mold. Cover and chill up to 1 week.

Makes 1 cup.

Mustard-Chive Butter

1 tablespoon dry mustard	½ cup plus 2 tablespoons unsalted butter, room temperature
½ teaspoon sugar	
2 tablespoons white vinegar	¼ cup minced fresh chives
¼ cup Dijon mustard	Salt and pepper to taste

Dissolve dry mustard and sugar in vinegar in a small bowl. Stir in Dijon mustard. Transfer mixture to a food processor, and add butter and chives. Process until thoroughly blended. Adjust seasoning. Serve on steaks, chops, chicken, and salmon.

Makes ⅔ cup.

Olive Butter

1   cup green or black olives, pitted
    Grated zest of 1 orange
2   tablespoons Cognac or brandy
2   shallots, finely minced
2   teaspoons finely minced fresh
    thyme or ½ teaspoon dried thyme

1   teaspoon finely minced garlic
1   tablespoon finely minced, drained
    anchovy fillets in oil
¾   cup unsalted butter, room
    temperature
    Freshly ground pepper to taste

Pulse olives in a food processor until just chopped; add orange zest and next 5 ingredients, processing until just combined. Add butter, and process until combined and lightly textured. Season with pepper. This is great on chops, steaks, tucked under skin of chicken before broiling, or blended into pasta or vegetables.

Makes 1½ cups.

Roquefort Butter

3   ounces Roquefort cheese
6   tablespoons unsalted butter, room
    temperature
2   tablespoons Cognac or brandy

1   teaspoon freshly ground pepper
¼   cup chopped walnuts or pecans
    (optional)

Process first 4 ingredients in a food processor until thoroughly blended. Fold in nuts, if desired. Delicious on grilled steaks, chops, and burgers.

Makes ¾ cup.

Green Chile Sauce

1   jalapeño, seeded and diced
1   garlic clove, crushed
¼   cup chopped green onions
4   husked tomatillos, diced
1½ cups chicken stock

2   New Mexico green or Anaheim chiles,
    roasted, peeled, seeded, and diced
¼   cup chopped fresh cilantro
1   tablespoon fresh lime juice
    Salt and pepper to taste
1   tablespoon whipping cream

Bring first 5 ingredients to a boil in a medium-size saucepan; reduce heat, and simmer until liquid is reduced to about 1 cup, 15 to 20 minutes. Pour stock mixture into blender; add chiles, cilantro, and lime juice, and process until smooth. Season with salt and pepper. Add cream, and process until blended. Serve warm. Store in refrigerator 1 to 2 days.

Makes 1½ cups.

Fresh Tomato Sauce

1 cup extra-virgin olive oil	2 (6-ounce) cans tomato paste
3 cups finely chopped onion	7 tablespoons fresh basil, finely
8 garlic cloves, finely minced	minced
1 cup finely diced carrot	2 teaspoons fresh oregano, chopped,
1 cup parsley, finely chopped	or ½ teaspoon dried oregano
1 cup finely diced celery	2 Bouquets Garnis
8 pounds tomatoes, peeled and	1 teaspoon salt
seeded	1 teaspoon ground white pepper

Heat olive oil in a large stockpot. Add onion, garlic, carrot, parsley, and celery, and cook over low heat without browning, about 20 minutes. Coarsely chop tomatoes, and add to sauce. Add tomato paste, basil, oregano, Bouquets Garni, salt, and pepper. Simmer sauce 1½ hours, stirring often. This may be used immediately or cooled and chilled in sealed jars 1 to 2 weeks. Or freeze in plastic containers 2 to 3 months. It may also be canned using traditional water bath method.

Makes about 4 quarts.

Bouquet Garni

¼ cup dried parsley	2 tablespoons dried marjoram
4 bay leaves, crumbled	2 tablespoons dried lovage leaves
2 tablespoons dried thyme	

Mix herbs together. Place 1 tablespoon mixture into a small muslin bag or in center of a 4-inch square of fine cheesecloth, doubled. Tie bag or gather up corners of square, and tie with kitchen string. Be sure to remove the bouquet before serving. Store bags in a jar with a tight-fitting lid. Use in soups and stews.

Makes 10 to 12 bags.

Mild Green Chile Sauce

2 tablespoons olive oil	2 cups chicken stock or broth
1 cup chopped onion	1 garlic clove, minced
4 tablespoons all-purpose flour	2 teaspoons salt
2 cups chopped mild green chiles	

Heat oil in a medium-size saucepan over medium heat until hot; add onion, and sauté until tender. Add flour slowly to onion, stirring constantly, until flour is browned and makes a roux. Add chiles, broth, and salt. Simmer 20 minutes.

Makes 4 cups.

_____ Red Chile Sauce _____

10 whole dried New Mexico chiles
1   tablespoon olive oil
1   cup finely chopped onion

2   garlic cloves, minced
    About 2 cups chicken stock
2   tablespoons lard or vegetable oil
    Salt to taste

Preheat oven to 250°. Place chiles in a heavy skillet, and roast them dry in the hot oven 3 to 4 minutes, being careful not to burn them. Fill a saucepan just large enough for chiles with water; bring water to a boil, and remove pan from heat. Add roasted chiles to the hot water, and, using a weight, keep them submerged until they are soft, 20 to 30 minutes. Remove chiles from water; stem, seed, and tear them into strips. Heat oil in a medium-size skillet; add onion, and sauté until browned, about 5 minutes. Process chile strips, onion, garlic, and 1 cup chicken stock in a food processor until smooth; pour mixture through a fine wire-mesh strainer. Heat lard in a heavy skillet; add chile mixture, and cook, stirring constantly, about 5 minutes. Add chicken stock until sauce is desired thickness. Add salt to taste. Cover and chill until ready to use. Store in refrigerator 2 to 3 days, or freeze.

Makes about 2 cups.

_____ Orange-Cilantro Hollandaise _____

1   cup fresh orange juice
4   shallots, minced
2   egg yolks
¾   cup unsalted butter, melted and
    warm

2   teaspoons grated orange zest
¼   cup minced fresh cilantro
    Salt and freshly ground pepper to
    taste

Cook orange juice and shallot in a small saucepan over medium heat until almost no liquid remains. Whisk eggs in a bowl; add shallot mixture. Place bowl in a pan of simmering water over medium heat, whisking constantly, until thick, 3 to 5 minutes. Remove bowl from heat. Add butter in a slow, steady stream to shallot mixture, whisking constantly. If sauce is too thick, add a little hot water. Add orange zest, cilantro, salt, and pepper, and serve immediately. Sauce may be held for 1 to 2 hours by putting it in a thermos that has been rinsed with boiling water and dried.

Makes about 1 cup.

Southwestern Eggs Benedict
This sauce is delicious over split Jalapeño Scones (see index) topped with smoked ham or salmon and poached egg. Try it over cooked fresh asparagus also.

Roasted Tomato Sauce

4 pounds very red summer tomatoes (12 to 16 medium-size)
1 pound sweet onions, chopped
5 garlic cloves, sliced
2 tablespoons green olive oil
1 teaspoon salt or to taste
3 tablespoons chopped fresh basil

Preheat oven to 375°. Peel tomatoes, catching all juice. Cut tomatoes into large chunks or wedges. Combine all ingredients, and spread evenly over a large baking dish with edges. Roast in oven for 2 to 2½ hours, stirring after 1 hour, then after every 30 minutes. Most of liquid will cook away, and tomatoes will melt into a soft, thick, slightly caramelized marmalade.

Makes 2 to 2½ cups.

Serve on pasta, with rice, on pizza or polenta, in soups, quesadillas, omelets, or with anything that goes well with tomatoes.

Taco Sauce

4 cups quartered tomatoes
1 tablespoon vegetable oil
1 cup finely chopped onion
2 garlic cloves, minced
1 teaspoon dried oregano
1 teaspoon dried ground cumin
1 teaspoon ground coriander
1 tablespoon tomato paste
1 jalapeño, seeded and minced
2 teaspoons sugar
1 tablespoon minced cilantro
2 teaspoons red wine vinegar
Salt and freshly ground pepper to taste

Process tomatoes in a food processor until pureed. Heat oil in a large skillet, and add onion and garlic; sauté until onion is translucent, about 3 minutes. Add oregano, cumin, and coriander, and sauté 2 minutes. Stir in remaining ingredients; reduce heat, and simmer, stirring often, until thickened, 15 to 20 minutes. Let sauce cool to room temperature; cover and chill up to 1 week.

Makes 2 cups.

—————Red Pepper Sauce—————————

1 garlic clove, minced	2 red bell peppers, roasted, peeled,
2 shallots, chopped	seeded, and diced
1 red jalapeño or serrano chile, diced	Salt and pepper to taste
1 cup chicken stock	

Bring first 4 ingredients to a boil in a small saucepan over medium-high heat; reduce heat, and simmer 15 minutes. Transfer mixture to a blender, and add bell pepper. Process until smooth. Add salt and pepper. Sauce may be made 2 to 3 days ahead and chilled and reheated.

Makes about 1½ cups.

—————Basic Pesto and Variations—————————

2 cups fresh basil leaves	¼ cup freshly grated Parmesan
½ cup fresh parsley leaves	cheese
½ cup olive oil	2 tablespoons butter, softened
3 tablespoons pine nuts	Salt to taste
2 garlic cloves, peeled	

Process first 5 ingredients in a food processor until pureed. Stir in cheese and butter; season with salt to taste. If pesto is too thick, add a spoonful or 2 of pasta cooking liquid just before serving.

If you are not going to use the pesto immediately, pour a thin layer of oil on top of pesto, and store in refrigerator. If you prefer to freeze sauce, add cheese and butter after thawing.

Mint Pesto
Substitute mint for basil and parsley, walnuts for pine nuts, and use sauce to coat leg of lamb, lamb chops, chicken, or as a spread for lamb or chicken sandwiches.

Rosemary Pesto
Substitute 1 cup rosemary for basil. Increase parsley to 2 cups. Use with beef, chicken, lamb, or potatoes.

Tarragon Pesto
Substitute tarragon for basil and walnuts for pine nuts. Good with chicken, fish, and vegetable salads.

Makes about 1 cup.

Parsley Pesto

3 cups firmly packed parsley leaves
3 garlic cloves, finely chopped
1 tablespoon capers, drained
3 tablespoons lemon juice
½ cup toasted pine nuts
½ cup freshly grated Parmesan cheese
⅛ teaspoon freshly ground pepper
½-¾ cup olive oil

Process first 7 ingredients in a food processor until smooth; add enough oil to make a thick paste. Great with chips, fresh baked potatoes, or pasta.

Makes 1½ cups.

Southwestern Pesto

4 cups loosely packed fresh basil
⅔ cup extra virgin olive oil
1 cup walnuts
3 garlic cloves
1 teaspoon salt
½ cup freshly grated Parmesan cheese
½ cup sun-dried tomatoes packed in oil, undrained
2 whole canned chipotle chiles

Process all ingredients in a food processor until a rough paste. Serve over pasta or over cream cheese on crackers.

Makes about 2 cups.

Spicy Pesto

6 tablespoons pine nuts, toasted
6 medium-size green chiles, roasted, peeled, and seeded
1 garlic clove
4-6 tablespoons olive oil
1 bunch fresh cilantro, leaves only
Salt to taste
Juice of 1 to 2 limes
1 large red bell pepper, roasted, peeled, seeded, and diced

Process first 5 ingredients in a food processor until a rough paste. Add salt and lime juice to taste, and stir in bell pepper.

231

Cilantro-Jalapeño Pesto

1   bunch fresh cilantro, rinsed and
    stemmed
2-3 jalapeños
½   cup pine nuts, almonds, walnuts,
    or combination

¼   cup olive oil
3   garlic cloves, crushed
    Juice of 1 lemon

Process all ingredients in a food processor until smooth; Serve on pasta or fresh vegetables.

Makes about 1 cup.

Sun-Dried Tomato Pesto

¾   cup chopped sun-dried tomatoes
    (not packed in oil)
1   cup boiling water
¼   cup freshly grated Parmesan
    cheese
5   large basil leaves

2   parsley sprigs
2   tablespoons pine nuts
2   garlic cloves, chopped
3   tablespoons olive oil
    Crostini

Soak chopped tomato in boiling water 10 minutes; drain. Process tomato, Parmesan, and next 4 ingredients in a food processor until blended. Add oil to mixture in a slow, steady stream until a smooth paste forms. Spread on Crostini.

Crostini
¼   cup olive oil
2   garlic cloves, quartered

1   baguette, cut into ¼-inch slices

Combine oil and garlic, and let stand 1 hour. Arrange bread slices on a baking sheet; broil 3 minutes or until slightly browned. Turn bread slices, and brush with oil mixture. Broil 1 minutes. Or preheat oven to 350°, and bake bread slices, oiled side up, 10 minutes or until lightly browned.

Soups & Sandwiches

Roswell Museum and Art Center

Roswell is distinguished by an active and serious art scene, and the Roswell Museum and Art Center is its hub. The original mission-style building, with its adobe walls, carved vigas, and tin chandeliers (built with the support of the Works Progress Administration) was opened to the public in 1937 and now houses the Founders' Gallery, dedicated to the original paintings of renowned regional artists Peter Hurd and Henriette Wyeth. The Museum and Art Center also is known for its collection of New Mexico modernist paintings, including those of Georgia O'Keeffe.

Special exhibits at the Museum feature exciting displays of contemporary art, often featuring work by artists in the Museum's Artist-in-Residence program, founded by local artist and businessman Donald B. Anderson. The Anderson Museum of Contemporary Art houses a large collection of works donated by artists involved in this nationally recognized program.

Permanent collections featured in the Museum include the Rogers Aston Collection of American Indian and Western Art, the Native American and Hispanic collections, and a re-creation of the workshop of Robert H. Goddard, Roswell native and "father of the modern rocket."

The Patricia Lubben Bassett Art Education Center, dedicated in April of 1998, has enabled the Museum to centralize its education facilities and provide an expanded space for art display, education, and experimentation. The Roswell Museum and Art Center, truly a jewel in the desert, serves a rich, diverse community and perpetuates the region's unique cultural identity.

Featured on page 233 "Roswell Museum and Art Center"

Beef Stock

3	pounds beef bones with some meat attached	3	parsley sprigs
2	onions, chopped	1	teaspoon thyme leaves, crumbled
2	carrots, washed and sliced	2	bay leaves
2	celery ribs, sliced	1	teaspoon peppercorns
3	quarts water		Salt and pepper to taste

Preheat oven to 400°. Place bones in a heavy roasting pan, and roast with no liquid for 20 minutes; add vegetables, and brown with bones an additional 15 minutes. Discard fat, and transfer ingredients to a stockpot. Add remaining ingredients (add more water if not enough to cover). Bring to boil, lower heat to simmer; cover with lid adjusted to allow release of steam. Simmer 6 hours. Strain through a colander, discarding bones and vegetables; Do not press vegetables while straining or broth will become cloudy. Chill broth, and skim off fat. Season to taste.

Makes 2 to 3 quarts.

This broth will keep up to 5 days and can be frozen.

Chicken Stock

1	(2- to 3-pound) chicken, cut up	1	teaspoon peppercorns
1	large onion, sliced	4-5	sprigs parsley
1	carrot, peeled and sliced	1	bay leaf
1	celery rib with top, sliced	8	cups water

Place all ingredients in a stockpot, and bring to a boil; reduce heat to simmer. Cover with lid adjusted to allow steam to escape; simmer 45 minutes. Remove chicken when cool enough to handle. Remove chicken from bone and set aside. Return bones and skin to pot; simmer 1½ hours. Strain broth; cool and chill at least 8 hours. Skim off fat. The stock can be kept up to 2 weeks but must be simmered for 10 minutes every 5 days to keep from going sour. Freezes well.

Makes about 6 cups stock and 3 cups chicken.

The chicken can be used in a number of ways or returned to stock with noodles, chopped onion, and carrot for a good chicken soup. A good addition to soup would be 2 tablespoons lime or lemon juice.

Basic Vegetable Stock

10 cups water
1 cup coarsely chopped onion
1 cup scraped and coarsely chopped carrot
1 cup coarsely chopped celery, including leaves
1 whole garlic bulb, papery outsides removed and tips cut off to expose flesh
1 (2- x ½-inch) strip lemon zest
2 bay leaves
1 sprig fresh thyme
1 tablespoon dried oregano
4 sprigs parsley
10 peppercorns
½ teaspoon cayenne pepper
1 clove
1 small cinnamon stick
¼ teaspoon salt

Bring all ingredients to a boil in a large stockpot; cover and reduce heat to simmer 1 hour. Remove from heat, and cool to room temperature. Strain broth through a fine wire-mesh strainer, pushing down on vegetables to release liquid. Chill until needed.

Makes 2 quarts.

This broth freezes well but must be used within 3 months.

Bisque of Butternut Squash and Apples

1½ pounds butternut squash, peeled and seeded
2 tart green apples, peeled and chopped
1 onion, coarsely chopped
⅛ teaspoon dried rosemary
⅛ teaspoon dried marjoram
½ teaspoon salt
2 teaspoons brown sugar
¼ teaspoon ground white pepper
1 quart chicken stock
4 tablespoons butter
2 tablespoons flour
2 egg yolks
1½ cups half-and-half

Bring first 9 ingredients to a boil in a large, heavy saucepan; reduce heat, and simmer 1 hour. Scoop squash and apples out of soup; process in a food processor until pureed, and return to soup. Melt butter in a separate saucepan, add flour, whisking to blend. Add soup in small portions to flour mixture through a wire-mesh strainer, whisking to blend; bring to a boil. Beat egg yolks with cream in a small bowl. Beat in a little of the hot soup; add yolk mixture to soup. Heat through but do not boil.

Makes 6 servings.

Special Vegetable Stock

4	unpeeled onions, cut into eighths	1	teaspoon dried marjoram
3	large celery ribs, quartered	½	cup mushrooms, chopped
2	leeks, white portion only	½	cup celery leaves, chopped
1	garlic bulb, peeled	1	zucchini, peeled and sliced
4	carrots, cut into 2-inch pieces	3	cups coarsely chopped tomatoes
1½	cups dry white wine	3	jalapeño chiles, seeded and
2	tablespoons olive oil		chopped
3	green onions, cut into 1-inch pieces	3	quarts cold water
⅓	cup fresh parsley, chopped, including stems	5	whole black peppercorns
			Salt to taste
¼	cup fresh basil, chopped, or 2 tablespoons dried basil		

Preheat oven to 350°. Place first 5 ingredients in a shallow pan, and add wine; bake, uncovered, for 1½ hours. Heat oil in large skillet; add caramelized vegetables and green onions, and cook, stirring constantly, 5 minutes. Add parsley and next 7 ingredients; cook, stirring constantly, 5 minutes. Add cold water and peppercorns; bring mixture to a boil. Reduce heat, and simmer, covered, 2 hours; uncover and simmer 30 minutes. Strain stock though a fine wire-mesh strainer lined with cheesecloth; add salt to taste.

Makes 10 cups.

 A Gala Silver Anniversary Concert and Reception was held on October 18, 1997 marking Maestro John Farrer's 25th year with the Roswell Symphony Orchestra. Concert-goers were delighted with a re-creation of the first program the Maestro ever performed in Roswell. We were especially fortunate to have The Honorable Senator Pete Domenici narrate "Lincoln Portrait", one of the evening's offerings.

Aztec Soup

1½ tablespoons olive oil
2 medium-size onions, peeled and sliced
6 garlic cloves, peeled
2 pounds ripe tomatoes, cored and cut into chunks
1½ tablespoons dried oregano
1½ tablespoons dried basil
1 tablespoon ground cumin
1 teaspoon ground black pepper
10 cups water
2 pounds meaty chicken pieces
3 bay leaves
1 epazote sprig (optional)
1 (6-ounce) can tomato paste
1 red bell pepper, seeded, cored, and thinly sliced

1 cup sliced celery
1½ cups diced zucchini
1 large carrot, peeled and thinly sliced
Salt to taste
1 medium-size potato, peeled and diced
1 cup vegetable oil
15 corn tortillas, cut into ¼-inch strips
½ pound fresh spinach, washed, stemmed, and cut into strips
1 avocado, peeled, cubed, and sprinkled with lemon juice to prevent discoloration
1 pound mozzarella or Monterey Jack cheese, shredded

Heat oil in a large skillet; add onion and garlic, and sauté until onion is translucent and soft. Add tomato chunks and next 4 ingredients. Cook over medium heat until tomato is soft, about 10 minutes. Process mixture in a food processor until smooth; set aside. Bring 10 cups water to boil in large stockpot, and add chicken pieces, bay leaves, and epazote. When water returns to a boil, skim off foam; add pureed vegetable mixture, and tomato paste. Simmer, uncovered, over low heat 20 minutes or until chicken is cooked and tender. Remove chicken pieces, and when cool enough to handle; discard skin and bones, and shred meat. Set aside. Add bell pepper, celery, zucchini, and carrot to broth; cook until tender, about 10 minutes. Remove vegetables, set aside, and salt broth to taste. While soup is cooking, parboil diced potato in salted water until tender; drain and pat dry on paper towels. Heat oil in a large skillet; add potato, and cook until browned. Remove from heat, drain, and set aside. In same skillet, fry tortillas until crisp; drain and set aside. To serve, divide vegetables and potato cubes among soup bowls. Add to each in order: tortilla strips, spinach, shredded chicken, avocado, and cheese. Pour boiling broth into soup bowls, and serve immediately.

Makes 12 servings.

Everything except the cubing avocado can be done in advance. Reheat vegetables in the soup; the other ingredients will be reheated sufficiently by the boiling broth.

Black Bean Soup

2	cups black beans, sorted and rinsed	¾	teaspoon ground cumin	
7	cups water	¼	teaspoon cayenne pepper	
1	tablespoon vegetable oil	¼	teaspoon ground coriander	
1	large onion, chopped	½	teaspoon dried oregano	
1	green bell pepper, seeded and chopped	½	teaspoon chile powder	
1	carrot, chopped	1	bay leaf	
2	celery ribs, sliced	1	teaspoon salt	
2	garlic cloves, minced		Freshly ground black pepper to taste	
4	cups water	¼	cup dry sherry	
4	cups chicken broth			

Bring beans and 7 cups water to a boil in a large stockpot over high heat; boil, uncovered, 2 minutes. Remove beans from heat, cover, and let stand 1 hour. Heat oil in a skillet over medium heat; add onion and next 4 ingredients, and sauté until tender, about 10 minutes. Drain beans, and return to pot with sautéed vegetables, 4 cups water, chicken broth, and next 6 ingredients. Bring mixture to a boil; reduce heat, and simmer, covered, stirring occasionally, until beans are tender, about 2¼ hours. Remove and discard bay leaf. Season soup with salt and pepper. Transfer to a food processor, and process until desired consistency. Return to stockpot, and reheat. Stir in sherry, and serve with your choice of hard-cooked egg, shredded Monterey Jack cheese, plain yogurt, chopped green onions, and lime wedges.

Makes 2 quarts.

Pomona Hallenbeck

Pomona Hallenbeck was born in Roswell, New Mexico, was educated at the Art Students League and Parsons School of Design in New York, and for many years has been active in the fields of illustration, painting, paper-making, and fiber arts. She divides her time between the Texas Hill Country, her working studio in Roswell, and Ghost Ranch, New Mexico, where she is a popular teacher of watercolor workshops.

The painting, "El Rio Hondo," is one in a series that chronicles the landscape, people, and history of the Pecos River and its tributaries, from the headwaters to its emptying into the Rio Grande, in south Texas. This project was many years in the making, and has resulted in a significant body of work that preserves, through art, an important area in our southwest.

Pomona's work has been exhibited in the United States, Mexico, and France, and her work is collected nationally and internationally. She has numerous awards and one-woman shows to her credit, and is listed in *Who's Who in American Art*.

El Rio Hondo
Artist – Pomona Hallendeck
8″ × 11″   1996
watercolor
Collection of the artist.
Photograph by Jose Rivera.

Cheese Soup

4 cups chicken stock
¼ cup butter
½ cup chopped onion
½ cup chopped celery
½ cup grated carrot
2 tablespoons chopped fresh parsley
Salt and freshly ground pepper to taste

4 cups milk
¼ cup all-purpose flour
1½ tablespoons cornstarch
1 cup shredded processed Cheddar cheese
¼ teaspoon baking soda
1-2 cups chopped cooked chicken (optional)

Place chicken stock in a large stockpot. Melt butter in a large skillet over medium heat; add onion, celery, and carrot, and sauté until tender. Add onion mixture to stock with parsley, salt, and, pepper. Add 3 cups milk to soup; blend remaining milk with flour and cornstarch. Add cornstarch mixture to soup. Add cheese and soda, and stir constantly until soup is thickened and smooth. Add chicken, if desired.

Makes 10 servings.

Chicken-Cilantro Soup

2 bay leaves
Stems from ½ bunch fresh cilantro
6 garlic cloves
4 quarts water
1 (3-pound) broiler-fryer, cut into serving pieces
1 medium-size plum tomato, chopped
1 teaspoon dried oregano
1 tablespoon dried basil
2 tablespoons ground cumin

1 fresh jalapeño
2 teaspoons salt
½ cup rice
2 cups diagonally sliced celery
2 cups diagonally cut green bell pepper
1½ cups julienned zucchini
1 medium-size onion, cut diagonally
1 cup diagonally sliced carrot
6 garlic cloves, chopped
Garnish: cilantro leaves, cubed tomato, cubed avocado

Place first 3 ingredients into a square of cheesecloth, and tie with string. Place in a large stockpot. Add 4 quarts water to pot, and bring to a boil. Add chicken, and cook until foam appears on surface; skim off foam, and discard. Add tomato and next 5 ingredients, and simmer 45 minutes. Add rice, and cook 15 minutes. Add celery and next 5 ingredients; boil 5 minutes. Remove pouch, and discard. Remove chicken, cool, and cut meat into bite-size pieces, discarding bones and skin. Return chicken to pot and cook until heated through. Garnish, if desired.

Makes 6 servings.

Chicken-Spinach Chowder

2	tablespoons butter	4	cups milk
1	onion, chopped	¾	cup whipping cream
1	garlic clove, crushed	½	bunch fresh spinach, chopped
2	cups chopped cooked chicken		Salt and ground white pepper to
2	potatoes, chopped and cooked		taste
3	chicken stock cubes		Garlic Croutons
¼	cup all-purpose flour		

Melt butter in a large stockpot; add onion and garlic, and sauté until soft. Whisk flour into onion mixture; add milk and cream, stirring until thickened. Add chicken stock cubes, potatoes, and spinach. Season with salt and pepper to taste, and sprinkle with croutons.

Makes 4 to 6 servings.

Garlic Croutons

6	bread slices, crusts removed	2	tablespoons olive oil
¼	cup butter	4	garlic cloves, crushed
		½	teaspoon garlic salt

Preheat oven to 350°. Cut bread into ½-inch cubes. Combine butter and remaining ingredients, and toss with bread. Arrange in a single layer on a baking sheet; bake for 15 minutes or until lightly browned.

Chilly Chile Soup

1½	cups chicken broth	¼	teaspoon ground cumin
⅓	cup minced onion	1	cup milk
1	garlic clove		Salt and ground white pepper to
½	pound green chiles		taste
1	(8-ounce) package cream cheese, softened		Red, yellow, and green bell peppers, julienned
1	cup sour cream		Garnish: sour cream

Bring broth and onion to a boil in a large saucepan; boil 5 minutes, and let cool. Process garlic and chiles in a food processor until finely chopped; add cream cheese, sour cream, and cumin, and process until blended. With processor running, add broth mixture in a slow, steady stream. Process until blended. Transfer to a large bowl. Stir in milk, salt, and pepper. Chill soup well. Garnish, if desired.

Makes 8 servings.

Chilled Tomatillo Soup

¼ cup olive oil
4 medium-size shallots, minced
12 medium-size green onions, white and green parts minced
1 pound husked tomatillos, quartered
1 quart chicken stock
1 teaspoon salt
½ teaspoon pepper
1 cup loosely packed minced cilantro
2 medium-size red jalapeños, minced (reserve 1½ teaspoons for garnish)
¼ cup sour cream

Heat oil in a large stockpot; add shallot and white parts of green onions, and sauté until softened. Add tomatillos and chicken stock; bring to a boil. Reduce heat, and simmer to blend flavors, about 6 minutes. Add salt and pepper. Pour soup through a fine wire-mesh strainer; transfer broth to a large bowl. Process solids in a food processor, adding green part of green onions, cilantro, and chiles. Process until smooth. Stir puree into broth in bowl. Cool soup to room temperature, and then chill. (Can be chilled overnight.) Top each serving with a dollop of sour cream and sprinkling of reserved chiles.

Makes 6 servings.

Lemon-Zucchini Soup

1 garlic clove
½ teaspoon salt
2 tablespoons butter
1 large onion, sliced
2½ pounds zucchini (4 to 5 large), cut into ¼-inch-thick slices
1½-2 cups chicken stock
Zest of 1 lemon
Juice of 2 lemons
Salt and pepper to taste

Mash garlic with ½ teaspoon salt to make a paste. Melt butter in a large, heavy saucepan over medium-high heat; add onion and garlic, and cook until onion is soft but not brown, about 6 minutes. Add zucchini; cover and cook, stirring often, until soft, about 15 minutes. Process mixture in a food processor until very smooth. Return to pan, and add chicken stock and lemon zest. Cook until heated through. Add lemon juice and salt and pepper to taste. Serve hot.

Makes 4 servings.

Cold Cream Of Vidalia Onion Soup

5 lean bacon slices (about ¼ pound), cut crosswise into ½-inch strips
½ cup unsalted butter
3 pounds Vidalia or other sweet onions, thinly sliced (about 10 onions)
8 garlic cloves
4 cups chicken broth
2 cups dry white wine

1 tablespoon fresh thyme or 1 teaspoon dried thyme
1 bay leaf
1 cup well-chilled whipping cream
1 cup Crème Fraîche
3 tablespoons fresh lemon juice
⅛ teaspoon Tabasco
⅛ teaspoon freshly grated nutmeg
2 cups Croutons
1 cup thinly sliced green onions

Cook bacon in a heavy stockpot until crisp, reserving drippings in pot; drain bacon. Add butter to reserved drippings; add onion and garlic, and cook, covered, over low heat, stirring occasionally, until lightly browned and softened, 25 to 30 minutes. Add broth, wine, thyme, and bay leaf to onion mixture, and simmer, covered, 20 minutes. Discard bay leaf. Process onion mixture in a food processor until blended. Pour mixture through a wire-mesh strainer, pressing hard on solids. Chill, covered, 3 to 4 hours or until cold. Whisk in cream, Crème Fraîche, lemon juice, Tabasco, nutmeg, salt, and pepper. Pour into chilled serving bowls, and sprinkle with bacon, Croutons, and green onions.

Crème Fraîche
2 cups whipping cream, room temperature
½ cup sour cream, room temperature

Whisk together, and let stand 24 hours in a warm, draft-free room. Keeps up to 2 weeks, if refrigerated.

Croutons
½ loaf Italian bread, crusts removed

Preheat oven to 350°. Cut bread into ½-inch cubes. Arrange in a single layer on baking sheets, and bake for 15 minutes or until toasted.

Makes about 2 cups.

Cold Curried Avocado Soup

8	very ripe avocados, peeled and seeded	3	(15½-ounce) cans chicken broth (or homemade)
⅔	cup fresh lime juice	¼	cup minced fresh parsley
2	garlic cloves, minced	¼	cup minced fresh cilantro
2	tablespoons mayonnaise	1	teaspoon Tabasco
1	teaspoon curry powder		Ground white pepper to taste
2	cups whipping cream		Garnish: fresh cilantro sprigs

Process first 5 ingredients in a food processor until smooth. Transfer mixture to a large bowl, and stir in cream and next 5 ingredients. Chill soup, covered with foil, up to 3 days. Stir before serving in chilled bowls. Garnish, if desired.

Makes about 10 cups.

Ripening Avocados
To hasten ripening, the avocado can be microwaved on MEDIUM (50% power)
2 minutes. Turn over, and microwave 1 minute longer.

Creamless Mushroom Soup

2	tablespoons butter	1	teaspoon thyme leaves
1	cup peeled, sliced carrots	2	pounds sliced mushrooms
1	cup sliced onion	6	cups chicken stock
1	cup sliced leeks, washed, white and light green parts only	1½	teaspoons salt or to taste
½	cup sliced celery	⅛	teaspoon pepper
		4	teaspoons minced chives

Melt butter in a large stockpot over medium heat; add carrot, onion, leeks, and celery, and sauté until tender but not brown. Stir in thyme and mushrooms, and cook until mushrooms are softened, about 5 minutes. Add chicken stock, salt, and pepper; simmer, covered, 30 minutes. Process soup in a food processor until pureed; adjust salt and pepper, and sprinkle with chives.

Makes 6 servings.

Creamy Garlic Soup

2   tablespoons peanut oil
1   leek, white and green parts cut into 1-inch pieces
8-10 garlic cloves, crushed
2   cups chicken stock
1   pound potatoes, peeled and cut into 2-inch pieces
1   teaspoon salt
½   teaspoon pepper

2   cups water
2   slices good white sandwich bread, crusts removed, cut into ½-inch cubes
1   tablespoon canola oil
1   cup milk
Salt and pepper to taste
Finely chopped chervil, chives, tarragon, parsley, or basil

Preheat oven to 400°. Heat peanut oil in a large saucepan; add leek and garlic, and sauté until softened. Add chicken stock, potato, 1 teaspoon salt, ½ teaspoon pepper, and 2 cups water; bring to a boil. Reduce heat to low, and simmer until tender, about 20 minutes. Toss bread cubes with canola oil, and spread on a baking sheet. Bake until toasted and golden. Pour soup through a wire-mesh strainer into a clean saucepan; process vegetables in a food processor until smooth with a little liquid. Return to broth, and add milk. Bring soup to a simmer; season with salt and pepper to taste. Serve with croutons and desired herbs.

Makes 6 servings.

Cream of Pecan Soup

2   tablespoons butter
½   cup finely diced onion
½   cup finely diced celery
3   garlic cloves, crushed
2   tablespoons tomato paste
8   ounces pecans, toasted

8   cups chicken stock or canned broth
1   whole chipotle chile in adobo sauce
2   tablespoons pure maple syrup
⅛   teaspoon Worcestershire sauce
Salt and pepper to taste
1   cup whipping cream

Melt butter in a heavy stockpot over medium heat; add onion and celery, and sauté until limp, 6 to 8 minutes. Add garlic, and sauté 1 minute. Add tomato paste, stirring well; set aside. Process pecans, 1 cup stock, and chipotle chile in a blender until smooth; add pecan mixture and remaining stock to onion mixture. Bring to a simmer, stirring often. Add maple syrup, Worcestershire, salt, and pepper, and cook 5 minutes. Reduce heat, and add cream, stirring to blend. Dollop each serving with Crème Fraîche (see index) and chopped chives, or pecan halves, or chipotle chile strips, if desired.

Makes 6 to 8 servings.

Garlic Soup

2	tablespoons olive oil	½	loaf stale French bread, in chunks
2	tablespoons butter	1	Bouquet Garni
2	pounds onions, coarsely chopped	2	cups half-and-half
1	cup chopped garlic		Salt and pepper to taste
6	cups chicken stock		Garnish: chopped green onions

Heat oil and butter in a large stockpot over medium heat; add onion and garlic, and sauté until a deep gold, about 30 minutes Add stock, bread chunks, and Bouquet Garni, and simmer 15 to 20 minutes. Remove garni, and process soup mixture in a blender until smooth Heat half-and-half in a small saucepan; add to soup with salt and pepper to taste. Serve immediately, or keep chilled 1 day to let flavors mellow. Garnish, if desired.

Makes 6 to 8 servings.

If you like garlic, you will love this. Even if you aren't crazy about garlic, you will only wonder what wonderful elixir is before you.

Make Bouquet Garni by tying together with cotton kitchen string: 10 sprigs fresh parsley, 5 sprigs fresh thyme, 1 bay leaf.

Gazpacho Blanco

3	cucumbers, peeled and seeded	1	green onion, white and green parts minced
2	celery hearts with stalks, leaves and all, chopped	1	garlic clove, minced
2	green bell peppers, halved and seeded	2	cups plain yogurt
2	tablespoons white wine vinegar	2	cups chicken stock
½	tablespoon salt		Garnish: chopped green onions, drizzle of extra virgin olive oil
2	dashes Tabasco		

Process first 6 ingredients in a food processor until smooth; stir in minced green onion and garlic, then yogurt. Add stock, and chill soup thoroughly. Garnish, if desired, or top with avocado chunks, fresh garlic croutons, or finely chopped tomato.

Makes 6 servings.

Buttermilk may be substituted for yogurt.

Lime-Chicken Soup

1	chicken breast	½	teaspoon dried oregano
5	cups cold water	½	teaspoon ground cumin
1	(28-ounce) can stewed tomatoes	1	bay leaf
½	onion, coarsely chopped	1	cup brown rice, cooked
2	garlic cloves, minced		Salt and pepper to taste
	Juice of 6 limes (1 cup)		

Place chicken in cold water in a large saucepan; slowly bring to a boil, skimming foam from top. Simmer until chicken is done, about 40 minutes. Remove chicken from broth, reserving broth. Shred chicken. Pour broth through a fine wire-mesh strainer into a clean stockpot; add tomatoes and next 6 ingredients. Bring mixture to a boil; reduce heat, and simmer 30 minutes. Add shredded chicken, brown rice, and salt and pepper to taste. Remove and discard bay leaf.

Makes 6 to 8 servings.

New Year's Stew

1	cup dried garbanzos	1	bay leaf
7	cups water	¼	cup rice
3¼	pounds turkey legs		Salt to taste
1	(28-ounce) can plum tomatoes, quartered, with liquid		Vegetable oil
		6	corn tortillas, cut into strips
2	onions, chopped	2	cups shredded Monterey Jack cheese
2	jalapeños, minced		
¼	cup chile powder	2	avocados, peeled, seeded, and sliced
1½	teaspoons dried oregano, crumbled		
1½	teaspoons coarsely ground pepper	2	tablespoons minced fresh parsley

Bring garbanzos and 7 cups water to a boil in a large stockpot; boil 2 minutes. Remove from heat, cover, and let stand 1 hour. Add turkey and next 7 ingredients to garbanzos; stir well. Cover and simmer until turkey is tender, about 1 hour and 15 minutes. Remove turkey from mixture. Simmer garbanzo mixture, uncovered, 40 minutes. Stir in rice, and simmer until garbanzos and rice are tender, about 20 minutes. Remove skin from turkey, and discard. Remove meat from bone, and cut into bite-size pieces; stir into stew. Season with salt. Heat oil in a large, heavy skillet; cut tortillas strips in half, and add to oil. Fry until golden brown on all sides. Drain on paper towels. Serve stew with tortilla strips, cheese, avocado, and parsley.

Makes 8 servings.

Smoky Bear Soup

3 tablespoons vegetable oil
1 cup chopped onion
3 garlic cloves, chopped
¼ pound garlic-flavored smoked pork sausage
5 cups beef stock

1 (16-ounce) can kidney beans, undrained
½ head cabbage, chopped
6 small new potatoes, quartered
2-4 tablespoons vinegar
1 cup tomato catsup
Salt and pepper to taste

Heat oil in a 3-quart saucepan over medium heat; add onion and garlic, and sauté until just translucent. Cut sausage into bite-size pieces, and add to onion mixture; cook until sausage is browned. Add stock and remaining ingredients; bring to a boil, stirring often. Reduce heat, and simmer, stirring occasionally, 35 to 45 minutes. Adjust salt and pepper.

Makes 6 to 8 servings.

Ranch Chicken Chowder

3 whole boneless chicken breasts, split and skinned (1¾ pounds)
3 tablespoons unsalted butter
1 medium-size onion, thinly sliced
1 large sweet potato, peeled and thinly sliced
4½-4¾ cups chicken stock

2 serrano chiles, seeded
½ teaspoon ground coriander
¼ teaspoon ground cumin
1 (16-ounce) can hominy, drained
⅔ cup fresh cilantro leaves
Garnish: sour cream

Cut chicken into ¾-inch cubes. Melt butter in a 5-quart saucepan; add chicken, and cook over high heat, stirring often, until no longer pink (do not overcook). Remove from pan with a slotted spoon, and set aside. Add onion and sweet potato to pan, along with 4½ cups stock. Cover and bring to a boil. Reduce heat, and simmer until vegetables are very soft, about 20 minutes. Pour through a wire-mesh strainer into a bowl, reserving broth. Process solids with serrano chiles, coriander, and cumin in a food processor until smooth. Return puree to pan with reserved broth, chicken, and hominy. To serve, cook soup just until heated through. Thin with remaining broth if too thick. Add cilantro, and adjust salt and pepper. Garnish, if desired.

Makes 7 cups.

Rio Grande Tomato-Basil Soup

3	tablespoons butter	1	tablespoon fresh thyme or
½	cup chopped yellow onion		1 teaspoon dried thyme
2	garlic cloves, minced	¼	cup chopped fresh basil or
3	tablespoons all-purpose flour		1 tablespoon dried basil
2	cups chicken broth	¼	teaspoon paprika
8	medium-size tomatoes, peeled, seeded, and chopped	1	bay leaf
3	sprigs parsley, chopped		Freshly ground black pepper to taste
1	teaspoon sugar		Light sour cream or plain nonfat yogurt
½	teaspoon salt		Garnish: basil leaf slivers

Melt butter in a large stockpot over medium heat; add onion and garlic, and sauté until tender, about 5 minutes. Stir in flour, blending thoroughly. Gradually add broth, stirring until bubbly and slightly thickened. Add tomato and next 8 ingredients; bring to a boil. Reduce heat, and simmer, covered, 30 minutes. Remove and discard bay leaf. Process mixture in a food processor until smooth. Top each serving with sour cream, and garnish, if desired.

Makes 4 cups.

To make basil slivers, stack 5 leaves on top of each other; roll up tightly lengthwise, and slice diagonally.

Sherried Tomato Soup

3	tablespoons butter	4	cups tomato juice
½	cup chopped onion	2	cups beef broth
½	cup coarsely shredded carrot	1½	cups dry sherry
¼	cup all-purpose flour	1	tablespoon chopped fresh parsley
1	teaspoon salt	1	tablespoon honey
⅛	teaspoon ground nutmeg		

Melt butter in a saucepan over medium heat; add onion and carrot, and sauté until tender but not browned. Stir in flour, salt, and nutmeg. Add tomato juice and broth, and cook, stirring constantly, until slightly thickened. Add sherry, parsley, and honey; simmer until vegetables are tender, 5 to 10 minutes.

Makes 6 servings.

Sierra Blanca Corn Chowder

2	bacon slices	½	teaspoon salt
¼	cup chopped onion	¼	teaspoon pepper
2	medium-size potatoes, cubed	2	cups chicken broth
2	cups fresh or frozen corn kernels, thawed	2	tablespoons all-purpose flour
½	cup chopped celery	2	cups milk

Cook bacon in a 3-quart saucepan until crisp; remove to paper towels to drain, reserving drippings in pan. Crumble bacon. Sauté onion in reserved drippings until soft but not browned; add potato, corn, celery, salt, pepper, and 1½ cups broth. Bring mixture to a boil. Reduce heat, cover, and simmer 15 to 20 minutes. Blend flour and remaining broth; add to soup mixture. Cook, stirring often, until thickened and bubbly. Reduce heat, and add milk; cook until heated through (do not boil). Serve topped with bacon.

Makes 4 to 6 servings.

Silky Two-Potato Soup

4	tablespoons unsalted butter	1	pound waxy potatoes, peeled and cut into 1-inch cubes
1	medium-size onion, coarsely chopped	½	teaspoon dried thyme
3	large mushrooms, coarsely chopped	1	bay leaf
½	cup tightly packed parsley leaves, chopped	1	tablespoon Worcestershire sauce
6	cups chicken stock or broth	1	cup whipping cream
1	pound sweet potatoes, peeled and cut into 1-inch cubes		Salt and freshly ground pepper to taste
			Garnish: chopped parsley or thinly sliced green onions

Melt butter in a medium-size saucepan over medium heat; add onion, mushrooms, and parsley, and sauté until soft but not browned. Add stock and next 5 ingredients; bring to a boil. Reduce heat, and simmer until potatoes are tender, 10 to 15 minutes. Process soup in a food processor until smooth; add cream, and season with salt and pepper to taste. Return to pan, and heat until nearly simmering. Garnish, if desired.

Makes 8 servings.

Pumpkin Soup

2	tablespoons butter	1	teaspoon salt
1	yellow onion, finely chopped	½	teaspoon dried ginger
2	tablespoons all-purpose flour	¼	teaspoon ground nutmeg
1	(2-pound) can pumpkin	2	egg yolks
5	cups chicken stock or broth	1	cup whipping cream
¼	cup vermouth		

Melt butter in a skillet over medium heat; add onion, and sauté until soft, 3 minutes. Stir in flour; add pumpkin, mashing into a puree. Add broth, vermouth, and salt; cover and simmer 15 minutes. Add ginger and nutmeg. Combine yolks and cream, and stir into soup. Heat just until hot. Serve immediately.

Makes 6 servings.

Spicy Vegetable Chile

¼	cup bulgur	2	red bell peppers, seeded and chopped
2½	cups (or more) boiling water	2	zucchini, chopped
¼	cup olive oil	1½	cups canned chopped tomatoes
2	small onions, chopped	½	cup well-drained canned garbanzos
½	cup chopped celery	½	cup well-drained canned kidney beans
½	cup chopped carrot	2	tablespoons chopped fresh basil or 2 teaspoons dried basil
1½	tablespoons minced garlic		
2	tablespoons tomato paste	1	tablespoon chopped fresh oregano or 1 teaspoon dried oregano
2	tablespoons chile powder		
1½	tablespoons ground cumin		Salt and pepper to taste
¼	teaspoon cayenne pepper		
¾	cup dry white wine		

Place bulgur in a medium-size bowl; pour ½ cup boiling water over bulgur. Cover and let stand until softened, about 15 minutes. Heat oil in a large, heavy saucepan; add onion, celery, carrot, and garlic, and sauté until tender. Add tomato paste, chile powder, cumin, and cayenne to onion mixture, stirring until spices are fragrant. Add wine and remaining 2 cups boiling water to mixture; bring to a boil. Add bell pepper, zucchini, and tomatoes; reduce heat, and simmer, stirring often, until all vegetables are tender. Add bulgur, garbanzos, kidney beans, basil, and oregano; simmer, stirring often, until thick. Season with salt and pepper to taste.

Makes 4 servings.

Sonoran Chile Verde

1	boneless pork shoulder roast (3 to 4 pounds)	1	teaspoon garlic powder
2	large onions, cut into large chunks	½	teaspoon pepper
2	(28-ounce) cans peeled whole tomatoes, drained	1	(28-ounce) can whole mild green chiles, cut into strips
1	teaspoon salt	1	tablespoon freshly ground cumin seed, or to taste

Cut roast into 1-inch cubes. Brown with onion in a large stockpot or Dutch oven. (Add a little oil if roast is very lean.) Add tomatoes and next 3 ingredients; cover and simmer 1 hour. Add chile strips and cumin; cover and simmer 45 minutes. If too thin, uncover the last 15 minutes.

Makes 4 to 6 servings.

Serve with warm flour tortillas. Freezes well and tastes even better the next day. This stew is very thick; if you prefer it soupy, don't drain tomatoes.

Tomato-Lentil Soup

4	tablespoons unsalted butter	1	cup chopped fresh parsley
2	cups chopped onion	½	cup dry red wine
2	cups chopped celery	4	garlic cloves, finely minced
2	(35-ounce) cans Italian-style plum tomatoes, undrained	½	teaspoon salt
6	cups chicken stock	½	teaspoon freshly ground pepper
½	cup dried lentils	¼	teaspoon ground cloves

Melt butter in a large stockpot over low heat; add onion and celery, and sauté until vegetables are wilted, about 10 minutes. Process tomatoes and their liquid in a food processor until pureed; add to onion mixture. Add stock and lentils to pot, and bring to a boil. Reduce heat, and simmer, uncovered, stirring occasionally, 20 minutes. Add ½ cup parsley, along with wine, garlic, pepper, salt, and cloves. Stir well, and simmer 25 minutes. Add remaining parsley, and simmer 5 minutes. Serve immediately.

Makes 8 servings.

————— Tortellini Soup —————

2 tablespoons butter
2-3 garlic cloves, minced
1 onion, chopped
8 ounces fresh mushrooms, sliced
7 cups chicken broth
1½ cups tomato-vegetable juice
1 (28-ounce) can tomatoes, un-drained
3 carrots, sliced

1 medium-size zucchini, finely chopped
2 teaspoons crushed basil
1½ teaspoons dried oregano
1 teaspoon dried marjoram
½ teaspoon dried thyme
1 (6-ounce) package fresh cheese-filled tortellini
Salt and pepper to taste
Freshly grated Parmesan cheese

Melt butter in a large stockpot over medium heat; add garlic, onion, and mushrooms, and sauté until tender. Add broth and next 8 ingredients; simmer until vegetables are tender. Add tortellini just before serving, and simmer 10 minutes. Add salt and pepper to taste, and sprinkle each serving with Parmesan. Serve with French bread.

Makes 6 to 8 servings.

For a variation, add chopped cooked chicken.

If using dried tortellini, cook according to package directions before adding to soup.

————— Zia Tortilla Soup —————

12 small corn tortillas or
   6 to 8 flour tortillas
   Vegetable oil for frying
1 tablespoon vegetable oil
1 large onion, chopped
2 garlic cloves, minced

6 cups chicken stock or broth
1 (14-ounce) can diced tomatoes
⅛ teaspoon Tabasco
3 cups shredded Cheddar or Monterey Jack cheese

Cut tortillas into strips. Heat oil in a heavy skillet, and fry strips until golden. Drain on paper towels. Heat 1 tablespoon oil in a large saucepan; add onion, and sauté until limp. Add garlic to onion, and sauté 30 seconds; add stock, tomatoes, and pepper sauce. Simmer, covered, 30 minutes. Add half of tortilla strips, and simmer until heated through. Serve topped with remaining strips and cheese.

Makes 6 to 8 servings.

Bottomless Lakes Tuna Salad Sandwiches

1   (6-ounce) can solid white tuna in water, drained and flaked
¼   cup sliced (¼-inch crosswise) fresh green beans, blanched
¼   cup chopped black olives
2   tablespoons chopped purple onion
2   tablespoons chopped fresh chives
2   teaspoons drained tiny capers

¼   cup mayonnaise
    Freshly ground pepper to taste
8   (½-inch-thick) slices peasant or sourdough bread, toasted
2   tablespoons extra virgin olive oil
2   red bell peppers, halved, cored, seeded and roasted

Combine tuna, beans, olives, onion, 1 tablespoon chives, capers, mayonnaise, and pepper in a bowl. Set aside. Brush 1 side of each toast slice with oil; lay a roasted bell pepper half on oiled side of 4 toast slices. Cover evenly with tuna mixture; sprinkle evenly with remaining chives. Top each with a toast slice, oiled side down. Cut sandwiches in half, and serve immediately.

Makes 4 servings.

To roast bell pepper:
Halve, core and seed peppers, flatten each half slightly. Lay skin side up on a baking sheet. Broil until skins are charred black. Seal in plastic bags 15 minutes to loosen skins. Remove from bags, and peel off skins.

Baked Quesadillas

4   flour tortillas
1   cup refried beans
1   cup diced, cooked potato
1   cup cooked beef (or wild game)
2   eggs, scrambled

1   cup red chile sauce (see index)
1   cup shredded Cheddar cheese
4   tablespoons sour cream
1   jalapeño, thinly sliced

Preheat oven to 350°. Place a tortilla on each of 4 ovenproof plates; spread each with refried beans. Layer potato, beef, eggs, chile sauce, and cheese over beans. Bake for 6 to 8 minutes or until cheese is melted and quesadilla is hot. Top each with sour cream and sliced jalapeño.

Makes 4 servings.

Garden Sandwich

1 loaf French bread, halved horizontally
1 garlic clove, halved
  Dressing
2 tomatoes, thinly sliced
1 tablespoon minced green onions
  Salt and pepper to taste

12 black olives, sliced
⅔ cup slivered green beans
½ cup slivered green bell pepper
½ cup sliced fresh mushrooms
½ cup thinly sliced zucchini
2 tablespoons minced fresh parsley

Rub cut sides of bread with garlic; drizzle half of Dressing over bottom half of bread. Cover bottom half with tomato, and sprinkle with green onions, salt, and pepper. Layer olives, green beans, bell pepper, mushrooms, and zucchini over green onions. Sprinkle with parsley, and drizzle with remaining Dressing. Cover with top half of bread. Tie loaf at intervals with kitchen string, and wrap tightly in foil. Weight sandwich with a heavy board or in refrigerator pan at least 2 hours. Unwrap and remove strings. Slice into 3-inch pieces.

Makes 6 servings.

Fresh basil can be used in place of parsley and gives a different and refreshing flavor. Experiment with other fresh vegetables or even beans. Can be made 1 day ahead.

Dressing

¼ tablespoon red wine vinegar
¼ teaspoon Dijon mustard
¼ teaspoon pepper

¼ teaspoon salt
¼ cup olive oil

Whisk together first 4 ingredients in a bowl; add oil in a slow, steady stream, whisking to blend.

Cap Rock Chicken Sandwich

2   (6-ounce) jars artichoke hearts, drained
1   onion, sliced
2   tablespoons chopped fresh basil
½   cup drained roasted red peppers in oil, sliced
2   tablespoons oil from peppers
7   ounces fresh asparagus spears, trimmed

4   boneless, skinless chicken breast halves
4   tablespoons butter
1   tablespoon olive oil
    Pepper to taste
8   (½-inch-thick) slices rye bread
1   bunch arugula, washed and stemmed
    Dijon Mayonnaise

Combine first 5 ingredients in a bowl, tossing well. Boil, steam, or microwave asparagus until just tender; drain well. Pound chicken between sheets of heavy-duty plastic wrap with a meat mallet until thin; cut in half crosswise. Heat 2 tablespoons butter and oil in a large skillet over high heat; add chicken, sprinkling with pepper, and cook until chicken is tender. Spread bread slices with remaining 2 tablespoons butter; top half of slices with arugula, half of chicken, asparagus, artichoke mixture, and Dijon Mayonnaise. Top with remaining half of chicken mixture and bread slices. Serve warm.

Makes 4 servings.

Dijon Mayonnaise
⅓   cup mayonnaise
1   tablespoon Dijon mustard

¼   teaspoon Tabasco
    Salt and pepper to taste

Combine ingredients in a bowl, blending well.

Mexican Chicken Burger

2	tablespoons vegetable oil	1	(6½-ounce) package corn chips
2	onions, sliced	½	head romaine lettuce, shredded
½	teaspoon ground cumin	1	cup chunky salsa (see index)
1	large avocado	⅓	cup sour cream
2	teaspoons lime juice		Fresh cilantro sprigs
	Salt and pepper to taste	⅓	cup chile sauce
1	(15-ounce) can refried beans		

Burgers

1½	pounds ground chicken	2	garlic cloves, crushed
1	tablespoon chopped fresh cilantro	6	green onions, chopped
1	tablespoon ground cumin	2½	cups stale breadcrumbs
1	teaspoon salt	1	egg, slightly beaten
¼	teaspoon chile powder	2	tablespoons vegetable oil

Heat 2 tablespoons oil in a large, heavy skillet over medium heat; add onion, and sauté until soft. Add cumin, and sauté until fragrant. Mash avocado with lime juice and salt and pepper to taste; keep tightly covered. Heat beans in a saucepan or microwave. For burgers, combine chicken and next 6 ingredients; add 1½ cups breadcrumbs and egg. Stir well. Shape chicken mixture into 4 large, flat patties, about 1 inch thick. Press remaining breadcrumbs onto patties, and chill 1 hour. Heat 2 tablespoons oil in a large skillet over medium-low heat; cook patties until well browned and cooked through. Arrange corn chips around edge of plates, and pile lettuce in center. Top lettuce with a burger, some of beans, onion mixture, salsa, avocado, sour cream, and cilantro. Drizzle with chile sauce. Recipe can be made a day ahead and reheated before assembly. Uncooked patties may be frozen.

Makes 4 servings.

New Mexican Egg Salad

12 hard-cooked eggs, peeled and chopped
4   celery ribs, chopped
5   green onions, white part and 2 inches green, sliced
2   jalapeños, minced
1   red bell pepper, diced
1   garlic clove, minced
1½ cups shredded Cheddar cheese

1   cup mayonnaise (or as needed)
    Juice of 1 lime
1   tablespoon ground cumin
1   tablespoon chile powder
    Salt and freshly ground pepper to taste
    Garnish: chopped fresh cilantro, avocado slices sprinkled with lime

Combine first 7 ingredients in a large bowl, stirring well. Blend mayonnaise and next 3 ingredients in a small bowl; gently fold mayonnaise mixture into egg mixture, adding more mayonnaise if dry. Season with salt and pepper to taste. Transfer to a serving bowl, and chill several hours to blend flavors. Garnish, if desired.

Makes 10 to 12 servings.

Basic Quesadillas

4   large flour tortillas
2   cups shredded Monterey Jack cheese

    Vegetable oil
    Fresh Salsa (see index)

Lay tortillas on a flat surface, and sprinkle each with ½ cup cheese. Fold over into semicircles. Brush a nonstick skillet with oil, and place over medium-high heat. Cook 1 quesadilla at a time until lightly browned and cheese is melted, about 2 minutes per side. Cut quesadillas into quarters, and serve with salsa.

Makes 4 servings.

Quesadillas can be stuffed with a variety of fillings, such as chopped cooked chicken, refried beans, sautéed green or red bell pepper, green chiles, sautéed onion, chopped green onions, chopped tomato, or sliced black olives. Any combination will taste good with cheese.

Olga's Cornish Pasty

2 cups all-purpose flour
½ teaspoon salt
2 ounces lard
2 ounces butter
½ pound beef sirloin or top round
steak, excess fat removed

Potatoes (or rutabagas)
Onions
Salt and pepper to taste
3 tablespoons butter

Preheat oven to 400°. Combine flour and salt in a large bowl; cut in lard with a pastry blender until texture of coarse meal. Add just enough ice water to hold dough together. Divide dough into 5 or 6 mounds. Wrap each separately in plastic wrap, and chill. When ready to use, roll each piece to about the size of a salad plate. Cut beef into ½-inch cubes. Cut potatoes and onions into thin slices, and season with salt and pepper to taste. Place potato and onion on 1 half of each dough round, leaving a border. Top with meat. Add a small pat of butter in center, topped by another layer of potato. Fold pasty over to cover filling; crimp edges with a fork dipped in milk. Prick top of pasty several times with fork. Bake on lightly floured baking sheets for 15 minutes; reduce temperature to 350°, and bake 30 minutes.

Makes 5 or 6 servings.

Pasties
Pasties are a traditional midday meal for Cornish miners. (The Cornish are Celtic people from southwest Britain.) Those who could not afford meat depended on additional potatoes or rutabagas. When the ancient mines closed in the mid 19th Century due to world competition, the Cornish emigrated to developing mining areas, especially in Australia and North America, including the copper mines of Arizona, Nevada, New Mexico, and Montana, bringing their pasties with them.

Onion Squares

3	cups all-purpose flour	3	tablespoons unsalted butter
2	tablespoons baking powder	3	cups coarsely chopped onion
1	teaspoon salt		Salt and pepper to taste
⅔	cup shortening	2	cups shredded Cheddar cheese
2	cups milk	1	cup sour cream

Preheat oven to 350°. Sift together first 3 ingredients; cut in shortening until texture of coarse meal. Add milk, and stir to create a soft dough. Turn dough out into a heavily floured sheet cake pan or baking sheet with sides; pat out until ½ inch thick. Melt butter in a heavy skillet until frothy; add onion, and sauté until golden. Add salt and pepper to taste to onion, then spread mixture over dough. Sprinkle cheese over top, and bake for 12 to 14 minutes or until dough is done and cheese is melted. Cut into squares, and serve immediately with sour cream.

Makes 6 servings.

Onion Squares can be served as a first course, followed by a light main dish. As lunch, they are wonderful with a tartly dressed salad and fruit for dessert. They can also be cut into much smaller pieces and served with a dab of sour cream as an appetizer.

Permian Basin Steak Sandwich

¼ cup plus 1 tablespoon olive oil
2 garlic cloves, minced
2 teaspoons dried oregano
2 teaspoons ground cumin
1 (2-pound) flank steak
  Salt and pepper to taste
2 firm but ripe avocados, peeled and chopped

1 (16-ounce) container thick, chunky salsa, well drained
1 (10- to 12-inch) round loaf sourdough bread
2 (7-ounce) jars roasted red bell peppers, drained and thinly sliced
7 ounces thinly sliced Monterey Jack or provolone cheese

Prepare grill (medium-high heat), or preheat broiler. Combine ¼ cup oil and next 3 ingredients in a small bowl. Rub mixture over both sides of steak. Sprinkle with salt and pepper to taste. Grill or broil steak to desired doneness, about 5 minutes per side for medium-rare. Transfer steak to work surface to cool. Cut steak across grain into thin strips. Toss avocado with salsa in a medium-size bowl; season avocado salsa with salt and pepper. Split bread loaf in half horizontally; scoop out center from each half, leaving 1-inch-thick shells. Brush cut surfaces of bread with remaining oil. Arrange steak in 1 bread shell, and top with bell pepper slices. Arrange cheese over peppers, and top with avocado mixture. Top with remaining bread shell. Wrap sandwich in foil, and chill at least 4 hours, or up to 8 hours. Cut into wedges.

Makes 6 servings.

Sunrise Breakfast Sandwiches

12 bacon slices, cooked until crisp
¼ cup chopped green onions
5 hard-cooked eggs, chopped
1 cup shredded Swiss cheese
⅓ cup mayonnaise

1 tablespoon Dijon mustard
  Salt and pepper to taste
  Butter
12 bread slices

Crumble bacon into a bowl; add green onions and next 5 ingredients. Butter bread for grilling. Divide bacon mixture evenly among 6 bread slices; top with remaining slices. Melt butter in a large skillet over medium-low heat; grill sandwiches, 1 at a time, until bread is golden, 4 to 5 minutes per side.

Makes 6 servings.

_____Southwest Shredded Beef Sandwiches_____

1   **3-3½ pound boneless chuck roast**
1   **(7-ounce) can diced green chiles**
4   **tablespoons ground cumin**
2   **tablespoons chile powder**
    Salt and pepper to taste
1   **tablespoon vegetable oil**
1   **cup chopped yellow onion**
1   **(10-ounce) can diced tomatoes and green chiles**

2   **(14½-ounce) cans stewed tomatoes**
1   **cup minced pickled jalapeño slices**
¼   **cup chopped fresh cilantro**
1   **teaspoon salt**
12 **onion buns, split**
    Shredded lettuce
    Shredded cheese

Preheat oven to 325°. Place roast on a sheet of heavy-duty foil. Combine green chiles, 2 tablespoons cumin, chile powder, salt, and pepper; spread mixture over roast, and wrap in foil, sealing well. Place roast in a roasting pan. Bake roast for 3½ to 4 hours or until meat is so tender it falls apart. Lift meat from drippings in foil, and allow to cool until ready to handle. Pour drippings into a small container, and skim off fat. Shred cooled roast into small strips with a fork. Set aside. Heat oil in a skillet over medium heat; add onion, and sauté until soft. Add reserved meat juices, shredded meat, diced tomatoes with chiles, stewed tomatoes, jalapeño slices, cilantro, remaining 2 tablespoons cumin, and salt. Mixture will be soupy. Simmer meat mixture gently, uncovered, over medium heat until thickened but saucy, about 30 minutes. Filling can be made ahead of time and chilled or frozen. When ready to use, thoroughly reheat by bringing it to a boil and simmering 5 minutes. Sprinkle buns evenly with some cheese, hot meat filling, more cheese, and lettuce.

Makes 12 servings.

Tangy Grilled Mushroom-Mustard Sandwiches

1	tablespoon olive oil	2	teaspoons chopped flat-leaf parsley
½	medium-size purple onion, sliced	4	sourdough bread slices or cracked wheat bread
½	teaspoon salt		
¼	teaspoon freshly ground pepper	4	teaspoons Dijon mustard
8	ounces fresh mushrooms, sliced (3 cups)	1	cup shredded Fontina cheese
			Unsalted butter, softened or melted

Heat ½ tablespoon oil in a medium-size skillet over medium heat; add onion, ¼ teaspoon salt, and ⅛ teaspoon pepper. Sauté onion until soft, about 5 minutes. Transfer to a bowl. Heat remaining oil in pan over high heat, and add mushrooms, ¼ teaspoon salt, and ⅛ teaspoon pepper; sear mushrooms until golden and a little crisp on edges. Add a little water to pan as mushrooms cook to loosen pan juices. Add mushroom mixture to onion mixture with parsley; toss to blend. Place bread on a work surface, and spread mustard on each slice. Pile vegetable mixture on 2 slices; press mixture into bread with palm of your hand. Sprinkle with cheese. Press remaining bread on top, and brush with butter. Heat a skillet over medium heat; add sandwiches, buttered side down, and brush tops with butter. Cook until golden, 4 to 5 minutes per side. Serve hot.

Makes 2 servings.

Desserts

Pecans

The pecan tree is not considered native to New Mexico, but some seedling-type pecan nuts were growing in the southern part of the state in the late 1800s or early 1900s. The Spanish explorer Cabeza de Vaca reported in his travels in Mexico that Indians subsisted entirely on this member of the nut family for two months at a time, when no other food was available.

Although pecans have been produced in New Mexico since 1920, economic conditions in the consumer market prevented commercial production until the 1960s. The first pecan orchard, of 720 acres, was planted in Roswell in 1960. Today, Chaves County has 100,000 pecan trees planted on 2500 acres, with the average annual production totaling 2.7 million pounds of harvested pecans.

Pecan trees are carefully pruned each year; the new branches bear the pecans. Although they must be watered regularly, pecan trees thrive in New Mexico's sunny, dry climate and provide welcome shade and shelter for native birds.

The oil found in pecans may be as beneficial to cardiovascular health as olive oil. In addition, pecans contain phytochemicals which may help fight some forms of cancer. The nuts also provide a lot more than crunch with an abundance of vitamins, minerals, and anti-oxidants.

When Alabama's pecan crop was completely destroyed by a hurricane, trucks were sent from there across the country to buy New Mexico pecans.

Featured on page 265 "Roswell Pecan Orchards"

Bourbon Cake

2½ cups cake flour
¾ teaspoon baking powder
½ teaspoon salt
1 cup butter, softened
1½ cups sugar

4 egg yolks, room temperature
1 large egg, room temperature
Juice and zest of 1 lemon
¾ cup sour cream
Garnish: fresh flowers

Syrup
¼ cup sugar

1½ ounces bourbon

Frosting
2 cups whipping cream

3 tablespoons sugar

Preheat oven to 350°. Butter and flour 2 (9-inch) round springform pans. Sift together first 3 ingredients into a large bowl. Beat butter and 1½ cups sugar at medium speed with an electric mixer until fluffy. Add egg yolks, 1 at a time, to butter mixture, followed by whole egg, beating until blended after each addition. Add flour mixture gradually, beating until blended. Fold lemon juice, zest, and sour cream into batter. Divide batter evenly into cake pans. Bake for 35 to 40 minutes or until a wooden pick inserted in center of layers comes out clean. Cool layers in pans 10 minutes; remove from pans, and cool completely on wire racks. For syrup, heat ¼ cup sugar and bourbon in a small saucepan over low heat, stirring until well blended. Cut each cake layer in half horizontally, and brush tops of layers with syrup. For frosting, beat cream at high speed with electric mixer until stiff peaks form, gradually adding 3 tablespoons sugar during beating. Spread first cake layer with whipped cream frosting; top with a cake layer. Repeat procedure with remaining layers and frosting. Garnish, if desired.

Makes 10 servings.

Chocolate Cheesecake

24 chocolate wafers, finely crushed	1½ pounds cream cheese, softened
¼ cup butter, melted	2 teaspoons cocoa
¼ teaspoon ground cinnamon	1 teaspoon vanilla extract
8 ounces semisweet chocolate squares or 1½ cups semisweet chocolate morsels	1½ cups sour cream
	1 cup sugar
	2 eggs

Preheat oven to 350°. Combine first 3 ingredients, and press over bottom of an 8-inch springform pan. Chill. Melt chocolate in top of a double boiler over hot water (not boiling). Beat cream cheese at medium speed with an electric mixer until fluffy; beat in melted chocolate, cocoa, vanilla, and sour cream. Beat in sugar. Beat in eggs, 1 at a time, until blended. Pour batter into crumb crust, and bake for 45 minutes. Cool cake at room temperature 1 hour, then chill at least 5 hours. (Cake will be soft at first, but will firm as it chills.) Cake freezes well.

Makes 16 servings.

New Mexico Chewies

1 pound dark brown sugar	¼ teaspoon salt
½ cup butter	1 teaspoon vanilla extract
3 eggs	1 cup pecans, chopped
1½ cups all-purpose flour, sifted	Powdered sugar
1½ teaspoons baking powder	

Preheat oven to 350°. Beat sugar and butter at medium speed with an electric mixer until fluffy. Add eggs, 1 at a time, beating until blended after each addition. Beat in flour, baking powder, and salt. Fold in vanilla and pecans, and blend well. Pour batter into a greased 13- x 7-inch pan. Bake for 30 minutes; sprinkle with powdered sugar, and cut into squares.

Makes 2½ dozen.

Chocolate Truffle Cake

5 ounces semisweet chocolate
   squares, chopped
6 tablespoons unsalted butter
2 tablespoons brewed coffee
2 tablespoons water
½ cup sugar
3 egg yolks

2 tablespoons all-purpose flour
½ teaspoon vanilla extract
5 egg whites
¼ teaspoon cream of tartar
⅛ teaspoon salt
   Raspberry Sauce

Preheat oven to 325°. Butter a 9- x 5-inch loaf pan, and line with foil or parchment paper. Combine first 4 ingredients in top of a double boiler over barely simmering water. Cook until chocolate and butter are melted; remove from heat. Whisk ¼ cup sugar into egg yolks; add to chocolate mixture. Whisk in flour and vanilla. Beat egg whites, cream of tartar, and salt at high speed with an electric mixer until soft peaks form. Sprinkle remaining sugar into egg white mixture, beating until shiny, stiff peaks form. Fold egg white mixture into chocolate mixture just until blended. Pour batter into loaf pan. Place loaf pan into a shallow baking dish, and add enough water to come halfway up sides of loaf pan. Bake for 1½ to 1¾ hours or until a wooden pick inserted in center comes out clean. Cool in pan. Turn cake out gently onto a plate. Use a heated knife for easy slicing. Serve with Raspberry Sauce.

Makes 4 to 6 servings.

Raspberry Sauce

½ cup water
½ cup sugar
4 cups fresh raspberries or unsweetened frozen raspberries, thawed

   Juice of 1 lemon
2 tablespoons framboise, kirsch, or
   Chambord

Bring water and sugar to a boil in a small saucepan; cook until sugar dissolves. Set aside to cool. Process raspberries in a food processor until pureed; pour through a fine wire-mesh strainer, discarding seeds. Pour cooled syrup into puree gradually to taste, depending on sweetness of berries. Add lemon juice and liqueur, if needed.

Makes 1½ cups.

Fruited Carrot Cake

½   cup chopped dried apricot
½   cup chopped dried peach
½   cup chopped dried Calimyrna figs
3   tablespoons bourbon
1¾ cups sifted all-purpose flour
2   teaspoons baking powder
1   teaspoon ground cinnamon
½   teaspoon salt
¼   teaspoon ground nutmeg
¼   teaspoon ground allspice

¾   cup pecans, toasted
3   large eggs
1½ cups sugar
1   cup unsalted butter, cut into
    8 pieces, room temperature
2   teaspoons vanilla extract
2   large carrots, peeled and cut into
    fourths
1   tablespoon powdered sugar

Preheat oven to 325°. Combine first 4 ingredients in a medium-size bowl; let stand 2 hours, stirring occasionally. (Or microwave, uncovered, in a 4-cup bowl on HIGH until fruit is plumped, about 20 seconds. Stir well.) Process flour and next 5 ingredients in a food processor about 5 seconds. Add pecans to flour mixture, and pulse until pecans are chopped. Transfer mixture to a sheet of wax paper. Process eggs and 1½ cups sugar in processor until thick and light, about 1 minute. Add butter and vanilla; process until fluffy, about 1 minute. Transfer egg mixture to a large bowl. Process carrots in processor until shredded; add shredded carrot to fruit mixture. Add ¼ cup flour mixture to carrot mixture, and toss to coat, separated fruit pieces. Stir fruit mixture gently into egg mixture. Fold in remaining flour mixture. Pour batter into a greased and floured 12-cup Bundt pan. Bake cake on middle oven rack for 50 minutes or until a wooden pick inserted in center comes out clean. Cool cake in pan on a wire rack 10 minutes. Turn cake out onto rack, and cool completely. Sift 1 tablespoon powdered sugar over cake, and serve. (Can be prepared 2 days ahead, wrapped in plastic wrap, and stored at room temperature.)

Makes 12 servings.

Jolt Cake

2 cups unsalted butter
1 cup brewed espresso
1 cup plus 2 tablespoons sugar
¼ teaspoon freshly grated orange zest
¼ teaspoon orange extract
2 tablespoons Grand Marnier

12 ounces semisweet chocolate squares, chopped
4 ounces unsweetened chocolate squares, chopped
8 large eggs, lightly beaten
Crème Anglaise

Preheat oven to 350°. Melt butter in a small saucepan over medium heat; stir in espresso and next 4 ingredients. Transfer butter mixture to a large bowl. Melt chocolates in top of a double boiler over barely simmering water, stirring occasionally. Stir melted chocolate into butter mixture, and add eggs, stirring until mixture is just combined. Line bottom of a buttered 9-inch cake pan with parchment paper. Butter paper. Spoon batter into pan; place pan in a baking dish, and add enough water to come halfway up cake pan. Bake cake on middle oven rack for 1 hour; remove from water bath, and cool on a wire rack. Cover loosely, and chill at least 3 hours. Run a thin knife around edge of cake, and dip bottom of pan in hot water 3 seconds. Invert a platter over cake, and invert cake onto platter with a sharp rap. Cut with a sharp knife dipped in hot water, cleaning knife after each slice. To serve, cover dessert plates with Crème Anglaise or chocolate sauce, and top with cake slices.

Makes 8 servings.

Crème Anglaise
6 egg yolks
3 tablespoons sugar

2 cups half-and-half, scalded
1 teaspoon vanilla extract

Beat egg yolks with sugar at medium speed with an electric mixer until mixture is light and falls in a ribbon from beaters. Add half-and-half in a stream, stirring constantly. Transfer mixture to a heavy saucepan, and cook over medium-low heat, stirring constantly, until thickened but not boiling. Remove pan from heat, and stir in vanilla. Strain custard through a wire-mesh strainer into a bowl. Set into a larger bowl of ice and water; cool, stirring occasionally. Refrigerate until ready to use.

Makes 3 cups.

Ted Robertson

Ted Robertson studied art at Colorado State University, Bergman Art School in Denver, Colorado, and spent three years in the U.S. Army as an illustrator for the 101st Airborne Division. He has conducted workshops since the '70's, and has numerous awards to his credit including a recent Best of Show in a national exhibit. He is an elected full member of the Pastel Society of America in New York City; the American Portrait Society in Los Angeles and a member of the Pastel Society of the Southwest, in Dallas, Texas. Mr. Robertson is listed in *Who's Who in American Art, Who's Who in the West,* and *Who's Who in the World,* as well as other biographical publications. His work hangs in public and private collections throughout the country and abroad.

Mr. Robertson is represented by McMahon Fine Art Gallery, Ruidoso, NM.

Hondo Oasis
Artist – Ted Robertson
18″ × 24″
pastel
Private collection

Hondo Valley Apple Cake

½ cup butter	2 teaspoons ground cinnamon
2 cups sugar	1 teaspoon baking soda
2 eggs	4 cups chopped apple
2 cups sifted all-purpose flour	1 cup pecans, chopped
1 teaspoon ground nutmeg	1 cup dates, chopped
½ teaspoon salt	Rum Sauce or Date Frosting

Preheat oven to 325°. Beat butter and sugar at medium speed with an electric mixer; add eggs, 1 at a time, and beat until blended. Sift together flour and next 4 ingredients; add to butter mixture. Fold in apple, pecans, and dates. Pour batter into an oiled and floured 14- x 10-inch pan. Bake for 1 hour or until a wooden pick inserted in center comes out clean. Serve with Rum Sauce, or frost with Date Frosting.

Makes 12 servings.

Rum Sauce

½ teaspoon ground nutmeg	1 cup sugar
2 tablespoons all-purpose flour	2 tablespoons rum or 1 teaspoon
1 cup water	vanilla extract
1 tablespoon butter	

Combine nutmeg and flour in a small saucepan; gradually stir in water, then butter and sugar. Bring mixture to a boil; cook 1 to 3 minutes. Remove from heat, and add rum. Serve hot over cake slices.

Date Frosting

2 cups sugar	½ package chopped dates
1 cup milk	1 cup chopped nuts
¼ cup butter	1 teaspoon vanilla extract

Cook sugar and milk in a saucepan over medium-high heat until soft ball stage. Add butter, dates, nuts, and vanilla to sugar mixture, stirring until spreading consistency. Ice cooled cake. Frosting may be frozen.

Roswell Pecan Cake

½ teaspoon ground nutmeg	3 eggs
2 cups all-purpose flour	½ cup bourbon or brandy
2 pounds pecan halves	½ teaspoon baking soda
1 cup unsalted butter, softened	½ cup water
1¼ cups sugar	Bourbon Crème Anglaise

Preheat oven to 300°. Combine nutmeg and 1½ cups flour in a small bowl. Toss remaining ½ cup flour with pecans in another bowl. Beat butter and sugar at medium speed with an electric mixer until fluffy; beat in eggs, 1 at a time, until blended. Beat in bourbon until blended. Dissolve baking soda in water in a small bowl. Beat half of flour-nutmeg mixture into batter; stir in baking soda mixture. Beat in remaining flour-nutmeg mixture; fold in pecans. Spoon batter into a greased and floured 10-inch tube pan, gently shaking to remove air pockets. Bake for 1 hour or until a wooden pick inserted in center comes out clean. Do not overcook. Serve with Bourbon Crème Anglaise, bourbon whipped cream, or vanilla ice cream.

Makes 12 to 14 servings.

Bourbon Crème Anglaise

1½ cups half-and-half	6 tablespoons pure maple syrup
1 tablespoon brown sugar	6 tablespoons bourbon
6 egg yolks	

Heat half-and-half and sugar in a small saucepan over medium heat just until sugar dissolves; remove from heat. Whisk egg yolks in a mixing bowl; beat in one-third of cream mixture. Whisk egg yolks back into cream mixture. Cook over low heat, stirring constantly, until just thickened. Do not boil. Remove to a clean bowl, and stir in syrup and bourbon. Cool completely.

Makes about 2½ cups.

Sponge Cake with Blueberry Sauce

3 (1- x ½-inch) strips orange peel	1 cup all-purpose flour
1 cup sugar	1 teaspoon baking powder
4 large eggs, separated	Powdered sugar
½ cup orange juice	Hot Blueberry Sauce

Preheat oven to 325°. Process orange peel and sugar in a food processor until peel is finely chopped, about 1 minute. Add egg yolks to processor, and process 1 minute, scraping down bowl. Pour orange juice through food chute, and process 10 seconds. Add flour and baking powder, and pulse 3 times. Beat egg whites at high speed with an electric mixer until stiff but not dry. Fold sugar mixture into egg whites. Pour batter into a 10-inch tube pan with removable bottom. Bake on middle oven rack for 40 to 50 minutes or until cake springs back when touched. Invert cake in pan onto a wire rack, and cool completely before removing from pan. Before serving, sprinkle cake with powdered sugar, and top with blueberry sauce.

Makes 12 servings.

Hot Blueberry Sauce

2 cups fresh or frozen blueberries (if fresh, sorted and washed)	¾ teaspoon grated lemon peel
	½ cup water
½ cup sugar	1 teaspoon cornstarch, dissolved in
1½ tablespoons fresh lemon juice	2 tablespoons water

Bring first 5 ingredients to a boil in a saucepan over medium-high heat; cook until berries begin to burst. Add cornstarch mixture, and boil just until sauce is thickened and clear, about 2 minutes.

Crème Caramel (individual flans)

¾ cup sugar	2 cups half-and-half
3 large eggs	1½ teaspoons vanilla extract

Preheat oven to 325°. Set out 6 custard cups. Heat ½ cup sugar in a heavy skillet over high heat, stirring with a wooden spoon until melted and amber in color, about 3 minutes. Quickly pour out sugar, dividing among custard cups. Arrange cups in a baking pan. Whisk eggs with remaining ¼ cup sugar in a large bowl; whisk in half-and-half and vanilla. Pour mixture into prepared custard cups. Pour hot tap water into baking pan to come halfway up sides of cups. Bake for 50 minutes or until a knife inserted in center comes out clean. Remove cups from pan, and cool. Cover and chill. To serve, carefully run a knife around edges of custards, and invert onto dessert plates.

Makes 6 servings.

_____ Apricot-Pecan Bars _____

⅓ cup butter
1½ cups packed brown sugar
½ cup honey
3 eggs
1¾ cups all-purpose flour
1 teaspoon baking powder

1 teaspoon salt
½ teaspoon ground cloves
1 (6-ounce) package dried apricots, finely chopped
1 cup chopped pecans
Lemon glaze (see note)

Preheat oven to 350°. Beat first 3 ingredients at medium speed with an electric mixer until creamed. Beat in eggs, 1 at a time, until blended. Combine flour and next 3 ingredients; beat into butter mixture. Fold in chopped apricot and pecans. Spread batter into a greased and floured 15- x 10- x 2-inch baking dish. Bake for 30 minutes; cool 15 minutes, and brush with lemon glaze. Cut into bars immediately.

Makes 20 servings.

To make lemon glaze, stir together ¾ cup powdered sugar and 4 tablespoons lemon juice.

_____ Cavern Molasses Cookies _____

¾ cup evaporated milk
2¼ teaspoons vinegar
½ cup dark molasses
3 cups all-purpose flour
2 teaspoons baking soda
1 teaspoon salt

1 teaspoon ground cinnamon
1 teaspoon ground ginger
½ teaspoon ground cloves
⅔ cup butter, softened
1 cup sugar
1 egg

Preheat oven to 375°. Combine first 3 ingredients in a small bowl; set aside. Combine flour and next 5 ingredients in another bowl; set aside. Beat butter and sugar at medium speed with an electric mixer until fluffy; add egg, and beat until well blended. Add flour mixture to butter mixture alternately with milk mixture, beating until smooth after each addition. Drop dough by tablespoonfuls, 2 inches apart, onto greased baking sheets. Bake for 12 to 15 minutes or until edges are lightly browned.

Makes about 5 dozen.

These cookies can be iced with vanilla frosting and topped with a walnut half.

Biscochitos

1	pound lard	1	teaspoon salt
1	cup sugar	2	tablespoons anise seed
2	large eggs	1	cup orange juice
1	teaspoon vinegar	½	cup sugar
7	cups all-purpose flour	2	teaspoons ground cinnamon
3	teaspoons baking powder		

Preheat oven to 350°. Cream lard with an electric mixer; add 1 cup sugar, eggs, and vinegar, and beat until blended. Combine flour, baking powder, salt, and anise seed in a large bowl; stir in shortening mixture. Gradually stir in orange juice to keep dough moist and intact. Roll dough out on a floured surface, and cut into desired cookie shapes. Place cookies on greased baking sheets. Combine ½ cup sugar and cinnamon; sprinkle on cookies. Bake for 10 to 12 minutes or until edges are lightly browned.

Makes 5 dozen.

In 1989, the New Mexico state legislature made biscochitos the state cookie. New Mexico became the first state to adopt an official cookie, indicating the importance that the state places on food.

This shortbread-like cookie is served at special occasions in New Mexico, such as weddings, Baptisms, and Christmas.

Lard is usually used, because it imparts a flakiness and flavor that cannot be achieved with butter or margarine. Not only is there loss of flavor, but also a gain in cholesterol, because butter contains twice as much cholesterol as lard.

Anise seed was introduced in the early 1800's by Spanish priests who brought spices from Spain to New Mexico via Mexico's Chihuahua Trail. The seed has a licorice flavor and is used in both sweet and savory dishes.

Lemon Biscochitos

2½ cups all-purpose flour
1 teaspoon baking powder
1½ cups plus 1 tablespoon sugar
1 cup unsalted butter, room temperature

2 large eggs
2 teaspoons fresh lemon juice
1½ teaspoons anise seed, crushed
½ teaspoon grated lemon peel
1 tablespoon ground cinnamon

Preheat oven to 350°. Sift together flour and baking powder into a medium-size bowl. Beat 1½ cups sugar and butter at medium speed with an electric mixer until fluffy; beat in eggs, 1 at a time. Beat in lemon juice, anise seed, and lemon peel. Stir flour mixture into butter mixture. Gather dough into a ball, and flatten into a disk. Wrap in plastic wrap, and chill until firm, about 2 hours. Combine cinnamon and remaining 1 tablespoon sugar in a small bowl. Roll out dough to ⅛-inch thickness on a floured surface. Cut into desired cookie shapes. Sprinkle cinnamon mixture over cookies. Bake on 2 large buttered baking sheets for 12 minutes or until golden. Transfer cookies to wire racks to cool.

Makes about 5 dozen.

Apricot Frozen Yogurt

1¼ cups sugar
1 cup water
½ pound dried apricots (1⅓ cups packed)

2 (16-ounce) containers plain yogurt
1 envelope unflavored gelatin
¼ cup cold water
Garnish: 2 fresh apricots, mint sprigs

Bring sugar and 1 cup water to a boil in saucepan, stirring until sugar dissolves; stir in apricots, and simmer, stirring occasionally, until apricots are softened, 20 to 30 minutes. Process apricot mixture in a food processor until pureed; cool mixture. Whisk puree and yogurt in a large bowl until combined. Sprinkle gelatin over ¼ cup cold water in a small bowl, and let stand 3 minutes. Set bowl in a pan of simmering water, and stir gelatin until dissolved. Whisk gelatin mixture into yogurt mixture, and freeze in an ice-cream freezer according to manufacturer's instructions. Transfer frozen yogurt to a large pastry bag fitted with a decorative tip; pipe yogurt decoratively into 8 brandy snifters. Cover with plastic wrap, and freeze at least 1 hour to overnight. Garnish, if desired.

Makes 8 servings.

If fresh apricots are unavailable for garnish, use other fresh fruit or dried apricots soaked in apricot brandy until soft.

Caramel-Nut Torte

⅔	cup butter	1	cup whipping cream, room temperature
2⅔	cups all-purpose flour		
1½	cups sugar	3	tablespoons honey
⅛	teaspoon salt	2	tablespoons kirsch
1	egg, lightly beaten	2¾	cups coarsely chopped walnuts
2	teaspoons rum	1	egg yolk, lightly beaten
1	teaspoon finely shredded lemon peel	1	tablespoon milk

Preheat oven to 350°. Beat butter at medium speed with an electric mixer until fluffy. Combine flour, ½ cup sugar, and salt; add to butter, beating until crumbly. Combine whole egg, rum, and lemon peel; stir into flour mixture until moistened. Divide dough into 3 equal portions. Pat 1 dough portion into bottom of a 10-inch springform pan. Pat another portion onto sides of pan to height of 1 inch. Roll remaining portion on wax paper into a ¼-inch-thick rectangle; cover. Chill crust and rolled dough 30 minutes. Melt remaining 1 cup sugar in a saucepan over low heat; slowly stir in cream. Cook, stirring constantly, until sugar dissolves. Add honey and kirsch. Stir in walnuts. Remove from heat, and cool 5 minutes. Spread walnut mixture in dough-lined pan. Cut rectangle of dough into ½-inch strips; arrange strips in a lattice design over pie. Pinch edges of crust to seal. Brush mixture of beaten yolk and milk over crust. Bake for 40 minutes.

Makes 16 servings.

Cold Brandy Soufflé

1	tablespoon unflavored gelatin	½	cup sugar
⅓	cup brandy (use a fine Cognac)	½	cup whipping cream
4	eggs, separated	¼	cup crystallized ginger, finely minced
1	teaspoon vanilla extract		

Dissolve gelatin in brandy about 5 minutes; place mixture in top of a double boiler over simmering water, stirring constantly, 5 minutes. Beat egg yolks until thick, adding hot brandy in a thin stream while beating. Stir vanilla into mixture, and chill about 10 minutes. Beat egg whites at high speed with an electric mixer until soft peaks form. Gradually add sugar, 1 tablespoon at a time, beating until mixture is very thick and shiny. Whisk one-third egg white mixture into yolk mixture; gently fold in remaining egg white mixture. Beat whipping cream until stiff peaks form; gently fold into egg mixture with ginger. Divide evenly among 6 dessert cups; cover with plastic wrap, and chill 1 hour or more before serving.

Makes 6 servings.

New Mexico Peach Ice Cream

2 cups half-and-half
2 cups whipping cream
2 vanilla beans, split
1 cup plus 6 tablespoons firmly packed brown sugar

8 egg yolks
4½ pounds peaches, peeled and pitted
3 cups sour cream

Scald half-and-half and whipping cream with vanilla beans in a heavy saucepan. Whisk together sugar and egg yolks in a large bowl until fluffy; gradually whisk in hot cream mixture. Return to saucepan. Stir cream mixture over medium heat until it coats a spoon, about 5 minutes. Do not boil. Pour through a fine wire-mesh strainer into a large bowl; cool completely. Process 3 pounds peaches in a food processor until coarsely pureed; fold into cream mixture, and stir in sour cream. Chill overnight. Coarsely chop remaining 1½ pounds peaches. Freeze cream mixture in an ice-cream freezer according to manufacturer's instructions, adding chopped peaches when almost set. Freeze in covered container several hours. If frozen solid, soften slightly in refrigerator before serving.

Makes 4 quarts.

Pear-Nut Torte

1 egg
¾ cup sugar
2 tablespoons all-purpose flour
1 tablespoon baking powder

¼ teaspoon salt
2 large ripe pears, peeled and cored
½ cup chopped nuts
1 teaspoon vanilla extract

Preheat oven to 350°. Beat egg and sugar at medium speed with an electric mixer until fluffy. Combine flour, baking powder, and salt, and stir into egg mixture. Cut pears into large cubes. Add to batter, along with nuts and vanilla. Bake in an 8-inch square baking dish for 35 minutes. Serve warm with ice cream or whipped cream.

Makes 6 servings.

Meringue with ———
——— Mexican Chocolate Filling

Meringue Shell

3   egg whites
¼   teaspoon cream of tartar
⅛   teaspoon salt

¾   cup sugar
½   cup chopped toasted pecans
    Chocolate Filling

Preheat oven to 250°. Beat egg whites at high speed with an electric mixer until soft peaks form. Sprinkle in cream of tartar and salt while beating. Gradually add sugar, and beat until stiff peaks form and sugar dissolves. Spread about two-thirds of mixture on bottom of a greased 8-inch pie pan. Spread remaining mixture on sides of pan. Bake for 2 to 2½ hours or until shell is golden. Cool shell. Sprinkle bottom of shell with pecans just before adding filling.

Chocolate Filling

2   (6-ounce) packages semisweet
    chocolate morsels
1   tablespoon instant coffee granules
¼   tablespoon boiling water

½   teaspoon ground cinnamon
1   cup whipping cream
1   teaspoon vanilla extract

Melt chocolate in top of a double boiler over simmering water (not boiling). Dissolve coffee granules in ¼ tablespoon boiling water; stir into chocolate. Add cinnamon, and beat with a mixer, as you would fudge, until creamy and cooled. Beat cream at high speed until stiff peaks form. Fold cream into chocolate mixture. Add vanilla, and pour into meringue shell without disturbing pecans. Chill. Serve with additional whipped cream and bitter chocolate curls. This is very rich, so serve in small portions.

Makes 10 servings.

_____ Peach Fajitas _____

4 cups peeled, sliced fresh peaches	Butter
½ cup sugar (brown or white)	Flour tortillas
1½ teaspoons instant tapioca	Cinnamon-sugar
⅓ teaspoon ground cinnamon	½ cup pecans, finely chopped
⅛ teaspoon ground cayenne pepper	Vanilla ice cream

Cook first 5 ingredients in a saucepan over medium heat, stirring constantly, until mixture comes to a boil. Remove from heat, and set aside. Heat a large skillet over medium-high heat; Melt 1 to 2 tablespoons butter in skillet, and add tortillas, frying on both sides. Add butter to skillet, if needed. Remove tortillas when cooked, and sprinkle with cinnamon-sugar. Fill tortillas with fruit mixture, fajita-style. Place filled fajitas on individual plates, and sprinkle with pecans; add scoops of ice cream to each plate.

Makes 6 to 8 servings.

Fresh peaches are always preferred, but frozen ones can be used. Tortillas should be fried just before using, but filling can be prepared ahead of time and chilled. Any fruit in season may be substituted for peaches.

_____ Pistachio Ice Cream _____

1 cup pistachios	1 cup whipping cream
2 cups half-and-half	1 teaspoon vanilla extract
⅔ cup plus 2 teaspoons sugar	1 teaspoon unsalted butter
4 egg yolks, beaten	

Process ⅔ cup nuts in a food processor until finely ground. Cook ground nuts and half-and-half in top of a double boiler over barely simmering water 15 minutes. Whisk ⅔ cup sugar into egg yolks; whisk in one-third of hot nut mixture. Whisk yolk mixture into remaining hot mixture, and cook, stirring constantly, until custard coats a spoon. Immediately place pan into a larger pan of cold water, and stir to cool. Stir in whipping cream and vanilla. Cover and chill 2 to 3 hours or until thoroughly chilled. Coarsely chop remaining ⅓ cup nuts. Melt butter and 2 teaspoons sugar in a small skillet over medium heat; add coarsely chopped nuts, and sauté until lightly browned. Let cool. Freeze custard in an ice-cream freezer according to manufacturer's instructions. When partially frozen, stir in sugared nuts, or sprinkle them over top at serving time.

Makes 1 quart.

Since this recipe is so much better before it gets too hard, let it stand at room temperature a few minutes before serving.

Pecos Valley Crisp

1	cup all-purpose flour	5-6	cups berries, cleaned and stemmed
1	cup sugar		
1	teaspoon baking powder	2	tablespoons all-purpose flour
½	teaspoon salt	½-¾	cup sugar
1	egg, beaten	½	cup butter, melted

Preheat oven to 375°. Generously butter an oval or 8-inch square baking dish. Combine first 4 ingredients in a large bowl, stirring well. Make a well in center of dry mixture, and add beaten egg. Stir mixture with a fork until it resembles coarse meal. If too dry, add a little more of another beaten egg. Place berries in another large bowl. Stir together 2 tablespoons flour and enough sugar to sweeten berries; sprinkle over berries, and carefully toss until berries are coated. Pour berry mixture into buttered dish, and spread evenly. Pat gently to compact. Sprinkle crumbly mixture evenly over top of berries. Drizzle with melted butter. Bake for about 40 minutes or until topping is golden. Serve warm with whipped cream or ice cream. Or serve at room temperature, when crust has absorbed berry juices.

Makes 6 to 8 servings.

Use any berry that is in season or a combination of berries.

Chocolate-Amaretto Pie

8	ounces semisweet chocolate squares	1	tablespoon sugar
2	large eggs, separated	1	cup whipping cream, whipped and chilled
¼	cup Amaretto	1	(9-inch) baked pie shell (regular, graham, or chocolate crumb)
⅛	teaspoon salt		

Melt chocolate in top of a double boiler over simmering water. Add egg yolks, 1 at a time, to warm (not hot) chocolate, blending thoroughly. Gradually blend in Amaretto with a rubber spatula. Add salt; set aside. Beat egg whites in a clean, dry bowl until they become dry and produce volume. Add sugar, and beat until stiff. Gently but firmly mix half of egg white mixture into chocolate mixture. Fold in remaining egg white mixture alternately with whipped cream. Pour mixture into pie shell, and chill. Top with additional whipped cream, and serve.

Makes 6 servings.

Spicy Apple Crêpes with Maple Cream

2 tart cooking apples	½ teaspoon ground cinnamon
1 tablespoon lemon juice	¼ teaspoon ground nutmeg
½ cup apple cider or water	¼ cup red currant or apple jelly
⅓ cup dark raisins or dried cherries	Dessert Crêpes (see index)
¼ cup sugar	Maple Cream

Peel, core, and chop apples into ¼-inch dice. Toss apple with lemon juice in a medium-size skillet. Stir in cider and next 4 ingredients. Bring mixture to a boil over medium-high heat. Reduce heat, and simmer, stirring occasionally, until apple is just tender, about 10 minutes. Stir jelly into apple mixture, and cook 5 minutes. Keep warm. Place a crêpe on each dessert plate. Spread 3 tablespoons apple filling over half of each crêpe. Fold crêpe over. Spoon 1½ tablespoons Maple Cream over center of crêpe. Serve hot or warm.

Makes 10 servings.

Maple Cream

½ cup low-fat (1%) cottage cheese	¼ cup maple syrup
¼ cup nonfat plain yogurt	

Process cottage cheese and yogurt in a food processor 2 minutes or until very smooth, scraping down sides of bowl 2 times. Stir in maple syrup. Chill at least 30 minutes.

Chocolate-Piñon Pie

8 ounces piñions (pine nuts)	1 cup plus 1 tablespoon sugar
7 ounces unsweetened chocolate squares	4 large egg yolks
	Zest of 1 orange
1 cup unsalted butter	4 large egg whites

Preheat oven to 300°. Process piñions and chocolate in a food processor until ground. Beat butter at medium speed with an electric mixer until creamed; add sugar, and beat until sugar dissolves. Add egg yolks to butter mixture; add zest and piñion mixture, and beat until blended. Beat egg white at high speed until stiff peaks form. Fold egg white, one-third at a time, into butter mixture. Pour batter into a buttered, floured 8-inch round cake pan lined with parchment paper. Bake for 45 minutes or until pie shrinks away from edges of pan. Cool and slice with a wet knife.

Makes 10 servings.

Musician's Tart

Crust

1¼	cups all-purpose flour	1	egg yolk
3	tablespoons sugar	½	teaspoon vanilla extract
1/16	teaspoon salt	6	teaspoons whipping cream, approximately
½	cup unsalted butter, chilled and cut into pieces		

Fruit Filling

1	(scant) cup dried pears, cored and coarsely chopped (4 ounces)	⅓	cup pear nectar
1	(scant) cup pitted dates, halved	¼	cup firmly packed dark brown sugar

Nut Topping

6	tablespoons unsalted butter	½	cup toasted whole almonds (about 2 ounces)
6	tablespoons firmly packed dark brown sugar	½	cup dry-roasted cashews (about 2 ounces)
3	tablespoons light corn syrup	1½	tablespoons whipping cream
½	cup pine nuts (about 2 ounces)		

Preheat oven to 350°. For crust, process first 3 ingredients in a food processor until blended. Add butter, and cut in by pulsing until mixture resembles coarse meal. Add yolk and vanilla, and pulse until blended. Blend in cream, 1 teaspoon at a time, until a soft dough begins to clump together. Gather dough into a ball; flatten into a disk, and wrap in plastic wrap. Chill 30 minutes. Roll dough into a 12-inch round between 2 sheets of wax paper. Transfer round to a 9-inch tart pan with removable bottom. Trim edges. Freeze crust 15 minutes. Line with foil. Fill crust with dried beans or pie weights. Bake crust for 10 minutes or until sides are set. Remove foil and beans; bake until crust is golden, about 20 minutes. Cool completely on a wire rack. For filling, bring all ingredients to a boil in a heavy saucepan. Reduce heat, and simmer 1 minute. Puree mixture in processor to form a thick paste. Cool completely. For topping, preheat oven to 400°. Cook first 3 ingredients in a heavy saucepan over low heat, stirring until sugar dissolves. Increase heat, and bring to a boil. Boil vigorously 1 minute. Remove from heat. Add nuts and cream. Spread fruit filling into crust, smoothing top. Set tart on a baking sheet. Spoon nut mixture over fruit. Bake tart for 20 minutes or until filling bubbles. Transfer to a wire rack, and cool 10 minutes. Loosen tart pan sides, but do not remove. Cool tart completely in pan. (Can be made 1 day ahead. Cover and let stand at room temperature.) Remove pan sides. Cut tart into wedges.

Makes 6 servings.

Musician's Tart

At one time, musicians who entertained in the Catalan countryside were paid with dried fruit and nuts. This came to be known as the "musician's dessert," which is still served to this day. Many places have updated the custom by turning the "pay" into a tart. Here is one rendition, with a rich caramel topping and sweet crust. It is a wonderful addition to a holiday meal or a dessert buffet.

Peaches-and-Cream Tart

9 soft coconut macaroon cookies, crumbled (about 2 cups)
1 cup ground pecans
3 tablespoons butter, melted
½ cup whipping cream
1 (8-ounce) package cream cheese, softened
⅓ cup sugar
2 teaspoons dark rum or orange juice
1 teaspoon vanilla extract
¼ teaspoon almond extract
2-4 medium-size peaches, peeled, pitted, and thinly sliced
2 tablespoons lemon juice
½ cup fresh raspberries (optional)
¼ cup apricot preserves
2 tablespoons honey

Preheat oven to 350°. For crust, combine first 3 ingredients in a large bowl. Press mixture onto bottom and up sides of an 11-inch tart pan with removable bottom (or a 12-inch pizza pan). Bake until golden (15 to 18 minutes for tart pan or 12 to 15 minutes for pizza pan). Cool on a wire rack. For filling, chill a medium-size mixing bowl and beaters. Beat whipping cream at high speed until soft peaks form; set aside. Beat cream cheese and sugar at medium speed until fluffy; add rum, vanilla and almond extracts to cream cheese mixture, and beat until smooth. Gently fold in whipped cream. Turn mixture out into cooled crust, spreading evenly. Cover and chill 2 to 4 hours. Before serving, toss peach slices with lemon juice, and arrange with raspberries over filling. Heat preserves and honey in a small saucepan over medium heat just until preserves are melted. Snip any large pieces of fruit in glaze, or strain out. Spoon glaze over fruit, and serve.

Makes 8 to 10 servings.

Pear Tart

Crust

1¾ cups all-purpose flour
¾ cup butter, chilled and cut into
 ½-inch pieces
¼ cup sugar

2 egg yolks
1 teaspoon water
1 teaspoon vanilla extract

Filling

1 cup plus 3 tablespoons sugar
6 tablespoons all-purpose flour
3 eggs
¾ cup butter

2 Bartlett pears, peeled, cored, and
 quartered lengthwise
 Powdered sugar

Preheat oven to 375°. For crust, process flour, butter, and sugar in a food processor 45 seconds, until mixture resembles coarse meal. Add yolks, water, and vanilla, and process until crumbly. Turn dough out, and shape into a ball; flatten into a disk, and wrap in plastic wrap. Freeze dough 20 minutes or refrigerate overnight. Knead dough slightly (do not overwork). Roll dough on a lightly floured surface to a 13-inch circle. Press into an 11-inch tart pan or pie plate; trim edges, and chill crust 15 minutes. For filling, combine sugar, flour, and eggs until smooth. Melt butter in a saucepan over medium heat until foamy. Slowly whisk melted butter into sugar mixture, and set aside. Cut pears lengthwise into ⅛-inch-thick slices. Gently open slices into a fan shape. Arrange pears in crust in flower pattern. Pour filling over pears. Bake for 1 hour or until lightly browned. Sprinkle with powdered sugar.

Makes 6 to 8 servings.

Pepper-Pumpkin Custard Pie

2 cups canned pumpkin	1 teaspoon freshly ground white pepper
1½ cups whipping cream	1 teaspoon vanilla extract
3 eggs	1 (9-inch) unbaked pie crust
¾ cup maple syrup	

Preheat oven to 350°. Combine first 4 ingredients in a bowl until smooth. Stir in pepper and vanilla. Pour filling into pie crust, and bake for 1 hour. Pie is done when a wooden pick inserted in center comes out clean. If center is firm, pie is done. Cool on a wire rack.

Makes 8 servings.

This pie can be completely changed by varying the seasonings. A more traditional pie would result from eliminating the pepper and adding all of the following:

1 tablespoon brandy	½ teaspoon freshly grated nutmeg
½ tablespoon ground allspice	½ teaspoon ground ginger

EVENT SOLD OUT! Roswell Symphony performances are always sold out because of the active community support. The only way one can get a ticket, if not a subscription subscriber is to hope someone will turn in one. There is always a waiting list of people wishing to attend a concert.

Sour Cream-Lime Tart

Crust

1½ cups graham cracker crumbs
½ cup sugar

6 tablespoons butter, melted

Filling

1 cup sugar
3 tablespoons cornstarch
1 cup whipping cream
⅓ cup fresh lime juice

¼ cup butter
1 tablespoon finely grated lime peel (2 to 3 large limes)
1 cup sour cream

Topping

1 cup whipping cream
¼ cup sugar

1½ teaspoons vanilla extract
¾ cup sour cream

Preheat oven to 350°. For crust, combine all ingredients in a bowl. Press onto bottom and up sides of a 9-inch pie plate. Freeze 15 minutes. Bake for 12 to 15 minutes or until lightly browned. Cool completely on a wire rack. For filling, combine sugar and cornstarch in a heavy saucepan; stir in cream, lime juice, butter, and lime peel. Bring sugar mixture to a boil over medium-high heat, whisking constantly. Reduce heat, and simmer, stirring until thickened and smooth, about 10 minutes. Cool mixture to room temperature, stirring occasionally. Fold in sour cream. Spread filling evenly into crust. For topping, beat cream, sugar, and vanilla at high speed with an electric mixer until soft peaks form. Gently fold in sour cream. Spread over filling. Chill pie at least 4 hours.

Makes 10 to 12 servings.

Whiskey Apple Pie

2 cups sliced, tart green apples, peeled, cored and cooked slightly in ¼ cup water until soft
1 cup brown sugar
¼ cup unsalted butter
3 large eggs, separated

4 ounces bourbon whiskey (more, if desired)
1 cup whipping cream
¼ teaspoon ground nutmeg
Butter Pastry
Whipped cream

Preheat oven to 425°. Stir hot apple, sugar, and butter; cool mixture slightly. Beat egg yolks; stir yolks, whiskey, cream, and nutmeg into apple mixture. Beat egg whites at high speed with an electric mixer until soft peaks form. Fold egg whites into apple mixture with a little more whiskey. Line a pie plate with Butter Pastry; pour filling into pastry, and bake for 8 to 10 minutes to set crust. Reduce temperature to 325°, and bake 30 minutes longer or until filling is just set. Cool pie, and cover top with whipped cream just before serving.

Makes 8 servings.

Butter Pastry
2 cups sifted all-purpose flour
¼ teaspoon salt
¾ cup very cold unsalted butter

Ice water to mix (about 2 tablespoons)

Sift flour and salt into a bowl. Quickly cut butter into flour until resembles fine oatmeal. Stir in ice water with a fork just until dry mixture absorbs water and holds together. Wrap dough loosely in plastic wrap, and chill 1 hour or more. Divide dough in half, and quickly and firmly roll each half out onto a floured surface to ¼-inch thickness. Use as needed.

Makes 1 (10-inch) double crust

U.F.O.s
Ungourmet & Unusual Food Offerings

The Roswell Incident

Few residents of Roswell can avoid the question of the existence of Unidentified Flying Objects - and particularly, what happened in July 1947 when a UFO allegedly crashed nearby. Now more than fifty years later, interest in the ongoing mystery has made Roswell "the UFO Capitol of the World."

Between June and October 1947, accounts of "flying saucers" appeared in a great number of states and were reported in local newspapers. During the first week in July of that year in Roswell, the area had its usual early summer onslaught of thunderstorms. One night during a particularly violent storm, ranch foreman Mac Brazel heard an "explosion louder than thunder," two nuns at St. Mary's Hospital saw a bright object "plunging to the ground," and a couple enjoying a romantic summer rendezvous watched as a blazing craft crashed into the side of Capitan Mountain.

A few days later, Mac Brazel drove into Roswell with some of the debris that he had found scattered on his ranch and turned it over to Chaves County Sheriff George Wilcox. Unable to identify the material, Sheriff Wilcox contacted Major Jesse Marcel, Intelligence Officer at the Roswell Army Air Field. In the meantime, news about Brazel's mysterious experience and discovery was printed in Roswell newspapers, aired on the radio, and discussed throughout the county.

What happened in the next few days is a matter of fierce study and debate. Many allege that the United States government became a primary player in one of the most egregious cover-ups in our history. In any event, Brig. General Roger Ramey of the Fort Worth Army Air Field pronounced that the debris came not from an alien spacecraft that crashed outside of Roswell, but a weather balloon.

Although many people around Roswell and the base questioned this explanation, general interest in the incident subsided for quite some time. Although some independent research into the 1947 incident got underway in the 1970's, it was not until the early 90's that The Roswell Incident was featured on the popular investigative television series Unsolved Mysteries. This program led authors Donald Schmitt and Kevin Randle to begin their own investigation, which culminated in the best-selling book *The UFO Crash at Roswell* (1991). Hollywood followed suit, with the production of "Roswell" in 1994, and by the time of the 50th Anniversary of the Roswell Incident in 1997, nearly every major network and cable channel had dedicated programming to the ongoing mystery of the events of July 1947.

Although no concrete proof that an alien ship crashed into the region north of Roswell in July of 1947 has yet been uncovered, Roswell's International UFO Museum and Research Center has amassed hundreds of witness statements, affidavits, accounts, and testimonies concerning this incident. Founded in 1992 to gather and disperse information on UFOs and related phenomena, the UFO Museum on Roswell's Main Street is the only institute of its kind in the country, and it offers a vast trove of documents to the serious researcher, easily understandable exhibits, videos, and programs to a casual visitor, and a truly extraordinary gift shop. Recognizing that constantly advancing technology has made the idea of space travel thoroughly possible, the same technology, on a small scale, has also given the public their own type of freedom - the freedom to ask questions, to find their own answers, and to form their own educated opinions.

Deon Crosby, Executive Director,
International UFO Museum and Research Center

Featured on page 291 "UFO's"

Alien Prickly Pear Jelly

3	cups peeled, chopped prickly pear (about 6 large)	2	cups sugar
2	cups water	¼	cup fresh lemon juice (optional)
		⅓	cup liquid pectin

Bring pear and water to a boil in a heavy saucepan over medium-high heat; reduce heat, and simmer 15 minutes. Transfer pear mixture to a blender, and puree. Strain back into saucepan. Add sugar to pan, and bring to a boil. Add lemon juice to taste. Add liquid pectin, and return to boil. Cook, stirring constantly, 1 minute. Pour into hot, sterilized jars; cool and refrigerate up to 1 month.

Makes 4 cups.

This jelly is a beautiful color, due to the deep shade of the fruit. Native Americans used the fruit as a dye for yarn. Not only is this delicious on bread, it may be thinned with red wine and served as a sauce for meat, or with a sweet white wine for a dessert sauce.

Antigravity Frantic Chicken

4-12	garlic cloves, coarsely chopped (number depends on your taste)	6	large chicken breasts (about 2½ pounds)
4	tablespoons olive oil		Salt and freshly ground pepper to taste

Place garlic and oil in a microwave-safe dish large enough to hold chicken in 1 layer. Microwave, uncovered, on HIGH 3 minutes or until garlic is lightly golden in spots. Add chicken and salt and pepper to taste, turning to coat. Microwave, uncovered, on HIGH 12 to 14 minutes, depending on thickness. (Chicken should show no pink in thick areas but should be moist.) Let stand 3 minutes. Add sauce of choice, such as tomatillo sauce (see index for sauces).

Makes 4 to 6 servings.

Celestial Prickly Pear Dessert Sauce

¼ cup sugar
1 tablespoon cornstarch
⅛ teaspoon salt
1 cup prickly pear puree

⅛ teaspoon almond extract
2 tablespoons lemon juice
1 tablespoon butter
   Ice cream, sherbet, or custard

Bring first 4 ingredients to a boil in a 2 quart saucepan over medium-high heat, stirring constantly; Cook until thickened and clear. Remove from heat. Add almond extract, lemon juice, and butter; Stir until butter is melted. Serve hot or cooled over ice cream, sherbet, or custard.

Makes about 1¼ cups

For prickly pear puree: Hold fruit with tongs or rubber-gloved hands, and rinse under cold running water. Still protecting your hands, cut off both ends of fruit, and split skins lengthwise. Peel skin back. Lift or scoop out pulp; process in a food processor until pureed. Pour through a wire-mesh strainer to remove any seeds or strings.

One large prickly pear yields ¼ to ⅓ cup puree.

Body Bag Pork Roast

1 (3- to 6-pound) boneless pork
   roast
   Garlic powder
   Cumin powder
   Cracked pepper
¾ cup red wine

½ cup red wine vinegar
¼ cup water
1 oven cooking bag
1 tablespoon all-purpose flour
½ tablespoon arrowroot
2 tablespoons water

Preheat oven to 325°. Lightly rub roast with seasonings. Place roast in cooking bag with flour; add wine, vinegar, and ¼ cup water. Place roast in a roasting pan according to cooking bag instructions. Bake for 25 minutes per pound. Remove roast from bag, and keep warm. Pour hot liquid from bag into a saucepan. Combine arrowroot and 2 tablespoons water; stir into juices. Cook gravy mixture over medium heat until slightly thickened. Slice roast, and serve with gravy.

Makes 3 to 6 servings.

Conspiracy Two-Tone Slaw

Dressing

⅔ cup buttermilk
⅔ cup low-fat mayonnaise
1½ tablespoons fresh lemon juice
1 teaspoon grated lemon peel

1 bunch green onions, thinly sliced on diagonal
¼ cup fresh dill weed

Whisk first 3 ingredients in a small bowl until blended; stir in three-fourths green onions and dill weed. Cover and chill. Can be prepared 1 day ahead.

Green Slaw

½ head green cabbage, cored and shredded
½ red or yellow bell pepper, cut into thin strips

½ cup shredded carrot
Salt and pepper to taste

Combine all ingredients with half of dressing; Cover and chill.

Red Slaw

½ head red cabbage, cored and finely shredded
½ green bell pepper, cut into thin strips

½ cup shredded carrot
Salt and pepper to taste

Combine all ingredients in a bowl with remaining half of dressing. Cover and chill.

Makes 8 servings.

Serve slaws side by side on lettuce leaves, and top with chopped fresh parsley and remaining green onions..

Close Encounter Marinated Green Chiles

1 cup sugar
1 cup white vinegar
1 garlic clove, chopped
1 tablespoon dill weed

½ teaspoon salt
1 (21-ounce) can green chiles cut into bite-size pieces

Combine first 5 ingredients; add chiles, and chill at least 24 hours. Store in refrigerator up to 7 days. Serve on crackers with a slice of Monterey Jack cheese.

Crash Site Chicken Chowder

3	whole boneless chicken breasts, split and skinned (1¾ pounds)	2	serrano chiles, seeded
3	tablespoon unsalted butter	½	teaspoon coriander
1	medium-size onion, peeled	¼	teaspoon ground cumin
1	large sweet potato, peeled	1	(16-ounce) can hominy, drained
4½-4¾	cups chicken stock	⅔	cup fresh cilantro leaves
			Garnish: sour cream

Trim fat from chicken; cut chicken into ¾-inch cubes. Melt butter in a 5 quart saucepan; add chicken, and cook over high heat, stirring often, until no longer pink. Remove chicken from pan with a slotted spoon, and set aside. Cut onion and sweet potato into thin slices; add to chicken drippings with 4½ cups stock. Cover and bring to a boil. Reduce heat, and simmer until vegetables are very soft, about 20 minutes. Remove vegetables, reserving liquid in pan. Process vegetables, chiles, coriander, and cumin in food processor until pureed. Return puree to reserved liquid in pan; add chicken and hominy. Cook until heated through, thinning with remaining stock, if needed. Stir in cilantro leaves, and garnish if desired.

Makes 7 cups.

Crop Circle Dip

1	medium-size eggplant (about 1 pound)	¼	cup lemon juice
1	small onion, quartered	1	tablespoon olive oil
1	garlic clove	1½	teaspoons salt
			Pita Triangles

Preheat oven to 400°. Prick eggplant 3 to 4 times with a fork; bake for 40 minutes or until very soft. Cool and pare eggplant; cut into cubes. Process eggplant and next 5 ingredients in a food processor until smooth. Serve with Pita Triangles or with vegetable.

Pita Triangles
Preheat oven to 400°. Separate pita rounds into 2 layers each. Stack 6 layers and cut into 8 wedges. Lay wedges in a single layer on a baking sheet. Bake for 7 minutes or until browned and dry. These keep several days in an airtight container.

Dummy Drop No-Bake Cookies

2 cups sugar	2-3 tablespoons cocoa
½ cup butter	½ cup crunchy or smooth peanut
½ cup milk	butter
1 teaspoon vanilla extract	3 cups oatmeal

Bring first 3 ingredients to a boil in a large, heavy sauce pan; cook 1 minute. Add remaining ingredients, stirring until blended. Remove from heat, and drop by teaspoonfuls onto wax paper. Cool.

Makes 4 dozen.

Enigma Fruit-and-Pecan Balls

½ cup dried apricots, coarsely chopped	¾ teaspoon freshly grated orange peel
½ cup pitted prunes, coarsely chopped	¾ cup pecans, toasted and finely chopped
¼ cup raisins, minced	¾ cup sweetened flaked coconut
3 tablespoons orange liqueur	¾ cup sugar

Combine first 5 ingredients in a large bowl; let stand, stirring occasionally, 1 hour. Process fruit mixture in a food processor until finely chopped; stir in pecans and coconut until mixture holds together. Shape by rounded teaspoonfuls into balls. Roll balls in sugar, and store in an airtight container lined with wax paper, separating each layer with wax paper. Balls will keep up to 2 weeks in a cool, dry place.

Makes about 36 balls.

Extraterrestrial Vegetarian Chopped Liver

¼ cup vegetable oil	1 cup walnuts, chopped
4 medium-size onions, chopped	6 hard-cooked egg whites, chopped
1 (15-ounce) can green peas, drained	Salt and freshly ground pepper to taste

Heat oil in a large skillet over medium heat; add onion, and sauté until rich dark brown in color. Let cool. Add peas, walnuts, and egg whites to onion stirring until blended. (Add more oil if mixture is dry.) Spoon mixture into a bowl, and season with salt and pepper. Cover and chill several hours. Serve at room temperature.

Flying Saucer Monster Cookies

12 eggs
2 pounds brown sugar
4 cups sugar
1 pound margarine
3 teaspoons vanilla
3 teaspoons white corn syrup

1 (3-pound) jar peanut butter
8 teaspoons baking soda
1 (16-ounce) package chocolate mini morsels
18 cups quick-cooking oats
1 (16-ounce) package M&Ms

Preheat oven to 350°. Combine ingredients in order listed in a dishpan, adding 1 ingredient at a time and blending thoroughly after each. Using a small ice-cream scoop or tablespoon, mound dough onto greased baking sheets, and flatten. Bake for 10 to 12 minutes. Cool before removing from pans. You can make half of recipe, using an electric mixer for creaming first 3 ingredients; transfer to dishpan, and stir in remaining ingredients by hand.

Makes about 12 dozen.

Be sure to start cookies in a HUGE bowl, roaster, dishpan, or tub.

Flying Saucers
Need about a zillion cookies? This recipe is for you! Mrs. Roger Staubach, wife of the famous Dallas Cowboys quarterback and alumnus of N.M.M.I., used to make these cookies for the team and was kind enough to share it.

Galactic Taco Soup

1½ pounds lean ground beef
1 onion, chopped
1 envelope taco seasoning mix
1 (8-ounce) can taco sauce
1 (15½-ounce) can chopped tomatoes, undrained
1 (10½-ounce) can tomatoes, undrained

1 can whole-kernel corn, undrained
1 (15-ounce) can pinto beans, undrained
1 (15-ounce) can jalapeño pinto beans, undrained
1 (16-ounce) can hominy, undrained

Brown beef with onion in a large skillet over medium heat; drain. Transfer beef mixture to a large stockpot, and add remaining ingredients. Simmer over medium heat until heated through.

Makes about 10 cups.

Impact Site Goulash

¼	cup shortening	2	teaspoons salt
2	pounds venison, cut into 1-inch cubes	2	teaspoons paprika
		½	teaspoon dry mustard
1	cup sliced onion	¼	teaspoon ground red pepper
1	garlic clove, minced	1½	cups water
¾	cup tomato catsup	2	tablespoons all-purpose flour
2	tablespoons Worcestershire sauce	¼	cup water
1	tablespoon brown sugar	3	cups cooked noodles

Melt shortening in a large skillet over medium heat; add venison, onion, and garlic. Cook until meat is browned and onion is tender. Stir in catsup and next 7 ingredients; cover and simmer 2 hours. Blend flour and ¼ cup water; stir into mixture gradually. Bring to a boil, and stir. Serve with noodles.

Any big game meat may be substituted for venison.

Makes 6 servings.

Interstellar Delight

1½	pounds lean ground beef	1	(16-ounce) container sour cream
1	envelope taco seasoning mix	½	cup chopped green onions
14	ounces salsa	1	(4½-ounce) can sliced black olives
9	corn tortillas		Chopped lettuce
2	cups shredded Cheddar cheese		Chopped tomato
2	small or 1 large can refried beans		

Preheat oven to 350°. Brown beef in a large skillet over medium heat; drain. Stir in taco seasoning according to package directions. Add salsa, and simmer 5 to 10 minutes. Put 3 tortillas in bottom of a 13- x 9- x 2-inch baking dish. Spread half of meat mixture over tortillas; sprinkle with ½ cup cheese. Top cheese with 3 more tortillas. Spread with refried beans. Cover beans with two-thirds of sour cream. Sprinkle with green onions and olives. Put remaining 3 tortillas over mixture, and cover with remaining meat mixture and cheese. Cover with foil, and bake for 20 to 30 minutes or until bubbly. Serve with lettuce and tomato and remaining sour cream.

Makes 6 servings.

——————— Mother Ship Bread ———————————

1 loaf French bread
¾ cup mayonnaise
½-1 cup freshly grated Parmesan
    cheese
1 cup shredded medium or sharp
    Cheddar cheese

5 green onions, chopped
3 garlic cloves, pressed
½ bunch fresh parsley, finely minced

Preheat oven to 450°. Cut bread lengthwise in half. Combine remaining ingredients, and spread on cut sides of bread. Bake for 8 to 10 minutes or until topping is bubbly and brown. Slice and serve immediately.

Makes 6 to 8 servings.

——————— Roswell Incident Salad ———————————

2 bunches fresh spinach, washed,
    drained, and torn into bite-size
    pieces
1 cup fresh bean sprouts
1 can sliced water chestnuts

2 hard-cooked eggs, cooled and
    chopped
4 bacon slices, cooked, drained, and
    crumbled
    Dressing

Toss together all ingredients.

Makes 6 to 8 servings.

Dressing
½ cup olive oil
⅓ cup sugar
⅓ cup catsup
¼ cup white wine vinegar
1 teaspoon paprika

1 teaspoon bottled steak sauce
1 tablespoon brandy
1 small onion, grated
    Salt and pepper to taste

Whisk together all ingredients.

Spaceship Veggies

3   tablespoons sherry vinegar or any good wine vinegar
1½ tablespoons lemon juice
1½ teaspoons Dijon mustard
½   garlic clove, minced
3   tablespoons nonfat yogurt
3   tablespoons olive oil
¼   cup chopped fresh herbs: basil, tarragon, thyme, chervil, parsley, dill, chives, singly or in combination
¼   teaspoon dried tarragon
    Salt and freshly ground pepper to taste
1   pound new potatoes, scrubbed, steamed or boiled until crisp-tender, and cut into bite-size pieces

½   head cauliflower, broken into florets and steamed 5 minutes
1   pint cherry tomatoes, red and yellow (if large, halve)
2   red bell peppers or 1 yellow or green and 1 red, halved, seeded, and cut into chunks
1   English cucumber, scored with a fork and sliced about ¼-inch thick
¾   pound medium-size mushrooms, stems removed and caps quartered
2   purple onions, sliced into rings
2   tablespoons sliced imported olives
1   cup cooked white beans, such as cannellini

Whisk together first 4 ingredients, blending well. Whisk in yogurt and oil. Stir in 2 tablespoons fresh herbs, dried tarragon, and salt and pepper to taste. Combine vegetables in a large dish; pour vinaigrette over vegetables, and toss well. Cover and chill at least 1 hour or up to 8 hours. Just before serving, remove vegetables from refrigerator, and add remaining fresh herbs. Toss and adjust seasonings. Arrange on a platter over lettuce leaves, and garnish with fresh herb sprigs.

Makes 20 salad servings or 30 appetizer servings.

Top Secret Cracker Toffee

1   cup butter
1   cup firmly packed brown sugar
1   package saltines

6-12 ounces semisweet chocolate morsels
Pecans, crushed or chopped

Preheat oven to 400°. Line a baking sheet with 1 piece of foil, and spray with cooking spray. Lay saltines, side by side, on foil. Bring butter and sugar to a boil in a saucepan; pour mixture over saltines, covering surface. Bake for 5 to 6 minutes. Remove from oven, and immediately sprinkle with chocolate morsels. When chocolate is soft, spread with a spatula to make smooth coating. Sprinkle nuts over top. Cool in refrigerator, and cut into bars.

Take Me To Your Leader Cookies

2 cups brown sugar	2 teaspoons salt
2 cups sugar	2 teaspoons baking soda
¾ cup butter, softened	3 cups uncooked oats
1 cup shortening	2 cups flaked coconut
4 eggs, beaten	2 cups raisins
2 teaspoons vanilla extract	1 cup chocolate morsels
3 cups all-purpose flour	1 cup pecans, chopped

Preheat oven to 350°. Cream sugars, butter, and shortening at medium speed with an electric mixer; beat in eggs and vanilla. Combine flour, salt, and soda, and beat into sugar mixture. Add remaining ingredients, and knead into mixture. Drop by heaping teaspoonfuls, 2 inches apart, onto greased baking sheets. Bake for about 8 minutes or until cookies are lightly browned. Cool on pans about 1 minute before removing to wire racks to cool. Store in airtight containers. Dough can be shaped into rolls, wrapped, and chilled several hours or longer, then sliced and baked.

Makes about 7 dozen.

These cookies are a great supply of quick energy for runners and for children.

Deep Space Barbecued Pork Roast

1 lean pork roast (size depends on your crowd)	1 small can mushroom stems and pieces, undrained
Your favorite barbecue sauce	1 envelope dry onion soup mix

Preheat oven to 250°. Pour barbecue sauce over roast; add mushroom pieces and soup mix. Wrap in foil, or place in covered baking dish. Bake until done.

Since nothing is measured and oven temperature is low, roast can be prepared in 2 minutes and cooked while one is at work, Christmas shopping, or taking house guests on a tour of your community. If using a very large roast, cook it overnight. All that is left to do is make a salad and enjoy!

The Great Cover-Up Barbecue Sauce

2   tablespoons butter
1   medium-size onion, diced
2   tablespoons vinegar or lemon juice
1   tablespoon brown sugar
1   cup chile sauce
1   teaspoon Worcestershire sauce

1   teaspoon dry mustard
½   cup minced celery
½   cup beef broth
1   teaspoon salt
¼   teaspoon ground red pepper
¼   teaspoon ground black pepper

Melt butter in a large saucepan; add onion, and sauté until tender, 5 minutes. Add vinegar and next 6 ingredients; bring to a boil. Reduce heat, and simmer 30 minutes. Add salt and peppers, and simmer 5 minutes. Use sauce on 3 pounds ribs or 2 chickens.

Sauce is best made a day or 2 ahead. It is very chunky.

Makes 2 cups.

UFO Phenomenon Macaroni Mousse

1   cup elbow macaroni
1   cup soft breadcrumbs
¼   cup melted butter
1   (4-ounce) jar diced pimientos, drained
1   tablespoon chopped fresh parsley

1   tablespoon onion flakes
1½ cups shredded Cheddar cheese
⅜   teaspoon salt
1½ cups scalded milk
3   eggs, well beaten
    Paprika

Preheat oven to 300°. Cook macaroni in a pan of boiling water according to package directions; drain. Put macaroni in a well-oiled baking dish. Combine breadcrumbs and next 6 ingredients in a bowl; pour scalded milk over top. Add eggs. Blend breadcrumb mixture well, and pour over macaroni. Sprinkle with paprika. Bake for 1 to 1¼ hours or until a knife inserted in center comes out clean.

Makes 6 to 8 servings.

Twilight Zone Pinto Bean Fudge

1   cup pinto beans, cooked, drained, and mashed
¾   cup unsalted butter, melted
1   tablespoon vanilla extract

¾   cup cocoa
2   pounds powdered sugar
½   cup nuts, chopped (pecans, walnuts, or your choice)

Combine first 4 ingredients in a large bowl; stir in sugar and nuts. Spread into a greased 13- x 9- x 2-inch pan. Store in refrigerator.

Keith W. Avery

Western artist Keith W. Avery is well known to horse enthusiasts throughout the United States. His paintings and drawings have appeared as covers on nationally circulated horse magazines such as the *Western Horseman*, and the *Quarter Horse Journal;* many of his paintings hang in private collections from coast to coast.

Having worked as a horse trainer and cowhand on Oklahoma, Florida, New Mexico, and Arizona ranches and through years of participating in rodeos and horse shows, he brings to his work an unquestioned authenticity. His love of horses was transferred to his easel during his early youth. Awards won in the National Scholastic art competition while a high school student earned him a scholarship to the Chicago Professional School of Art.

A World War II veteran and graduate of New Mexico State University, Keith taught for several years at the Judson Ranch school in Scottsdale, Arizona, and in Lowell, Michigan, High School. He is a recipient of an honorary doctor of letters degree from NMSU.

Keith received the Governor's Award, New Mexico's highest artistic honor for "Excellence and Achievement in the Arts." Recognized as the "dean of New Mexico cowboy poets, and called the "premier painter of the working cowboy," Keith as the first cowboy poet selected by the National Endowment for the Arts to represent New Mexico at the National Cowboy Poetry Gathering in Elko, Nevada in 1986.

Keith and his wife, Carol, have been married 51 years. Two of their three children, CLA and David, make their homes in Roswell., Their daughter, Jane, resides in Michigan.

Homeward Bound
Artist – Keith Avery
24″ × 30″
oil on canvas
Private collection

ACHIOTE: Tiny brick-red seeds of the annatto tree. It is often used as a coloring agent (Cheddar cheeses). Seeds have an earthy, musky taste.

ANISEED: Seed of the anise plant. It adds a sweet licorice flavor to baked goods, both sweet and savory.

CHAYOTE: Pale green, pear-shaped vegetable. Chayote has a mild, white flesh and tastes similar to zucchini. It is used raw in salads or as a substitute in any recipe calling for summer squash.

CHEESES, MEXICAN:

Asadaro: Mild, soft cheese with flavor of provolone and texture of mozzarella. Asadaro melts well. Substitute mozzarella or provolone.

Cotija: Hard, dry, aged, full-flavored cheese. Substitute feta, Parmesan or dry Monterey jack.

Manchego: Rich, mellow table cheese. Substitute white Cheddar, Swiss or Gouda.

Oaxaco: Similar to mozzarella; melts easily. Substitute mozzarella.

Queso Fresco: Tangy flavored cheese with crumbly texture. Substitute feta.

Ranchero: Fresh cheese, good for table or cooking. It has the texture of farmers cheese and the taste of Monterey jack.

CHILES, DRIED:

Ancho: Most commonly used dried pepper made from the green poblano. It is mild to medium pungency, has a smoky favor, and is sweeter than most dried chiles.

Cayenne: Usually dried and ground to powder form. Provides pungent heat and a slightly acid flavor.

Cascabel Chile: Small round shaped pepper which is medium hot with slightly acid quality. It is often used in uncooked salsas.

Chile Caribe: Crushed form of New Mexico dried red chile pods along with the seeds. May be sold under the name of Dried Red Pepper Flakes.

Chipotles: Dried, smoked jalapeño chiles, tobacco colored, with a rich, sweet, smoky flavor and a very pronounced heat.

Chipotles in Adobo: Canned chipotle chiles in sauce of tomatoes, vinegar, garlic, onion and spices.

Preparation of Dried Chiles:

Dried chiles have an intense flavor and may be stored indefinitely in airtight containers. To use dried chiles, toast in a dry skillet 3 or 4 minutes or until flexible. Remove ribs, stems and seeds. Depending on recipe, tear chiles to pieces or grind in a blender, or soak them, weighed down, if necessary, in very hot (not boiling) water for 20 to 30 minutes or until soft. To use soaked chiles in a sauce, puree them with a little of the soaking water.

CHILES, FRESH:

Anaheim: Bright green chile about 6 inches long. It is very mild in flavor.

Habanero: Slightly spherical chile about 1½ inches in diameter. Color ranges from dark green to bright red. Habaneros are the hottest of all chiles, so use with caution. They are also available in dried form.

Jalapeño: Bright green tapered chile about 2 inches long and 1 inch wide. They are the most common hot chile used in the USA and may be added to almost anything, even desserts. Ripe jalapeño is bright red and slightly sweeter than the green chile.

New Mexico Green: Medium green in color and about 7½ inches long and 1½ inches wide. There are several types of New Mexico chiles with varying degrees of heat—from mild to hot. When New Mexico chiles are used, it is always assumed they have been roasted and peeled.

New Mexico Red: Ripe form of the New Mexico Green. It is usually roasted, is dark red and sweeter in flavor than the green chile. It provides crisp heat. The traditional method of storing these chiles is to tie them together in strings called ristras.

Poblano: Dark green, triangular and thick fleshed chile about 4 inches long and 2½ inches wide. Roasting brings out smoky, earthy flavor. It is often stuffed.

Serrano: Small, thick-fleshed cylindrical chile with a tapered end. It is slightly hotter and smaller than a jalapeño.

Preparation of Fresh Green Chiles:
Char or blister until blackened over a grill or under the broiler. Remove chiles and place in plastic bag to steam for 15 to 20 minutes. The skins will then peel off easily. Remove stems, ribs, and seeds. The flavor will be more intense if the chiles are not rinsed with water. Use according to your recipe. Green chiles may also be frozen after they have been blackened. The skins may be removed before freezing, but chiles will have more flavor if peeled when ready to use them. At that time, peel, stem, and remove ribs and seeds.

CHILI POWDER and POWDERED CHILE: Chili powder is a seasoning made of dried red chiles, garlic, oregano, cumin and other herbs. Powdered chile is the ground form of one particular chile. Both have a short shelf life.

CHORIZO: Highly seasoned, fresh pork sausage. Must be cooked before eating. It is usually removed from its casing and crumbled before cooking.

CILANTRO: Green herb also known as Chinese parsley or fresh coriander. It has a pungent, sweet odor and adds a distinctive flavor to salsas and other dishes.

Storage of Cilantro
Choose unwilted bunches of cilantro. Wash and drain well. Re-cut stem ends and place in ½ inch water. Cover with a plastic bag and store in the refrigerator for a week or more. The stems have as much flavor as the leaves, so use all but the coarsest ones.

CORNHUSKS: Outer wrappings of fresh corn that are dried. They are used in making tamales.

CUMIN: Has a spicy, nutty flavor and is often used with chile powders and curries. It is sold as whole seeds or ground into a powder. The best flavor comes from toasting and grinding the seeds.

GRITS: Coarsely ground dried hominy.

HOMINY: Whole dried corn kernels that have been soaked in slaked lime or lye to remove tough outer hulls. The processing improves the nutritive value. Yellow and white hominy is available canned and is available fresh or dried in some markets. Dried hominy must be soaked before using.

JICAMA: Root vegetable with fibrous brown skin and crisp white flesh. This slightly sweet, nut flavored, crunchy vegetable is usually eaten raw although it retains its water chestnut-like texture when cooked.

MASA: Dough made from dried, specially processed corn that has been ground. It is used to make tortillas or tamales.

MASA HARINA: Flour made from dried corn. When combined with liquid it is used to make tortillas and tamales.

NOPALES: Fleshy oval pads of prickly pear cactus that taste much like a green bean. The thorns must be scraped away before using.

NOPALITOS: Dried or sliced nopales available either canned or pickled.

PEPITAS: Dark green hulled pumpkin seeds. Use in salads or main dishes, or eat toasted and salted as a snack.

PIÑON NUTS: Delicate flavored seeds from cones of the Piñon tree. Skinned piñons resemble small white corn kernels and are often roasted and used in cooking.

PRICKLY PEAR FRUIT: Purple-red pear shaped fruit of the prickly pear cactus. It has a smell similar to a melon and has a sweet subtle flavor. Must be peeled (very carefully) and the tough black seeds removed from the soft flesh before eating or cooking.

REFRIED BEANS: Cooked beans which have been mashed and then fried in lard.

TEQUILA: Colorless liquor distilled from the sweet sap of the century plant.

TOMATILLO: Looks like a small green tomato with thin brown husks. They have a slightly tart but mild flavor with hints of lemon and apple. Use raw or cooked.

TORTILLA: Bread of Mexico. Tortillas are made from either corn (masa) or wheat flour, pressed, then quickly cooked on a hot skillet.

Index

• SAVORING THE SOUTHWEST, AGAIN •

Savoring the Southwest Again

P.O. Box 3078
Roswell, New Mexico 88202-3078
(505) 623-7477 or 1-800-457-0302

Please send me _____ copies of *Savoring the Southwest Again*

Savoring The Southwest Again .... @ $22.50 each

Shipping and Handling—Continental USA .... @ $ 3.50 each

Gift Wrap .... @ $ 2.00 each

Make checks payable to RSG Publications

Name _____

Street _____

City _____ State _____ Zip _____

PRICES SUBJECT TO CHANGE

Savoring the Southwest Again

P.O. Box 3078
Roswell, New Mexico 88202-3078
(505) 623-7477 or 1-800-457-0302

Please send me _____ copies of *Savoring the Southwest Again*

Savoring The Southwest Again .... @ $22.50 each

Shipping and Handling—Continental USA .... @ $ 3.50 each

Gift Wrap .... @ $ 2.00 each

Make checks payable to RSG Publications

Name _____

Street _____

City _____ State _____ Zip _____

PRICES SUBJECT TO CHANGE